Baedeker's

COSTA BRAVA

Imprint

Cover picture: Rocky bays on the Costa Brava

98 colour photographs
19 maps, plans and diagrams, 1 large map

Text: Peter M. Nahm, Ostfildern-Kemnat
Editorial work: Baedeker's editorial staff
Design and layout: Creativ GmbH, Ulrich Kolb, Stuttgart
General direction: Dr Peter Baumgarten, Baedeker Stuttgart

(Source of illustrations: Ancora (4), Baedeker-Archiv (4), Historia-Photo (3), Nahm (91), Sanz-Vega (2), ZEFA (1)

Cartography: Christoph Gallus, Lahr; Franz Kaiser, Sindelfingen;
Gert Oberländer, München, Mairs Geographischer Verlag GmbH & Co., Ostfildern-Kemnat (large map)

Translation: Alec Court

Following the tradition established by Karl Baedeker in 1844, buildings, works of art, beauties of nature and views of particular merit, together with hotels and restaurants of outstanding quality are distinguished by one or two asterisks.

To make it easier to locate the principal places listed in the A–Z section of the guide, their coordinates on the large map of the Costa Brava are shown in red at the head of each entry; e.g. Barcelona K 1-2.

Because of the large numbers involved only a selection of hotels, restaurants and shops can be given; no reflection is therefore implied on establishments not included.

In a time of rapid change it is difficult to ensure that all the information given is entirely accurate and up-to-date, and the possibility of error can never be entirely eliminated. Although the publishers can accept no responsibility for inaccuracies and omissions, they are always grateful for corrections and suggestions for improvement.

1st edition 1989

US and Canadian Edition
Prentice Hall Press

Licensed user: Mairs Graphische Betriebe GmbH & Co., Ostfildern-Kemnat bei Stuttgart

Printed in Italy By Sagdos, Milan

0–13–055880–X US and Canada
0 86145 676 9 UK
3–87504–565–3 Germany

Contents

Preface

This pocket guide to the Costa Brava is one of the new generation of Baedeker guides.

These pocket-size regional guides, illustrated throughout in colour, are designed to meet the needs of the modern traveller. They are quick and easy to consult, with the principal sights described in alphabetical order and practical details about times of opening, how to get there, etc., shown in the margin.

Each guide is divided into three parts. The first part gives a general account of the area, its history, prominent personalities and so on; in the second part the principal places are described, and the third part contains a variety of practical information designed to help visitors to find their way about and make the most of their stay.

The new guides are abundantly illustrated and contain numbers of newly drawn plans. In a pocket at the back of the book is a large area map and each entry in the main part of the guide gives the co-ordinates of the square on the map in which the particular place is situated. Users of this guide should have no difficulty in finding what they want to see.

Facts and Figures

Note

In this book the terms "Catalonian" and "Catalonia" are used insofar as they refer to the geographical and political identity of the autonomous region of Catalonia (Catalunya). Catalan refers to the common ethnic roots of the people, their language, their traditions and their culture. For example the independent entity of the Balearic Islands and of the adjoining area of Roussillon in France, the Côte Vermeille to the north of the Pyrenees, are not called Catalonian but simply Catalan.

General

Outline of the area

In this guide the coastal area in the extreme north-east of Spain is described. Primarily this is the Costa Brava, the "wild coast", which extends from the French-Spanish border as far as the mouth of the River Tordera, not far south of Blanes. Here the Costa Dorada ("golden coast") begins and extends as far as Barcelona, the capital of the Spanish autonomous region of Catalonia (Spanish: Cataluña; Catalan: Catalunya). Not far south-west of here lies the monastery of Montserrat, which is the southern terminus of the

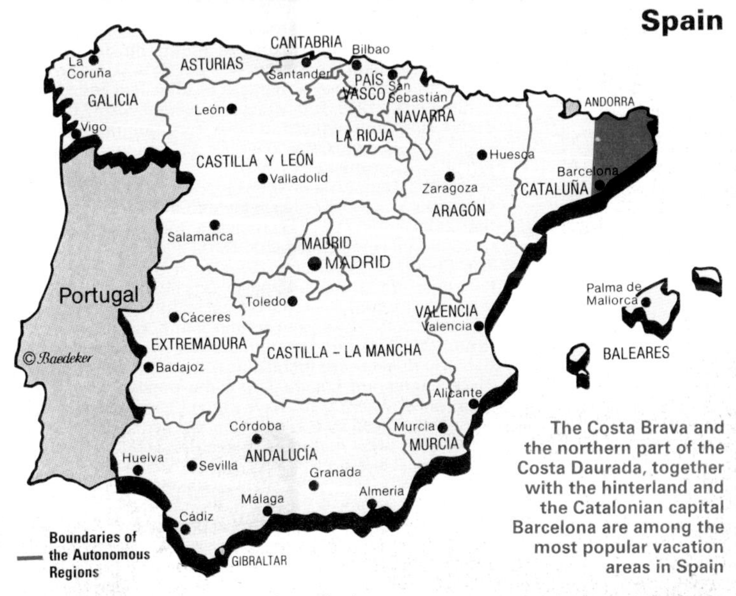

The Costa Brava and the northern part of the Costa Daurada, together with the hinterland and the Catalonian capital Barcelona are among the most popular vacation areas in Spain

◄ *Tossa de Mar: watch-tower above the bay*

route here described (see page 29) but which is outside the area included in the touring map. In the north the most important places in part of the Catalan speaking part of France (as far as Perpignan) are included. In the west the area ends approximately near the main highway which leads from Barcelona via Vich and Ripoll to the Spanish frontier at Puigcerdá or Bourg-Madame. Thus the area in question has an extent of about 180 km/110 miles from north to south and 130 km/80 miles from east to west.

Region, Provinces

The autonomous region of Catalonia (the organ of government is the Comunitat Autonoma Catalunya/Comunidad Autónoma Cataluña), with 31,930 sq. km/12,324 sq. miles and almost 5.7 million inhabitants (14% of the total Spanish population), is divided into four provinces (Lieida/Lérida, Girona/Gerona, Barcelona and Tarragona). The Balearic Islands (Mallorca, Menorca, Ibiza, Formentera and their neighbouring isles) belong ethnologically, historically and philologically also to Catalonia but they form an independent autonomous region. The area which is dealt with in this guide includes in Spain the coastal areas of the provinces of Girona and Barcelona and in France part of the region Languedoc-Roussillon which forms part of the Département Pyrénées-Orientales.

Statute of Autonomy

Efforts to acquire autonomy within the whole country began in those regions where the inhabitants differed in language and culture from the Castillian speaking Spanish. As well as the Catalans there were also the Basques and the Galicians. Primarily because of mounting discontent a regionalisation of the country was begun and this process, which entered its practical phase in 1979, had been largely completed by 1983. Today Spain is divided into 17 Comunidades Autónomas (autonomous communities), each of which has its own single chamber parliament and its own regional government.
Within the framework of Spanish policy of decentralisation Catalonia gained its provisional autonomy in 1977 and on the 22 December 1979 its complete autonomy. The organ of government is the Generalitat de Catalunya.
The Statute of Autonomy has also had an effect on the language. While literary Spanish (Castillian, Lengua Castellana) was formerly the only official language, and was preferred for both spoken and written communication, Catalan (Spanish: Catalan; Catalan: Català) dialects (e.g. the Balearic dialect) are increasingly gaining ground. Many place names are bilingual with the Catalan form taking preference; where signs have not yet been altered help is sometimes given by means of areosol paints. In this guide the Catalan place names are given first and determine the alphabetical order.

Note

Since Castillian place names are at present more familiar to foreign tourists than the Catalan names an alphabetical list will be found on page 214 giving the Spanish place names and their Catalan equivalents. Further details about the language can be found on page 14.

The Landscape

Catalonia is the most northerly of the Mediterranean regions of Spain, different in character and historical development from Castile and the interior. The Catalonian Mountains run parallel to the coast, linking the eastern Pyrenees with the hills bordering the Meseta on the north-east. Originally a continuous range they were later divided by tectonic disturbances into isolated masses, such as at Montseny (2745 m/5727 ft) in the north and the famous Montserrat (1241 m/4073 ft), with its monastic buildings, in the south.
Between the main range of mountains and the lower coastal chain extends the Catalonian Longitudinal Valley, a syncline filled with late Tertiary deposits. This is the heart of the region, densely populated and covered with olive groves, vineyards, market gardens and, especially around Girona, plantations of cork-oaks. The rivers flowing down from the Pyrenees, particularly the Llobregat, cut through the hills in narrow gorges; their abundant flow of water, long used for irrigation, is now also harnessed to provide electric energy for industry. In the west Catalonia extends also into the Ebro basin.
In the Pyrenees, to the south of the main ridge, is a region of sparse population and rugged mountain scenery. In the east the range descends in separate ridges to the uplands of Empordà (Ampurdán), where olive groves, vineyards and woods of cork-oak fringe the base of the hills. The Costa Brava owes its name, the "wild coast", to the cliffs which reach down to the sea, and dividing the coastline and forming in many places wild and romantic landscapes. The Costa Dorada is considerably flatter and more monotonous; its broad almost level sandy beaches extend as far as Barcelona.
The Catalonian capital Barcelona, situated in the fertile area around the mouth of the Llobregat, has developed into a major centre of commerce and industry; however, it must be said that in the outlying catchment areas the quality of the sea-water and of the beaches has greatly deteriorated.

Climate

The climate on the Catalonian Mediterranean coast is more equable than in the interior. Compared with those of the Atlantic west coast of the Iberian peninsula summer temperatures are about 6–7 °C/10–12 °F higher and the water temperature some 4–6 °C/7–10 °F higher. In summer strong land and sea breezes develop on the coast. The wind blowing from the sea during the day can penetrate as far as 50 km/30 miles inland and even there modify the heat of the day. Precipitation on the coast decreases as one goes south; the maximum rainfall is in October with a second rainy period in May; the lowest precipitation is in July and August. In winter the north is influenced by a cold and dry north-east wind called the Tramontana.

Water temperatures

The surface water temperature of the sea in April is 14–15 °C/57–59 °F, in May about 17 °C/62 °F, in June 20 °C/68 °F, in July and August 23–25 °C/73–77 °F, in September 23–24 °C/73–75 °F and in October 21 °C/70 °F.

Catalan wind rose

Plants and Animals

Plants

The southern flank of the Pyrenees which was thickly forested until comparatively recent times, has been biologically impoverished by clearances and felling. Most of the area is covered with scanty shrubs (gorse, thyme, rosemary, lavender) as well as stone- and cork-oaks. As a result of the intense summer heat and consequently frequent extensive fires (which because of the relatively low density of population can scarcely be effectively controlled), a thick and intensive vegetation is scarcely to be expected. In the higher areas in the interior there are extensive cattle pastures. The commonest cultivated crops are olives, figs, currant and almond trees, vines, cereals and potatoes. The absence of vegetation has, in extensive areas, led to visible and continuing erosion of the land, for example on the Montserrat. The Sierra de Montseny is more extensively afforested.

On the north side of the Pyrenees vegetation is considerably more luxurious and varied. Here oaks, beech and chestnut trees flourish. In the area of the coast can be found palms, agaves with their characteristic bunches of leaves and fruit, as well as the ubiquitous cactus fig (opuntia) which was introduced from the tropics and from the New World. Cultivation of vines on a large scale is carried on in the area of Barcelona and further south. On the French side the wines of the Banyuls region have an excellent reputation.

Bougainvillea . . .

. . . and cactus fig

Animals

Side by side with the clearance of the forest went the impoverishment of the fauna, since the traditional habitat was extensively destroyed. Thus today there are few animal species. They correspond in large measure to those in the rest of the Mediterranean area and in Central Europe. On the higher slopes chamois, ibex and occasionally bears can be seen; there are foxes, linxes, wild cats, wild boar, birds of prey (including several species of eagle), owls and, in wet areas, water fowl, wading birds and marsh birds (cranes, herons, flamingos, great crested grebes, various species of duck and geese). There are also reptiles (snakes, lizards) and insects.
The large variety of Mediterranean fish and aquatic mammals is also in decline. Encounters with large spined perch or cephalopods, which were common when diving was in its infancy in the 1950s, now seldom occur. The reasons are increasing pollution of the water by poisons from the environment and unrestricted subaqua fishing. Fortunately underwater fishing using breathing apparatus is now forbidden.

Population

The population of Catalonia is about 5,660,000, corresponding to approximately 15% of the entire population of Spain. Like the Spanish, the Catalans are almost without exception members of the Roman Catholic Church. The largest conurbation of the region and at the same time the second largest in the whole country is Barcelona; the province of the same name reaches a density of population of 594 per sq. km/228 per sq. mile which is also the second highest figure in the country.

In type and nature the Catalan differs considerably from the Castilian. He is considered to be realistic, pragmatic, honest, lively and industrious; nevertheless, his individualism borders on stubbornness. The industry and drive of the Catalan can be ascribed to the fact that Catalonia is the most forward-looking and economically leading area of Spain and also one of the densest populated regions. The Catalan is thoroughly convinced of this special status; if asked for his nationality he will first state that he is a Catalan and secondly a Spaniard. This feeling of being different certainly leads to a tendency towards political separation which is not necessarily the fault of the Catalans themselves. It can be observed that workers who come to this highly developed region from other parts of the country find that Catalan is the idiomatic language used by people concerned with the economy and so these incomers prefer to remain apart as a Castilian speaking and less privileged group.

Language and Literature

Official languages

As in the rest of Spain Castilian (Castellano) is the first language of administration and business in Catalonia. In addition, since 1975, Catalan (Català) has been recognised as a second official language in business and education; it is daily growing in importance and has largely overtaken Castilian, the Spanish literary language, in everyday use.

North of the Pyrenees border, in parts of the French region of Languedoc-Roussillon, the Catalan language is used but here it has not yet obtained an official status.

Catalan

Catalan is an independent romance language which shows considerable difference from Castilian and reveals a large influence of Provençal in its vocabulary. In contrast to Castilian Catalan does not turn the main Latin vowel into a diphthong (Latin: portus; Castilian: puerto; Catalan: port; Latin: bonus; Castilian: bueno; Catalan: bo); final vowels disappear (Castilian: dulce; Catalan: dulc; Castilian: muerte; Catalan: mort). As well as the Spanish verbs ending in -ar, -er and -ir Catalan has a further conjugation ending in -re (prendre =, as in French, to take). As examples of the influence of Provençal on the vocabulary can be given words such as "table" (Castilian: mesa; Catalan: taula), "cereal" (Castilian: trigo; Catalan: blat) or "window" (Castilian: ventana, Catalan: finestra).

Pronunciation of Catalan

As in Portugese unstressed a and e are almost swallowed, unstressed o is like a short u. The Castilian j, which is pronounced like the ch in the Scottish word "loch" before an a, o and u, as well as a g before e and i, are both pronounced in Catalan like j in the French word "journal". Ll, which in Castilian is pronounced like lli in "million", in

Catalan it is almost like the y in "yacht". Where double-l is to be pronounced as two separate l's, it is often divided by a hyphen (example: sil-labe = syllable). The Spanish letter ñ, which is pronounced something like the ni in onion, is replaced by ny, otherwise y is not used and the sound is always written as an i. Ch is always pronounced like a k and in recent times it is often written simply as c. Letter x is almost always pronounced as if it were sh. The Castilian sound ch (as in church) is often replaced by tx and at the end of a word by ig. Z and c before e and i are not lisped as in Castilian but pronounced like a voiced s and, in contrast to Castilian, there is a double-s (massa) in Catalan. Rules for stress correspond to those in Spanish, although in the ending ia where the i is stressed no accent is used (Castilian: María; Catalan: Maria). The grave (è) or acute (é) accents are used according to pronunciation of the vowel; a grave accent is always used on an à, an acute always on ú and í; on e and o an open vowel has a grave accent (cafè, arròs) and a closed vowel an acute (consomé, fórmula).

Catalan Literature

The first known examples of Catalan literature date from the 12th c. Historical works and chronicals play a large part; translations from classical antiquity and from scientific works of the Moorish culture are common. On the other hand the belles-lettres genre is not very prominent.
The courtly troubadour poetry of Provençe had great influence on Catalan authors who lived in the 12th and 13th c. and it was at this time that many Provençal words and expressions found their way into Catalan. A leading figure of the Catalan language and culture is Ramón Llull (latinised: Raimundus Lullus; 1235–1316) who was born in Mallorca. He was a man of extensive education; under his influence Catalan had a great impetus as a cultural language, a status which until today it has not been able to maintain. Lullus wrote his important tracts and poems for the entire western world in Latin and Arabic and also in the idiom of his homeland and thus his works were not confined to an elite of educated people but were also capable of being understood by those who spoke the ordinary language of the people, that is Catalan. This idiom was so moulded and formed to a lasting degree by Lullus that a Catalan can read his writings today without difficulty. Lullus' work "Libre de Cavalleria", on the theme of the chivalrous life-style, was taken up by Joanot Martorell who brought the Catalan novel of chivalry to perfection ("Tirant lo Blanch", *c.* 1455).
From the 15th c. the orientation of the Pyrenees peninsula became directed strongly towards Castile and the Castilian language (even today standard Spanish is called Castellano). Thus the Catalan language suffered a similar fate to Provençal which was swamped by northern French. Catalan has much in common with Provençal and although it kept its importance as a spoken language, in the fields of writing and especially in literature it was superseded by Castilian. From 1714 its use was even officially forbidden by the king. This effectively prevented the spread of original Catalan literature and a fresh start was possible only with the emergence in the Romantic period of "Renaixença" ("born again"), i.e. a looking back to its former significance. Catalan found its way into intellectual and literary circles,

received support from sponsors and became an object of ongoing philological and linguistic research. The linguist Maria Anguiló (1825–97) wrote the first "Lexicon of Classical Catalan" and Tomás Forteza (1838–89) published a "Gramática Catalana". Nineteenth century literature is chiefly devoted to subjects taken from bourgeois circles. Of note are Jacint Verdaguer i Santaló (1845–1902), an important writer of epics, who is thought much of today, Emili Vilanova (1840–1905), humorist and comic author, and Pere Corominas (1870–1939; pseudonym Enrique Mercader), who was a political and philosophical writer as well as a freedom fighter in the Spanish Civil War.
As a result of the regionalisation in Spain and of the clashes characterised by separatist movements of the late 1970s, Catalan which had been allowed as an official language from 1975 received a new impetus. Today there are books, magazines and newspapers in Catalan. The third television programme broadcasts a considerable part of its programmes in the Catalan language. Street and place-name signs have been exchanged and every bookshop sells Català-Castellano dictionaries. The number of examples of this renaissance is endless. However, it is not necessary for visitors to Catalonia to learn Català if they have a knowledge of Spanish. Every Catalan on the mainland is bilingual. As far as the older generation is concerned this is a relic of the time of the Franco dictatorship and the compulsion to use Castilian, but in centres of tourism knowledge of foreign languages at least at information offices, travel agents, hotels, restaurants and the larger shops is usual.

Trade and Industry

Agriculture

The basic economic conditions of Catalonia are not so good as might be expected when compared with the high standard of living. Only a small part of the area is useful for agriculture, in particular the Empordá (Ampurdán) plain, where grapes both for the table and for wine, as well as olives, cereals and potatoes thrive.
The rearing of livestock (cattle, sheep) to any great extent is principally confined to the Pyrenees. With a workforce of only 6.4% of the total, Catalonian agriculture is well below the EEC average of 8.2%.

Fishing

Fishing in the Mediterranean is still important, although the amount and quality of edible fish has been restricted in many places owing to increasing pollution of the water by harmful substances and by over-fishing (especially underwater fishing which was uncontrolled for years and widely practised). Today only 0.4% of all employees are active as professional fishermen.

Minerals

Industry

The region has few minerals. Supplies of coal and ore are very small. The only large deposits are of potash (calcium carbonate; used in the production of glass and soap). Thus a many-sided finishing and improvement industry has developed using imported raw materials. Notable are paper fabrication, metalwork (engine and vehicle building; growth industries), textiles (cotton in Barcelona, wool in

Sabadell and Tarrasa, although their importance has recently declined), leather and cork working (a high export potential). Barcelona is the centre of the Spanish printing industry (28% of the total revenue). The town of La Bisbal, north of Girona, has a great deal of ceramic industry (both artistic and technical ceramics). The industry of Catalonia accounts for 25% of the total industrial production of Spain and the largest firms are situated in the conurbation of Barcelona.

Energy

The reservoirs and dams on the rivers coming from the Pyrenees play a great part in the production of energy.

Tourism

The Mediterranean coasts of Catalonia are one of the oldest areas of post-war tourism in Europe. The infrastructure is correspondingly well developed; there are hotels of all categories and at all price levels as well as many leisure establishments and service undertakings, together with an unusually large number of camp sites. Provision for transport (air, road and rail) is excellent. In 1986 a total of 14.3 million foreigners visited Catalonia (including those who were in transit to other Spanish regions). About 90% of visitors come by car. The most important airport of the region (and also the second most important in the country) is the airport of Barcelona; Girona is principally used by charter aircraft. The greatest number of foreign visitors (43%) are from France; then come Germans, Italians, British and Dutch. Although the summer was once the favourite period for holidays it has been noticed recently that an extension of the season into spring and autumn is growing.
Tourism accounts for some 15% of the total gross income of Catalonia; almost a quarter of all Spanish income in this sector is received in this region.

Road traffic

The backbone of road traffic is the motorway/highway (subject to toll) which runs parallel to but a little way inland from the coast between Salses (on the northern edge of the large map) and Barcelona, crossing the French/Spanish frontier at Le Perthus – La Jonquera/La Junquera. It gives access to the large towns of Perpignan, Figueres/Figueras and Girona/Gerona. From the various exits there are many lateral roads to the coast which is never farther away than 35 km/22 miles in a straight line.
A better prospect for the motorist is to use the national roads near the coast. In the area of the Costa Brava these are usually very winding and hilly. On the Costa Daurada/Costa Dorada the national road runs almost in a straight line right by the sea and parallel to the railway, a fact which unfortunately hinders access to the beaches.

Rail traffic

A main line railway links the Spanish border town of Portbou with Barcelona. A short way south of Girona the line divides; the western branch follows the valley of the Tordera up towards Granollers, while the eastern branch heads for the mouth of the River Tordera reaching the Mediterranean near Malgrat and from then following the coast.

Air traffic

The most important airport in Catalonia is Barcelona with an annual turnover of some 5.5 million passengers. There

are direct services from all the major cities of Europe and also from overseas; all destinations within Spain can be reached from Barcelona by air.
Girona/Costa Brava with about 500,000 passengers a year, is an airport with more regional importance and is used from abroad principally by charter flights. The Spanish national airline Iberia flies on most of the international routes and shares the inland services with the smaller airline Aviaco.

Shipping

Catalonia has four large ports: Barcelona, Palamós, Sant Feliu de Guíxols and Tarragona (although the last named lies outside the area described in this guide). The volume of freight in 1985 was about 7.8 million tonnes; Barcelona has one of the largest container terminals in the Mediterranean as well as storage warehouse and loading facilities for oil, liquid gas, bulk goods, textile products, etc.

Barcelona: a Gaudi creation in the Parc Güell ▶

Famous People

Pau (Pablo) Casals
(29.12.1876–22.10.1973)

Pau (Spanish: Pablo) Casals was born in the Catalonia province of Tarragona. From 1919 he led his own orchestra in Barcelona and with the French pianist Alfred Cortot (1877–1962) and the violinist Jacques Thibaud (1880–1953) he formed a trio from time to time. After the outbreak of the Spanish Civil War Casals emigrated in 1937 to France, without, however, entirely turning his back on his Catalan homeland. His place of exile was the little town of Prades in the valley of the Têt only about 25 km/15 miles north of the Spanish/French frontier and he remained here continuously from 1950 to 1956. He founded the festival which still takes place annually in the nearby monastery of Saint-Michel-de-Cuxa. From 1956 Casals lived in Puerto Rico in the Antilles where he also founded a music festival, a symphony orchestra and the conservatoire.
Pau Casals is one of the most important cellists of his time. Concert tours took him to all parts of the world. He was instrumental in reviving the solo works of Johann Sebastian Bach; at the same time he appeared as a conductor and was a composer principally of sacred music.

Salvador Dali
(b. 11.5.1904)

Born in Figueres (Spanish: Figueras), Salvador Dali is one of the most productive and versatile but also one of the most enigmatic artistic personalities of our time. He was a student of the Academy of Art in Madrid at the early age of 17. On tours of Italy he studied closely Renaissance and Baroque art. Echoes of mannerism are often to be found in his work. Between 1929 and 1935 he belonged to the group of Surrealists which was formed in Paris and which had its basis in the literature of the time. At the end of the 1940s Dali lived almost exclusively in the little coastal town of Port Lligat north of Cadaqués but, after the death of his wife Helena (née Diakonoff; known as "Gala") in 1982, he avoided this home. King Juan Carlos granted him, in the same year, the title of Marqués de Dali de Pubol (the artist had an estate in the village of Pubol north-east of Girona).
Salvador Dali's considerable output includes paintings, drawings, sculptures, collages and ensembles of surprisingly imaginative quality. He is outstanding by reason of his virtuoso mastering of differing techniques and in a positive sense by an irreverent approach to themes and motifs. His paintings, notable mostly for a minute and meticulous attention to the representation of detail, are compositions which often appear to have their origin in a tormented world of dreams and hallucinations. The artist left the greater part of his works to his home town of Figueres and there they form the basis of the world-famous Dali Museum.

Antoni (Antonio) Gaudi
(25.6.1852–10.6.1926)

Antoni (Spanish: Antonio) Gaudi, born in Reus (Tarragona province) is far and away the most famous Spanish architect of the recent past. He received his technical education in the College of Architecture in Barcelona and that at a time when historicism and especially neo-Gothic was the quintessence of all architecture in that part of Europe. Gaudi felt himself strongly attracted towards Gothic, even though he was critical of many of its technical details, such as the use of buttresses which he wanted to see replaced by a principle of sloping supports. His ideal was the revival of a light colourful Mediterranean Gothic, and elements of the Gothic form are those which stand out in many of his works. By the use of historic patterns and interwoven floral forms of art nouveau his creative achievement was to produce a new style which can be classed as Spanish "modernismo", which is also a literary movement. The principal works of Antoni Gaudi are to be found in Barcelona, the capital of Catalonia. Here he built dwellings (Casa Milá, Casa Batiló) and churches which reveal on the one hand Gothic forms and on the other a striking similarity with the architectural designs of Rudolf Steiner. Gaudi received a great deal of support from Count Eusebi Güell, who had a house built for him on the south-western outskirts of the old town of Barcelona (Palau Güell). The best known of Gaudi's architectural works is the Templo de la Sagrada Familia in the north of the Catalonian capital. The architect devoted to this building by far the greater part of his working life yet even today this huge "Church of the Poor", as its builder called it, remains incomplete.

Christopher Columbus
(Spanish: Cristóbal Colón,
Italian: Cristofora
Colombo;
1451–20.5.1506)

For a long time several Mediterranean towns competed for the honour of being the birthplace of the discoverer of America; more recent research makes it appear certain that he was born in Genoa. No one can be sure of the exact date of birth of Christopher Columbus; it was between 25 August and 31 October 1451. From an early age he was concerned with seafaring and maritime trade and in 1476 came to the Portuguese capital and port of Lisbon. Here he investigated the possibility of following to India the route which had been suggested since ancient times, but had found little encouragement from the royal household. So with the intention of going to France, he crossed Spanish territory and in the Monastery of La Rábida received from the confessor of the Spanish Queen Isabella a letter of recommendation. She concluded an agreement with him which had as its object the planned voyage and gave him the rank of a high admiral and viceroy of the territories he discovered together with one tenth of the expected booty. On 3 August 1492 the fleet consisting of the caravels "Santa Maria", "Pinta" and "Niña" left the port of Palos de la Frontera on the southern Atlantic coast of Spain and steered westwards with the expected aim of arriving in India. For three weeks the sailors saw only sky and water and hope for landfall became smaller and smaller. Unrest became noticeable among the crew but after Columbus had altered course to the south-west an island came into view which Columbus, who was the first discoverer to land on it, called San Salvador (in all probability it was Watling Island in the Bermuda group). On the same voyage Columbus reached Cuba and Haiti where he left behind a group of 39 volunteers. Then he returned to Spain in order to bring the news of his success personally to the king and queen. Three other voyages followed, without bringing the discoverer any great moral or material advantages in Spain, where people were disappointed by the fact that it was not the fabulous rich India at the end of the route but, as they said, uncultivated rough land inhabited only by poor wild people and this promised no economic advantages. In addition the discontented participants on his voyages of discovery saw fit to denounce their commander and create for him an unfavourable atmosphere. This became so bad that during his third voyage to Hispaniola (Haiti) he was taken prisoner and brought back to Spain; however, he defended himself successfully before the king and queen and was rehabilitated. However, lasting success was denied to him. Even the New World which was discovered by Columbus was not named after him but after one of his less important contemporaries, the Italian Amerigo Vespucci.

Aristide Maillol
(8.12.1861–27.9.1944)

Aristide Maillol came into the world only a few kilometres north of the French/Spanish frontier at Banyuls-sur-Mer. He began his career as a painter; first as a pupil of the aristocratic conventional Alexandre Cabanel. Under the influence of French post-impressionism (especially by Paul Gauguin) he developed a flat linear style of painting which was translated into other representative media (for example wall hangings). Only when he was forty did he turn to sculpture, the art form which was to make him famous. In this field he was self-taught. The characteristic skill of Rodin, who was then the master of all sculpture, left him almost unimpressed. Maillol turned to models of classical antiquity without, however, slipping into historicism. He worked chiefly in bronze and stone and among his works were nude figures of monumental simplicity. A good part of modern sculpture is based on Maillol's stylistic principles. In his later years the artist lived on a little estate near his birthplace on the Côte Vermeille and here he is buried.

Joan Miró
(20.4.1893–25.12.1983)

Joan Miró, born in Montroig near Barcelona, received his earliest artistic impetus from the French realists and especially from the newly arrived Cubism. He learned about this in Paris to which he paid his first visit in 1919. A little later he was one of the signatories to the surrealist manifesto, and in 1923 he turned aside completely from traditional painting and also from his former efforts in cubism in order to develop his own characteristic style. In Miró's paintings powerful, often curiously graphic and symbolic lines with intensive colours are added to compositions in which the abstract is completely lacking and which suggest many sided objective associations. The artist was also continuously occupied with graphic techniques and with ceramics and sculpture. Miró lived mostly in Paris until 1940, but when German troops entered the French capital in that year he sought refuge again in Spain. In 1944 Paris was freed by Allied forces and Miró returned to France. After the end of the war he moved to the island of Mallorca where he died on Christmas Eve 1983.

Hyacinthe Rigaud
(Hyacinthe Rigau y Ros;
(18.7.1659–29.12.1743)

Born in Perpignan Hyacinthe Rigau y Ros, known as Rigaud, was the most important portrait painter in the time of high Baroque. In 1680 he moved to Paris where his portraiture, at first still influenced by Dutch painters, was highly esteemed. He was soon head of the flourishing undertaking in which a great number of fellow workers finished the paintings which were conceived by him. He knew how to take into account the prevailing taste and demands of the aristocracy by an ambience of splendour and by distancing

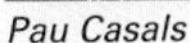

Pau Casals

Antoni Gaudi

Charlie Rivel

the subject with allegorical features. His portrait dating from 1701 of Louis XIV, the legendary "Sun King", is famous.

Charlie Rivel
(José Andrea Rivel; 28.4.1896–26.7.1983)

Charlie Rivel, born in Cubellas near Barcelona, delighted visitors to the circus throughout his life. The descendent of a Spanish family of artistes, he was one of the "quiet" clowns whose humour was never coarse and who awakened in his audience a slight feeling of sadness and pity, when faced with the deeply tragic and malicious way in which things can behave. This makes the clown appear very human – all too human – in his misfortunes. Charlie Rivel, whose trademark was an almost cubic red nose and a very long pullover which covered the whole of his body, was well aware how to make his public understand him without using any words; the onomatopoeic sounds with which he accompanied his appearances were a means of expression of which he was an absolute master.

Antoni (Antonio) Tàpies
(b. 13.12.1923)

Antoni Tàpies born in Barcelona, is one of the most important artists of the modern school. His first works were strongly stamped by the representatives of surrealism, especially of Joan Miró with whom he had a close relationship. At the beginning of the 1950s Tàpies learned in Paris the new style of tachismus (from the French tache = spot, spot of colour). This was a variation of the informal art style which moves from surrealism into total abstraction. His subjects – he worked frequently with coloured mortar, ceramics and such like materials – more plastic than artistic, draw their life from a very unusual symbol and sign language. Tàpies is also notable as a graphic artist and illustrator.

History

At the beginning of recorded history the Iberians are settled on the east coast of Spain; in the opinion of some researchers these are the ancestors of the Basques and probably related to the Berbers of North Africa. In the 6th c. B.C. the Celts arrive from the other side of the Pyrenees and in course of time mingle with the Iberians to become the Celtiberians. Their chief settlement is situated in the north-east of the Spanish uplands.

700 B.C. onwards — A number of ports on the east coast of Spain, including Emporion (now Empúries/Ampurias), are settled by Greek colonists mainly Ionians from the Phocaean colony of Massalia (Marseilles).

600 onwards — The Cathaginians begin to drive out the Greeks.

236–203 — After the First Punic War the Carthaginians extend their colonial power to the north as far as the Ebro; the area of present-day Catalonia remains in the zone of influence of the Roman Empire.

201 — Under a peace treaty with Rome Carthage gives up its Spanish possessions. A little later (197 B.C.) Rome founds the provinces of Hispania Citerior with its capital Tarraco (Tarragona) and Hispania Ulterior (in the area of modern Andalusia). The complete subjection of the peninsula, however, is hampered by the uprising of the Celtiberians (143–133 B.C.). Nevertheless the Romanisation both from the points of language and civilisation makes progress.

82–72 — The Roman praetor Sertorius, a supporter of Marius, tries to establish an independent Celtiberian state.

27 — Spain is divided into the provinces of Hispania Terraconensis (in the north-east around the present town of Tarragona), Hispania Lusitania (in the west, between the Duero and the Guardiana) and Hispania Baetica (originally Hispania Ulterior).

19 — The entire Iberian peninsula is fully incorporated into the Roman Empire by the Emperor Augustus.

A.D. 100 onwards — Beginning of the Christianisation of the Iberian peninsula.

414 — The Visigoths (West Goths) led by King Athaulf advance into Catalonia (Gotalonia).

466–84 — King Eurich, ruler of the Visigoth kingdom of Tolosa, defeats the Suevi and establishes Visigothic rule throughout Spain (except the north-west).

587 — The conversion of the Arian Visigoths to orthodox Catholicism is followed by their rapid amalgamation with the Romanised population.

714 onwards — Spain (with the exception of the upland regions of Asturias,

Galicia and the Basque country) is a province of the Umayyad Caliphate of Damascus.

756 — The Umayyad having been driven from Gaul by Charles Martell flees to Spain and founds the Emirate of Córdoba which extends over the whole of the peninsula. A period of great economic prosperity and cultural achievement begins.

After 778 — The territories conquered by Charlemagne in Spain develop into the provinces of Catalonia (with its capital Barcelona) and Navarra.

985 — Almansor ("the Victorious"), the grand vizier of Caliph Hisham II, conquers Barcelona. The farthest expansion of Moorish military power in Spain.

1130 — Alfonso VII of Castile becomes Emperor and gains the domination of the whole of the Christian state of Spain yet his kingdom disintegrates through division of the inheritance.

1137 — Catalonia is united with Aragón.

1212 — In the battle of Las Nava de Tolosa the combined armies of Castile, Aragón and Navarra inflict a decisive victory over the Almohad caliph.

1307 onwards — The Cortes (the representive bodies of the clergy, the secular noblity and the cities) of Aragón, Catalonia and Valencia) meet together.

1469 — The marriage of Ferdinand II of Aragón and Isabella of Castile leads to the union of the two previously rival kingdoms. Under the rule of the Reyes Católicos ("catholics monarchs") the transition to an absolute monarchy takes place.

1492 — The conquest of Granada ends the Reconquista (recovery by the Christian kingdoms of the Iberian peninsula). Isabella supports the plans of Christopher Columbus whose voyages of exploration and discovery make possible the establishment of the Spanish colonial empire in America.

1516 — Charles I, a Habsburg, becomes king of Castile and Aragon. After the death of his grandfather Maximilian I he inherits the Habsburg territories and becomes in 1519 Holy Roman Emperor as Charles V (coronation in Rome in 1530). He is now ruler of Spain, the Netherlands, Sardinia, Naples, Sicily, Milan, Franche-Comté and numerous American colonies.

1556 — After the abdication of Charles V, his son, Philip II, assumes power and takes over the leadership of the Counter-Reformation in Europe and with the help of the Inquisition he fights heresy in Spain.

1571 — In the naval battle of Lepanto (Greek: Naupaktos), a port at the entrance to the Gulf of Corinth, the Turkish fleet is annihilated by Spanish warships, helped by Venice and the Holy See. The commander of the Spanish forces is Don

	Juan of Austria, a half brother of Philip II. The naval victory assures Spanish domination in the Mediterranean.
1640	The Catalan states rebel against the crown; the revolt is not suppressed until 1652.
1659	Under the Peace of the Pyrenees the war with France which has lasted since 1635 is ended. In the treaty Spain gives up territory including Roussillon and the Cerdagne to France. Thus the Catalan cultural sphere which extends on both sides of the Pyrenees is divided.
1701–13	In the War of the Spanish Succession the Bourbon claimant, Philip of Anjou, a grandson of Louis XIV, fights for recognition against the Austrian Habsburgs, Great Britain and the Netherlands.
1714	Philip V removes all the privileges which until now the Catalans have possessed. The Catalan language is excluded from official use.
1788–1808	Under the influence of his favourite Manuel de Godoy, Charles IV leads Spain into total dependence on Napoleon I. After Godoy has been overthrown by an uprising in Aranjuez (near Madrid) Napoleon compels both Charles IV and Ferdinand VII to abdicate and establishes his brother Joseph Bonaparte as regent. A revolt by the people of Madrid against the French forces marks the beginning of a Spanish national rising. However, in his Spanish campaign Napoleon occupies the capital of Madrid and thus makes possible the return to the Spanish throne of Joseph who in the previous year fled in the face of Spanish resistance. The following rule remains until Wellington's victory over the French at Vitoria in 1813.
1814	Ferdinand VII returns to the throne, rejects the liberal constitution of 1812 and rules as an absolute monarch.
1834	Introduction of a moderately liberal constitution.
1834–39	First Carlist War. Don Carlos, Ferdinand VII's brother, declares himself king (Charles V) in opposition to the regency of the Queen Mother, Maria Cristina of Naples, during the minority of Isabella II. He is supported by the Basque provinces as well as Aragon and Catalonia, but the enterprise fails and in 1839 he is forced to flee to France.
1847–49	The Second Carlist War and republican risings aggravate internal conflicts.
1872–76	The Third Carlist War initiated by Don Carlos's grandson against King Amadeo I, a son of Victor Emanuel II of Italy, and against the First Republic set up in 1873 by the Cortes. At the same time socialist uprisings occur.
1890 onwards	Autonomist movements in Catalonia, Galicia and the Basque country.
1906	The first Congress of the Catalan Language takes place in Barcelona. One of its aims is the standardisation of Catalan

which has been used from the 17th and 18th c. only as an oral means of communication.

Tho founding of the Institut d'Estudis Catalans (Institute of Catalan Studies) is an indication of the growing importance of the Catalan language which is increasingly becoming more accepted in official places. — 1907

Workers' uprising in Barcelona. — 1909

Spain remains neutral in the First World War. — 1914–18

General Primo de Rivera establishes a military dictatorship with Alfonso XII's approval. Dissolution of the Cortes. — 1923

After a Republican victory in the local government elections Alfonso XIII leaves the country. Beginning of the Second Republic. The Liberal and Progressive constitution envisages among other things a regional autonomy for Catalonia (this is put into effect in 1932). The Catalan language is approved for official and educational use; an increasing number of newspapers, books, etc., appear in Catalan. — 1931

Election victory for CEDA (Confederation of the Autonomous Party of the Right). During the next three years there is a succession of government crises and serious disturbances which lead to the dissolution of Parliament. — 1933

The Spanish Civil War breaks out, following the murder of the monarchist Member of Parliament Calvo Sotelo and the military rising by General Francisco Franco y Bahamonde in Spanish Morocco. With other generals he forms an alternative government in Burgos. — 1936–39

The Franco dictatorship annuls the autonomy granted to Catalonia in 1932. — 1939

In spite of its links with the Berlin–Rome axis, Spain remains neutral during the Second World War. — 1939–45

A national referendum approves Franco's plan to restore the monarchy at a later date. — 1947

Spain enjoys a considerable economic upturn thanks to mass tourism.
The Costa Brava is one of the first areas to be developed. — From 1960

In the monastery on Montserrat the first ecclesiastical monthly magazine in Catalan since 1939 is published. — 1966

Strikes in Catalonia. — 1972–73

On Franco's death Prince Juan Carlos becomes King of Spain as Juan Carlos I. Catalan, Basque and Galician are recognised as teaching and official languages. — 1975

After a plebiscite a new constitution comes into force; Spain becomes a constitutional monarchy. — 1978

In a referendum the Catalans decide on far-reaching self- — 1979 government for their region. In November the Spanish Lower House grants by a majority a Statute of Autonomy for Catalonia.

1980 — A regional parliament is elected in Catalonia. Other Spanish regions seek a statute of autonomy.

1986 — Spain becomes a member of the European Community. In the eastern Pyrenees and on Montserrat a large part of the vegetation is destroyed by heath and forest fires.

1987 — On 19 June the militant Basque separatist organisation ETA causes an explosion in a large store in Barcelona; 15 people are killed and many injured.

Suggested Tour

Time-table

The visitor who wishes to follow the route described here (with all the detours it totals approximately 1100 km/ 685 miles from and to Salses, situated to the north of Perpignan – on the upper edge of the enclosed touring map) and who also wishes to have enough time for the major sights, should count on spending about four weeks including getting to the area by using the convenient and speedy motorways. The Catalonian capital of Barcelona on its own needs a stay of about a week if all its numerous attractions are to be seen.
It is recommended that the route is followed in the order given, since by driving along the Costa Daurada and the Costa Brava in a northerly direction the sun is at your back and the best light is on the coast.

Note

Places which have a main heading in the A to Z section appear here in **bold type**. In the routes described only the Catalan place names are given; the Spanish (Castilian) form can be found in the A to Z section under the appropriate text. An alphabetical list of Spanish place names with the corresponding Catalan forms can be found on page 214.
All the places mentioned here, whether they are under a main heading or are places in the vicinity of the chief resort, can be found in the index on page 221.
The visitor who prefers not to follow the complete route but to choose a base will find in the Practical Information Section an alphabetical list of main resorts with suggested excursions in the immediate surroundings.

Getting to Catalonia by car

Whichever route is taken from northern France it is advisable to make for Dijon and then to follow the motorway (Autoroute du Soleil) through the Rhône valley to Valence. Continue to Orange where the Autoroute Languedocienne or Autoroute Catalan branches off in a south-westerly direction; then via Nîmes, Montpellier, Béziers and Narbonne to the exit for Leucate, where the motorway is left. Now the visitor should take the national road RN9 which runs parallel with it towards the south along the west bank of the Etang de Leucate to **Salses**.
From Salses we drive to **Perpignan** the capital of Catalan France, and continue in a southerly direction through the estuarial plain of the Têt at the foot of the Pyrenees. Ascending the valley of the Têt we reach **Céret** and **Amélie-les-Bains** before crossing the Col d'Ares/Collado de Ares into Spain. Then via **Camprodón** and **Sant Joan de les Abadesses** to **Ripoll** where the Romanesque façade of the church is famous.
We now follow the valley of the Riu Ter as far as **Vic** where the episcopal museum and the cathedral should be visited. At Tona we turn south-east and traverse the upland countryside of the **Montseny** before driving parallel to the motorway to **Granollers** via **Caldes de Montbui** and on to **Barcelona** the capital of the province of the same name and also of the whole of Catalonia.
From Barcelona a day's excursion to **Montserrat** with its famous monastery and its curious rocky landscape is

Sant Pol de Mar: bathing beach

strongly recommended and the visitor with enough time can, on the outward or the return journey, make a detour via **Sant Cugat** with its pretty Romanesque-Gothic church and reach the capital again via the Tibidabo.

The next stretch of the route runs mainly along the Spanish Mediterranean coast towards the east. Detours will take in interesting parts of the interior. In the area of the principally flat and sandy **Costa Daurada** we pass the industrial town of **Badalona** and the resorts of **Mataró, Arenys de Mar, Sant Pol de Mar, Calella de las Costa** and **Malgrat**; a short way inland is the picturesque village of **Tordera**.

On the far side of the Riu Tordera, the estuary of which forms the boundary between the provinces of Barcelona and Girona between the Costa Daurada and the rocky, romantic **Costa Brava**, lies **Blanes** which has a fine botanical garden. Then come the very popular **Lloret de Mar**, **Tossa de Mar**, known because of its elevated walled old town, and finally **Sant Feliu de Guíxols** with its Romanesque church.

A detour now takes us inland to **Caldes de Malavella**, with the remains of Roman baths and a spa establishment as well as to **Santa Coloma de Farners** which is also popular as a spa. The provincial capital of Girona with its great cathedral is well worth visiting. To the east, in the area of the estuary of the Riu Ter, lies the old Iberian settlement at **Ullastret** and the pottery town of **La Bisbal**. Near **Palafrugell** and **Begur** the coast has many beautiful bays; farther on is the ancient little market town of **Pals** and – again by the river – the town of **Torroella de Montgrí** at the foot of a hill crowned with a castle. Not far from here can be found the

resort of **L'Estartit** with its off-shore island Islas Medas and the archaeological site of **Empúries**.
We now turn farther inland and reach **Banyoles** with its beautiful lake of the same name and then the well-preserved village of **Besalú** and finally passing **Castellfollit de la Roca** magnificently situated on a rocky headland, we arrive at the town of **Olot** in an old volcanic zone.
Now we return through Besalú to **Figueres**, the birthplace of the surrealistic painter Salvador Dali to whom a highly original museum is dedicated. Nearby lies **Peralada** with an old castle and a casino. A detour leads to the village of **La Jonquera** near the frontier.
To the east of Figueres near **Castello d'Empúries** with its Romanesque-Gothic church, the modern "lagoon town" of **Empúria Brava** has been established. A little way inland from the Golf de Roses we reach **Roses**, a well-known resort with the remains of an old fort. The road now winds its way through the mountainous inland area of the peninsula to the white town of **Cadaqués** and then to **Port de la Selva** situated on a beautiful sandy bay. Not far south-west of here in the mountains stands the former abbey of **Sant Pere de Rodes**. We continue to the resort of **Llança** and go through **Portbou** the Spanish frontier town where the Costa Brava ends.
The **Côte Vermeille** which geologically forms the northern continuation of the Costa Brava has a similar landscape. **Elne** possesses a Romanesque church which is well-worth seeing and the tour we have described finally finishes at Perpignan.

Sights from A to Z

Note

Spanish places in this section are arranged alphabetically according to their Catalan names where these exist; in the headings the Catalan name is placed first followed by the high Spanish (Castilian) form. Thus for example the provincial capital, known previously as Gerona, will be found under the heading "Girona/Gerona".
The same principle is adopted when describing each place for the names of streets, squares, museums, etc., which generally can be found under their Catalan name; the Spanish name follows and is used in the text so that it is recognisable.
For some time tourists have been better acquainted with the high Spanish forms than the Catalan names which have only recently come into official use. In order to make it easier to find places an alphabetical list of Spanish place names with their corresponding Catalan forms can be found on page 214.

Aiguablava

See Begur/Bagur

Amélie-les-Bains D5

Country: France
Département: Pyrénées-Orientales
Altitude: 230 m/755 ft
Population: 4000

Location

Amélie-les-Bains is situated near the French-Spanish border in the valley of the Tech, about 35 km/22 miles SW of Perpignan.

The Town

The present resort of Amélie-les-Bains extends over the Tech which rises near the Franco-Spanish frontier pass at Col d'Ares/Collado de Ares. The town, which has a favourable climate, owes its name to Queen Amélie, the wife of the "Citizen-king" Louis Philippe (1830–48). The mineral springs are used as a remedy for diseases of the respiratory tracts and for rheumatism; in the modern pump room can be seen remains of a bathing establishment of Roman date. Near the town there is an open-air theatre.

Ceret

See entry

◀ *Cliffs on the Costa Brava*

Arles-sur-Tech

D4

Location
3 km/2 miles SW of Amélie-les-Bains

By following the valley of the Tech upstream from Amélie-les-Bains we reach the little town of Arles-sur-Tech above which rises the 1778 m/5835 ft high Puig de l'Estelle which can be seen to the right of the road. Iron ore is obtained on its southern flank and is transported to Arles-sur-Tech on a freight railway 2 km/1 mile long.

Former abbey

In the middle of the town stand the remains of an abbey, founded about 900 with a church which is intact. On the left of the main doorway can be seen two old sarcophagi (one dating from the 4th c. A.D.) and above them in the wall the epitaph of Guillaume Gaucelme dating from 1204. Notable in the arch over the doorway is Christ in a Mandorla surrounded by symbols of the four evangelists; above this is a little round arched window ornamented with arabesques. The interior of the church is rather dark, the side aisles are fairly wide and have large side chapels; on the contrary the nave is somewhat narrow and high and with a ceiling reminiscent of an upturned ship's keel which is an early transitional feature towards Gothic.
From the church door the late Romanesque/early Gothic cloister is reached through the side aisle of the monastic church.

Saint-Sauveur

Near the former abbey stands the little single-aisled church of Saint Sauveur (early Gothic) with its massive square

Gorges de la Fou

Crucifix in Prats-de-Mollo

tower; its interior is of little interest. The great Baroque altar was clearly designed on Spanish models.

*Gorges de la Fou

Continuing upstream for a little over 2 km/1 mile we come to the entrance to the Gorges de la Fou; they are situated a little way from the main road (signpost; fairly narrow minor road). The gorge which was only completely reconnoitred in 1926 is considered one of the narrowest of its type. In places it is less than a metre wide.
The part of the gorge which can be visited is 1.4 km/ ¾ mile long. It takes about an hour to walk it in both directions. At the entrance protective helmets are supplied; children should be constantly supervised and if possible led. Dogs are not allowed in the gorge.
The path leads along a narrow wooden walkway directly above the bed of the stream and between vertical rock walls 100 m/330 ft high. Noticeable are huge stone blocks wedged in the wall of the cliffs (at 390 m/426 yds and 790 m/864 yds) and two caves some 12–27 m/13–29 yds long at 800 and 1160 m/875 and 1270 yds. In these caves the remains of stalactites can be seen. At the end of the gorge the stream foams down in several cascades.

Prats-de-Mollo D3–4

Location
23 km/14 miles SW of Amélie-les-Bains

The little resort of Prats-de-Mollo, divided into a lower town (ville basse) and an upper town (ville haute) has a picturesque situation in the valley of the Tech and is dominated by

Prats-de-Mollo, an upland spa

the stately fortified church. The entire centre of the village is a pedestrian zone.
Administratively Prats-de-Mollo is united with the mineral spa of La Preste which lies 8 km/5 miles W at an altitude of 1130 m/3709 ft.

Lower town

This is entered through the Porte de France on the through road from where we follow the main road as far as a branch on the right where there is a flight of steps leading up to the church. At the upper end stands a cross with the symbols of the Passion of Christ (the sword of St Peter with the ear of Malchus which he had cut off; the nails of the cross; Judas's thirty pieces of silver, etc.
The church tower is a relic of the Romanesque building which was replaced early in the 17th c. by a Gothic church. The entrance is in the right-hand wall of the nave overlooking the valley; over the doorway, which has its original iron fittings, hangs a large whalebone as a votive offering. The interior (only open in the afternoon) has a Baroque altar depicting the lives of the saints Justus and Rufinus, the patronal saints of the little town.
Within the wall a battlemented walk leads round the apse of the church; on the mountain side a gate, once protected by a moat and a drawbridge, leads out of the ring of walls. From the hillside there is a particularly good panorama over the church buildings which resemble a battlemented fortress. Here can be seen Fort La Garde, built in the 17th c. (not open to the public).

Upper town

To the W on the far side of the stream which separates the two parts of Prats-de-Mollo lies the upper town. In the 12th c. the Dukes of Besalú were rulers here; in the centre stands the so-called "House of the Kings of Aragón".

Col d'Arès/Collado de Ares

Beyond Prats-de-Mollo the road winds its way uphill and affords magnificent views of the town and of the mountain scenery of the Pyrenees. After travelling 14 km/8 miles, for the most part through green pastures, we reach the Col d'Arès/Collado de Ares (summit 1513 m/4966 ft), the frontier crossing between France and Spain (formalities normally between 8 a.m. and 4 p.m.). To the S the road continues to Camprodón (see entry).

Ampuriabrava

See Empúria Brava

Ampurias

See Empúries

Arenys de Mar

J4

Country: Spain
Province: Barcelona
Altitude: sea level
Population: 10,000

Arenys de Mar: the fishing harbour

Location

Arenys de Mar is situated in the central section of the Costa Daurada (Spanish: Costa Dorada) about half way between Barcelona and the mouth of the Riu Tordera.

The Town

The main road leads through the centre of the town towards the beach. In summer cars may be parked in the dried-up river bed which traverses the town. Here a tour is sign-posted.

*Lace museum

Leaving the river bed parking place we walk S and in a few yards reach the Carrer de l'Eglesia, where in No 43, a fine building dating from 1772, is the Museu Marés de la Punta (lace museum; open Tues. and Thur. 6–8 p.m., Sat. 11 a.m.–1 p.m., Sun. 11 a.m.–2 p.m., entrance fee). Several storeys are devoted to a large collection of decorative materials, lace mantles, liturgical vestments, samples (so-called "pillow lace") and tools for handworking as well as cross stitch work including some more coarse traditional items.

Parish church

Following the road towards the sea we soon reach the Parish Church of Santa Maria. The present building was begun by the French in 1584 and completed in 1628. The main altar by Pau Costa, begun in 1704, is probably the most outstanding Baroque altar in Catalonia; it can be viewed daily from 11 a.m.–1 p.m. and from 5–7 p.m. Entrance is by a little doorway in the right-hand wall of the nave.

Casa Consistorial

From the church it is only a few steps to the lower end of the main street which with its shady plane trees and street cafés provides a picturesque sight. Here in the Plaza de la Vila, the main square of the old town centre of Arenys de Mar, stands the rectangular building of the Casa Consistorial with two wings; it houses the local administration offices and the library. On the façade of the left wing is a little fountain decorated with coloured tiles and above it on a plaque is a short summary of the history of the town.

Arenys de Mar, beach and harbour

The bathing beach is situated on the far side of the main road (underpass); dogs are prohibited. On the northern side of the town can be found the large marina and the equally interesting fishing harbour.

There are other beaches along the coastal road to the N, with a number of camp sites, hotels, bars and discotheques on both sides.

Caldes d'Estrac/Caldetas de Estrach

Location
3 km/2 miles SW of Arenys de Mar

The greater part of the pretty little residential town of Caldes d'Estrac (Spanish: Caldetas de Estrach) is situated on the sea side of the main road and the railway line. It has a long attractive promenade and a fairly clean beach of coarse sand divided up by artificial breakwaters. The thermal springs of the place reach a temperature of 41 °C/105 °F but there are no spa facilities.

Canet de Mar

Location
4 km/2½ miles NE of Arenys de Mar

Canet is also one of the popular resorts of the Costa Daurada (Spanish: Costa Dorada) because of its large sandy beach and its numerous hotels. The little town of 8000 inhabitants is cut off from the sea by the road and the railway line; it is centred around the bed of the river which has been concreted over and which in summer is generally dry. The church, dedicated to St Peter and St Paul (Sant Pere i Sant Pau), is Gothic; a short way inland stands the Castell Santa Florentina which was built as long ago as the 10th c.

Badalona

K2

Country: Spain
Province: Barcelona
Altitude: sea level
Population: 202,000

Location

Badalona to the N of Barcelona lies on the far side of the Riu Besós and has now become practically part of the capital.

The Town

The industrial town extends for some 5 km/3 miles along the flat coast where the water is polluted by flourishing factories. In the old town centre stands the Church of Santa Maria dating from the 17th c. (pictures of the Baroque painter Antoni Viladomat). Remains from Roman times can be found in the archaeological museum (Museu de Badalona; Plaça Assemblea de Catalunya 1).

Sant Jeroni de la Murta/San Jerónimo

Location
3 km/2 miles NW of Badalona

A pleasant excursion from Badalona is to Sant Jeroni de la Murta (Spanish: San Jerónimo) with a monastery dating from the 14th c. (15th c. cloister).

Montgat/Mongat

Location
3 km/2 miles NE of Badalona

In Montgat (Spanish: Mongat) stands a castle which was important in the Wars of Liberation against Napoleon (1788–1808).

Banyoles/Bañolas F5

Country: Spain
Province: Girona
Altitude: 172 m/565 ft
Population: 11,000

Location

Banyoles (Spanish: Bañolas) on the shore of the lake of the same name, is a favourite local recreation centre. It lies in the interior on the SW end of the Empordà (Spanish: Ampurdàn) a mere 20 km/12 miles N of Girona.

The Town

Market place

The centre of the narrow but charming old town (best visited on foot) is the Plaça Major (main square; market) which is fringed by plane trees and surrounded by old houses with arbours.

Archaeological Museum

A short way E of the market place we reach the little Plaça de la Font ("fountain square"). Here in an old building is the Archaeological Museum (officially Museu Arqueologic Comarcal; open weekdays 10 a.m.–1 p.m. and 4–7 p.m; entrance fee) with many prehistoric finds from the vicinity. The admission ticket is also valid for the Museum Darder (ethnology, natural history).

Sant Esteve/San Esteban

Away from the town centre to the E stands the Church of Sant Esteve (St Stephen) which was originally built in the

Porqueres: a chapel by the lake

9th c. It was destroyed by French troops in 1655 and was completely rebuilt in classical style. It once formed part of a Benedictine monastery. The interior houses a beautiful Gothic reredos (called Retaule de la Mare de Deu de l'Escala), made in the years 1437–39 by the stone mason Joan Antigo. It consists of twelve individual scenes grouped around a statue of the Virgin.

Llac de Banyoles/Lago de Bañolas

The Llac de Banyoles (Spanish: Lago de Bañolas) extends to the W of the town and is the largest natural lake in Catalonia. It is one of the favourite recreation areas of the people living in and around the provincial capital of Girona. Its banks are lined with woods of poplar, willow and oak; there are beaches for bathing, camp sites and many facilities for water sports.

Porqueres/Porqueras

At the SW end of the lake lies the little village of Porqueres (Spanish: Porqueras) which has a pretty Romanesque church. The single-aisled interior boasts some beautiful capitals with relief decoration.

Barcelona

K1–2

Country: Spain
Province: Barcelona
Altitude: sea level up to 532 m/1746 ft (Tibidabo)
Population: l,800,000 (conurbation about 3,500,000)

Location

Barcelona lies on the Costa Daurada (Spanish: Costa Dorada) between the mouths of the Riu Besós and the Riu Llobregat.

General

Barcelona, both the new and the old capital of Catalonia, is the seat of a university, the see of a Bishop and, after Madrid, is the most important town in Spain. It is the principal industrial and commercial centre of the country, one of the largest Mediterranean ports and has an important international airport.
The town has an exceptionally favourable position on a broad coastal plain which rises gradually from the sea to the ridge of Tibidabo and is bounded on the NE by the Montaña Pelada and on the SW by Montjuïc (Spanish: Montjuich). Beyond the Montaña Pelada lies the valley which the Riu Besós has carved through the hills; to the S of Montjuïc the Riu Llobregat reaches the sea after flowing through a wide and fertile valley, the market garden of Barcelona.
The old town is bounded by the harbour and by broad ring roads ("Rondas") which occupy the line of the former town walls. On the highest point of the town centre, the 12 m/ 40 ft high Monte Tabor stands the cathedral, surrounded by narrow medieval streets. The principal street is the broad Rambla which is lined by trees and which divides the old town into two parts.
The new parts of the town (ensanches) with their avenues lined with plane trees and their stately houses were largely built to a regular plan. A number of attractive and modern residential quarters extend from the Montjuïc as far as the Montaña Pelada encircling the town; industry and trade are concentrated in the NE.

History

Generous local tradition ascribes the foundation of the town in 218 B.C. to the Carthaginian general Hamilkar Barkas.
Barcelona first appears in history under the Iberian name of "Barcino" and in the time of Augustus became a Roman colony under the style of "Julia Faventia", later "Augusta" and later still "Pia". The Visigoths captured "Barcinona" in 414 and 531 and made it temporarily their capital. The Moors took "Bardschaluna" in 716; Louis the Pious conquered the town in 801 and made it the capital of the Spanish "march" which had already been founded in 778 by Charles the Great. During this period, also after the union of Catalonia with Aragón, Barcelona ranked with Genoa and Venice as one of the leading commercial cities of the Mediterranean. In 1492 the ships of Christopher Columbus (Spanish: Cristobal Colón), the "Santa Maria", the "Niña" and the "Pinta" sailed from here on their voyage of discovery which was intended to find a passage to India but during which they discovered America. The power of the city, however, was destroyed by the union with Castile in the 15th c. and particularly by the exclusion of Catalonia by trade with the New World. During the War of the Spanish Succession Barcelona supported the cause of Archduke Charles of Austria from whom it hoped for greater freedom. When the French stormed the town in the autumn of 1714 a great part was destroyed.
During the reign of Charles III, who opened up trade with

America in 1778, Barcelona began to prosper again and was able to establish its old pre-eminence in the course of the 19th c. In 1888 and again in 1929 Barcelona was the venue of international exhibitions.
After 1931 when Spain was declared a republic, Catalonia was granted independent status (until 1939) and Barcelona was the seat of the regional government. During the Spanish Civil War, in which a number of old churches were burned down, Barcelona was held by the Republicans until 1939. In 1975 Catalan was recognised as a language of education and administration. In October 1979 the Catalans voted in a referendum for far-reaching autonomy of their region. A little later the Spanish parliament accepted a statute of autonomy for Catalonia and the following year the regional parliament was elected.
The year 1992 will have a double significance for Barcelona; firstly the XXV Olympic summer games will be held here and this has already led to considerable building activity (Olmypic stadium); also the 500th anniversary of Columbus's voyage of exploration will be celebrated.

Note

There is so much to see in the great city of Barcelona that a single tour is not sufficient. In the following pages the most interesting sights of the city are collected under the names of the different districts.
Because of the large volume of traffic and the lack of parking places and also from the considerable risk in the inner city of a vehicle being broken into, a risk that cannot be denied, it is sensible to see the sights without using a car. The extensive system of public transport, especially the underground (Metro) where trains run at very frequent intervals, makes it easy to reach anything in the city which deserves a visit.

Port Area

Port

The port (Catalan: port; Spanish: puerto) which, including the outer harbour, covers an area of about 300 ha/ 740 acres, ranks with those of Gigón and Bilbao as one of the largest and most modern in Spain, handling some 40 million tonnes of freight annually. The main imports are coal, corn and cotton. The principal exports are wine, olive oil and cork. Passenger ferries link Barcelona with the Balearic Islands (Mallorca, Minorca) and with Pityusen (Ibiza). Embarkation from the north mole or the Estación Maritima (signposted). A trip around the harbour is an interesting experience; the motor boats moor at the breakwater near the Columbus column.

Columbus Monument

Location
Plaça del Portal de la Pau

In the Plaça del Portal de la Pau (Spanish: Plaza de la Paz) rises the 60 m/197 ft high Columbus monument (Monumento a Cristobal Colón) which was erected in 1888. The iron column is completely covered with allegorical figures.

Barcelona: Passeig de Colom ▶

View of the international port from Montjuïc

Open
Weekdays 9.30 a.m.–1.30 p.m., 4.30–8.30 p.m.
Sun. and public holidays 11.30 a.m.–7.30 p.m.

Entrance fee

At the base can be seen a row of reliefs depicting important events in Columbus's life and voyages of discovery. On the top of the column is an 8 m/26 ft high statue of Christopher Columbus.
Inside the column there is a lift, but the view from the top is restricted; the entrance is on the harbour side of the base at the top of some steps. Here there is also an information kiosk of the municipal tourist bureau (Patronat Municipal de Turisme).

"Santa Maria"

A short way from the Columbus monument a reproduction (1951) of the "Santa Maria" is moored. This was Columbus's flagship on his first voyage to America (1492), the object of which was to find a passage to India. The ship can be viewed (fee) daily from 9 a.m. to 2 p.m. and from 3 p.m. until sunset.
To the S of the monument stands the stately but somewhat overdecorated building of the Aduana (customs office).

** Marine Museum

Location
Plaça del Portal de la Pau

Open
Tues.-Sat. 10 a.m.–2 p.m., 4–7 p.m. Sun. and public holidays 10 a.m.–2 p.m. closed on Mon.

Beyond the Passeig de Colom (Spanish: Paseo de Colón), the harbour area from the inner city, lies the extensive arcaded complex which once served as a marine arsenal for the royal fleet (Reales Atarazanas) and which was situated in the area of the former docks (Catalan: Drassanes, Spanish: Darsenas). Here can be found the marine museum (Catalan: Museu Maritim; Spanish: Museo Maritimo). The

Reproduction of the "Santa Maria"

Entrance fee

wharf was established as early as the middle of the 13th c. and extended in the 18th c. to twelve separate yards. Here the galleys of the Crown of Aragón were built, maintained and repaired. When, however, after the discovery of America marine interest shifted to the Atlantic the importance of these shipyards quickly declined and the buildings were used as warehouses, powder magazine and as barracks for soldiers. In 1936 it was officially resolved to build a museum here. From 1976 the whole complex was made a protected monument. To the S a remnant of the old town wall has been preserved.

The museum, which is constantly being extended, illustrates all aspects of the sea and shipping: ships, model ships, nautical apparatus, tools, weapons, diagrams and illustrations.

The large hall is dominated by the excellent life-size replica of the galley "Real". This was the flagship of the fleet which overcame the Turks under the command of Don Juan of Austria at Lepanto (Greek: Naupaktos) which gave Spain dominance in the Mediterranean. What was believed to be the original figurehead, the "Christ of Lepanto", can now be seen in the cathedral (see page 57). The occasion for the construction of the replica (1960) was the approaching 400th anniversary of the victory. In the same hall there are numerous diagrams illustrating subterranean topography of the globe, the characteristic winds of the Mediterranean and what they are called in Mediterranean languages, the migration of the more important fauna of the sea, the maritime food chain and sailors' knots and tackle; there are also

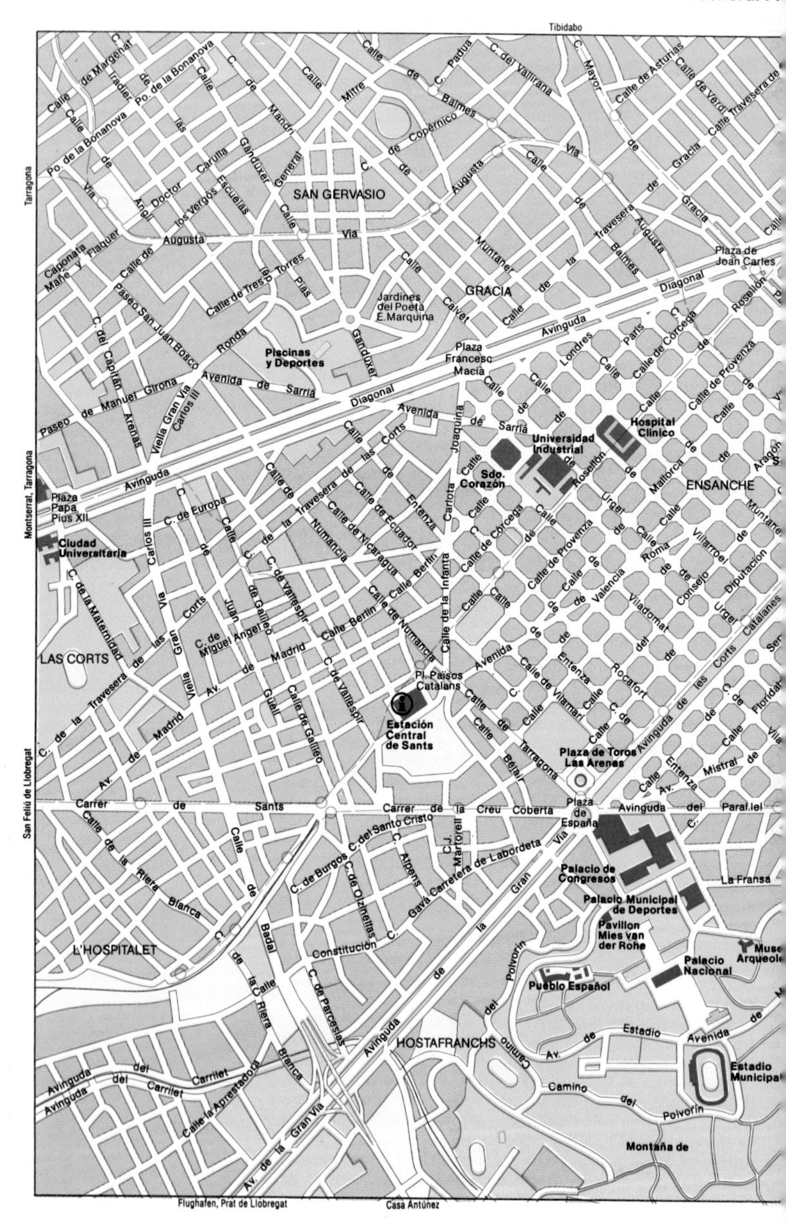
Tibidabo
Tarragona
Montserrat, Tarragona
San Feliú de Llobregat
Flughafen, Prat de Llobregat
Casa Antúnez
SAN GERVASIO
GRACIA
ENSANCHE
LAS CORTS
L'HOSPITALET
HOSTAFRANCHS
Plaza de Joan Carles
Jardines del Poeta E.Marquina
Piscinas y Deportes
Plaza Francesc Macia
Hospital Clinico
Universidad Industrial
Sdo. Corazón
Plaza Papa Pius XII
Ciudad Universitaria
Pl. Països Catalans
Estación Central de Sants
Plaza de Toros Las Arenas
Plaza de España
Palacio de Congresos
Palacio Municipal de Deportes
Pavillon Mies van der Rohe
Palacio Nacional
Pueblo Español
Estadio Municipa
Montaña de
La Fransa
Avinguda Diagonal
Carrer de Sants
Carrer de la Creu Coberta
Avinguda del Paral.lel
Gran Via
Calle de Mallorca
Calle de Valencia
Calle de Aragón
Calle de Provenza
Calle de Corcega
Calle de Roselon
Calle Berlin
Calle de Numancia
Calle de Entenza
Calle de Tarragona
Calle de la Infanta Carlota
Calle de Galileo
Calle de Badal
Calle de la Riera Blanca
Calle de Balmes
Calle de Muntaner
Calle de Calvet
Via Augusta
Ronda General Mitre
Avenida de Sarriá
Paseo de Manuel Girona
Carretera de Labordeta
Camino del Polvorín
Avenida de Estadio

Parque Güell
Sabadell, Gerona
Badalona
Sagrada Familia
Plaza de las Glorias
PUEBLO NUEVO
Plaza de Toros Monumental
Diagonal
Plaza Mossén J. Verdaguer
Cementerio del Este
N. S. de la Concepción
Plaza de Tetuán
Estación del Norte
Arco del Triunfo
Palacio de Justicia
San Pedro
Pal. de la Música
Parque de la Ciudadela
Mus. Zool.
Museo Martorell
Museo de Arte Moderno
Zoo
Coliseum
Teatro Barcelona
El Corte Inglés
Plaza de Cataluña
Santa Ana
Palacio Real Mayor
BARRIO GOTICO
Catedral
Spitzen-museum
Museo Picasso
Pal. Episc.
Pal. Generalitat
Canónigos
S. María del Mar
Estación de Francia
Belén
Casa de Misericordia
Pal. d. l. Virreina
Biblioteca Central
Lonja
Teatro Liceo
Plaza Real
La Merced
BARCELONETA
Com. d. Marina
Pl. Portal de la Pau
Mon. a. Colón
Santa María
Museo Marítimo
San Pablo
Aduana
Mar Mediterráneo
Torre San Sebastián
Muelle de Barcelona
Muelle Nuevo
Aéreo
Funicular
Estudios T.V.E
Estación Marítima
PUEBLO SECO
Teleférico
Port
Muelle de Poniente
Muelle de Levante
Castillo de Montjuich
Muelle de Contradique
Barcelona
200 m
© Baedeker
Prat de Llobregat
Metro

a number of fishing boats including one from Màlaga with their typical features and variants of local decoration, naval weapons, torpedoes and mines.
On the right side of the large hall in the small hall there is a specialised collection concerning sailing vessels.
In reaching the sailing ship section the visitor crosses a small external courtyard and in the adjoining range of buildings are models of various types of boats and ships, paintings and drawings, seals and stamps and moulds of commemorative medals of the Salón Nàutico Internacional, tools and equipment (compasses), two large dioramas, ships engines, etc. In the balcony, various methods of naval construction and the associated tools are shown in model form. On the same level as the great hall can be seen works of art concerning shipping, including pottery with ships motifs, a little silver model of the "Santa Maria" (Columbus's flagship), model ships of all kinds in glass – these are on sale everywhere in the town and are popular as souvenirs – and ships in bottles.

*Harbour Cable Car

Operational
Daily 11.30 a.m.–8 p.m.

The entire pool of the main harbour is spanned by a cable car (Catalan: Transbordador Aeri; Spanish: Funicular Aéreo). The terminus on the harbour side is the Torre de San Sebastian on the new mole; this is a 96 m/315 ft steel lattice mast. The midway station is formed by the 158 m/519 ft high Torre de Jaime I. The funicular ends on the flank of Montjuïc (see page 61). A trip in the cable car provides an excellent view of the inner city.

Passeig de Colom/Paseo de Colón

From the Columbus monument the Passeig de Colom (Spanish: Paseo de Colón), 42 m/46 yds wide and lined with palms leads NE to the main post office. In this street there are many ships chandlers where pretty little brass articles can be bought.

La Merced

A little way N of this street in Carrer de la Mercé (Spanish: Calle de la Merced) stands the handsome domed church La Merced, built in the mid 18th c. with the much venerated statue of the "Virgen de la Merced" (13th c.), patroness of Barcelona, on the high altar.

Exchange

The road ends at the main post office (correos; 1928) and a short way to the N stands the Lonja (exchange), a foundation of 1832, with a fine Gothic exchange hall (Sala de Contractaciones).
Around the square (Catalan: Pla del Palau, Spanish: Plaza del Palacio) on the N, the centre of Barcelona's maritime trade, there are a number of offices and commercial houses including the Govern Civil (Gobierno Civil; civil administration). A little farther N and to the right is the Estació (Spanish: Estación de Francia; the so-called French station).

Flagship of Don Juan d'Austria ▶

a number of fishing boats including one from Màlaga with A little to the W in the cramped old town stands the Church of Santa Maria del Mar (see page 60) and the Picasso Museum (see page 60).

Parc de la Ciutadella/Parque de la Ciudadela

The Municipal Park (Catalan: Parc de la Ciutadella, Spanish: Parque de la Ciudadela) is a 30 ha/74 acre extensive park on the NE edge of the old town. It was laid out on the site of the former citadel, with avenues of trees, terraces, flower beds, ornamental ponds and various monuments. In the park are the zoo, two museums and administrative offices including the parliament of the autonomous region of Catalonia.
At the northern corner of the park is an artificial fantastic grotto, the Cascade del Parque, with fountains.

Museu de Zoologia/Museo de Zoologia

Location
Passeig dels Til-lers

Open
Tues.–Sun. 9 a.m.–2 p.m. and 4–7 p.m.

Entrance fee

The Zoological Museum is situated at the corner of the Municipal Park. The somewhat peculiar building, in pseudo-Moorish style, was erected for the international exhibition of 1888 and is popularly known as the "Castell dels tres dragons" (the three dragon castle). The ground floor houses temporary exhibitions and in addition there is a very extensive collection of insects and the skeleton of a whale and a mammoth; in other glass cases mussels, snails and stuffed birds can be seen. A staircase leads to the upper floor which houses the main part of the permanent collection. This consists principally of birds and stuffed mammals (some of which are accompanied by a skeleton of the species). In addition there are molluscs, fish, reptiles and amphibia preserved in alcohol. At the end of the main hall behind a glass door can be found a collection of shells and shellfish (mussels and snail shells). All the stock is used for research and education. Although the furnishings of the museum are antiquated it is excellently kept and arranged and has a great nostalgic charm.

Museu de Geologia/Museo de Geologia

Location
Passeig dels Til-lers

Open
Tues.–Sun. 9 a.m.–2 p.m.

Entrance fee

The Geological Museum (also called the Museu Martorell after its founder) is associated with the Institute of Natural Science. The entrance to this neo-classical building is in the gabled central part of the front facing the park. The rooms to the left of the entrance hall are devoted to minerals, especially precious and semi-precious stones (including copies of the best known large diamonds made from crystal) and in addition exhibits on the setting of precious and non-ferrous metals. The minerals are arranged primarily according to their chemical construction. At the end of the room where pieces of agate can be seen in X-rays is a darkened room with minerals exposed to long or short

ultra-violet light (interesting light effects). To the right of the entrance hall are rooms primarily containing fossils.

Palm house

Adjoining the Geological Museum stands the palm house with its exotic flora.
In the centre of the road roundabout near the park gate a monument commemorates Don Juan Prim (general and statesman; 1814–70).

*Zoo

The zoo occupies the eastern part of the Municipal Park. It is astonishing what a varied and comprehensive layout has been attained with skill and imagination in a small area. Of especial interest among the exhibits is a huge white gorilla, a very rare pale variety of this species. Well arranged are the reptile house and especially the dolphinarium in which there is also a killer whale (Orcinus orca). The pool is circular and surrounded by an aquarium two storeys high (in the upper storey sea water, in the lower fresh water). Visitors can view the dolphinarium through plate glass windows. Another fine feature is the bird house with a special department for nocturnal birds.
There are several refreshments kiosks and picnic tables in the zoo grounds (some of them near the imitation of the Montserrat in the central area); a huge skeleton of a whale is on view in the open.

Open
daily 9.30 a.m.–7.30 p.m.
Dolphin show: daily 12.30 and 4.30 p.m. Sun. and public holidays noon, 1 and 4.30 p.m.
Killer whale show: weekdays 11.30 a.m., 12.30, 1.30 and 6 p.m., Sun. and public holidays 11.30 a.m., 12.30, 1.30, and 6 p.m.
Children's zoo daily 11 a.m.–7 p.m.

Entrance fee

Feeding the animals is forbidden

Museu d'Art Modern/Museo de Arte Moderno

Open
Tues.–Sat. 9 a.m.–7.30 p.m., Mon. 3–7.30 p.m., Sun. and public holidays 9 a.m.–2 p.m.

Entrance fee

The Museum of Modern Art has since 1945 been housed in the extreme left wing of the Palau de la Ciutadella (Spanish: Palacia de la Ciudadela) where the Parliament of Catalonia (regional parliament) is also situated. The Municipal Palace was built in the 18th c. as an arsenal, the museum wing was added about the turn of the century.
The term "Museum of Modern Art" is somewhat confusing for the exhibits go back in time via Historicism to the Romantic period. Correspondingly in the older sections, most of which are arranged in chronological order, the themes are conventional (portraits, genre scenes, landscapes, a few large historic paintings). Of interest is the Art Nouveau department (furniture, pictures, sculpture) also Expressionism and early modern works and sculptures from the first third of the 20th c. Then the visitor goes up a staircase to the upper floor and here can be seen a graphic collection with a great number of extremely wicked caricatures.
The Department of Contemporary Art, which occupies a small area, also shows works of the Catalan artists Miró and Dalí.
In all the museum provides a representative and fairly restricted survey of Spanish art (especially Catalan) since about 1830 but is of interest more from the standpoint of art history than from general interest.
Associated with the Museum of Modern Art is the Library of the Museum of Art (Biblioteca dels Museus d'Art).

*Ramblas

Bordered by plane trees, the Ramblas, the principal line of boulevards of the inner city lead NW from the Columbus Monument (see page 42) to the Plaça del Portal de la Pau. They have a total length of 1180 m/¾ mile and link the port district with the Plaça de Catalunya (Spanish: Plaza de Cataluña; see page 55), the largest and busiest square in Barcelona. They continue to the Avinguda de la Diagonal (Spanish: Avenida de la Diagonal), the broad traffic artery of the new town which cuts diagonally across the rectangular grid of streets.
To the E of the Ramblas lies the Barri Gotic (Spanish: Barrio Gótico = Gothic quarter; described on page 56) which is the centre of the old town. As well as a flower market and a bird market the Ramblas have a considerable number of book and newspaper kiosks. There are also many restaurants and cafés with tables in the open air.

Ramblas de Santa Mónica

Near the Columbus Monument starts the Ramblas de Santa Mónica. At their nearer end on the left can be seen the naval headquarters; a short way farther on, on the right side lying a little way back from the street, is the Museo Cera de Barcelona (waxworks museum; daily 11 a.m.–1.30 p.m. and 4.30–7.30 p.m.; entrance fee).

Gate of the covered market

Flower market in the Ramblas

Rambla dels Caputxins/Rambla de los Capuchinos

Palau Güell/Palacia Güell
Museu de les Arts de l'Espectacle/Museo de Arte Escénico

Not far W of the Rambla dels Caputxins, which continues this line of main streets, there stands in Carrer Nou de la Rambla the Palau Güell (1885–89) a stately old unconventional building by Antoni Gaudi. This now houses the theatrical museum (officially Museo de les Arts de l'Espectacle; Tues.–Sun. 10 a.m.–1 p.m. and 5–7 p.m.) with sketches for costumes and scenery, a ballet department, library, etc. Because of restrictions on space the major part of the stock is in store.

Plaça Reial/Plaza Real

Level with this building on the right, there is a passageway leading from the Rambla to the Plaça Reial, a beautiful enclosed square with classical houses where the ground floors have arcaded passages.

The shortest way to the Barri Gotic (see page 56) is along Carrer Ferran Jaume I (Spanish: Calle Fernando Jaime I) a short way N of the Rambla and turning to the right.

Gran Teatre del Liceo Sant Pau del Camp

Farther on, on the left of the Rambla, stands the Gran Teatre del Liceo (1848) which can seat 500 people. Carrer de Sant Pau leads to the Romanesque Church of Sant Pau del Camp (Spanish: San Pablo del Campo), which was built in 1117 outside the town of that time (therefore it is called del Camp = in the fields). The beautiful main doorway is very fine and adjoining the church to the S is a charming little cloister dating from the 13th c.

Scampi in the covered market

Santa Maria del Pi

The Rambla dels Caputxins ends at the junction of Plaça de la Boqueria. From here Carrer del Cardenal Casanyas leads N to the Plaça del Pi (Spanish: Plaza del Pino) in which stands the 15th c. Church of Santa Maria del Pi (Spanish: Santa Maria del Pino). On its W side is a large rose window; the interior contains beautiful modern stained glass.

Rambla dels Flors/Rambla de las Flores

Mercat/Mercado

The Rambla de Sant Josep (Spanish: Rambla de San José) joins the Plaça de la Borqueria. In the morning a colourful flower market is held here which accounts for the street being called Rambla dels Flors (Spanish: Rambla de las Flores). Also on the left-hand side can be found the market hall (Mercat) with its large variety of produce. In the centre is a fine fish market where a great variety of fish, mussels, crustaceans, etc., can be obtained.

Palau de la Virreina/Palacio de la Virreina

It is only a short way from the market hall to the former palace of the vicereine, which can be recognised by the two modern bronze equestrian statues on either side of the doorway. The building was erected between 1772 and 1777 as a residence for the former viceroys of Peru and named after the vicereine who, after her husband's death, lived here until 1791. On the façade can be seen Classical motifs but the interior decoration is Baroque.

Museu d'Arts Decoratives/ Museo de Artes Decorativas

The palace now houses the Museum of Applied Art (open Tues.–Sat. 9 a.m.–2 p.m. and 4.30 –9 p.m., Sun. and public holidays 9 a.m.–2 p.m., closed Monday mornings). On view are furniture, wrought iron work, glass, clocks and porcelain from Gothic times. From time to time temporary exhibitions on various themes are mounted.

Museu Gabinet Postal

In the same building as the Museum of Applied Art is also the Postal Museum (officially Museu Gabinet Postal) which includes a stamp collection, articles illustrating postal history and a specialist library.

Where the Rambla crosses Carrer del Carmen the gloomy and heavy Baroque façade of the Jesuit Church of Nuestra Señora de Belén (1681–1729) can be seen.

Rambla dels Estudies/Rambla de los Estudios

Rambla Canaletes/Rambla Canaletas

The Rambla dels Estudies, the setting for a morning market of birds and ornamental fish, leads into the Rambla Canaletes, providing a link to the Plaça de Catalunya (Spanish: Plaza de Cataluña).

*Plaça de Catalunya/Plaza de Cataluña

The busy Plaça de Catalunya forms the end of the inner city Ramblas and of the centre of the old town. In the wide spacious square with its open green spaces and water basins are the headquarters of many large banks (on the NW side the square is dominated by the building of the Banco Español de Crédito); on the E side the huge building of the telephone administration (Telefónica). Visitors who wish to make use of one of the seats in the square – there are also seats in other squares – should note that they are subject to a small charge. Beneath the street lies the most important junction of the city Metro system (including a line to Tibidabo (see page 72); the station can be reached from all sides of the square.

El Corte Inglés

On the N side of the Plaça de Catalunya stands the department store "El Corte Inglés" which is worth visiting. Foreign customers can obtain the services of an interpreter by telephoning (there are instructions on the phone). On the ninth floor is a self-service restaurant with a glazed observation terrace which is recommended as a pleasant place for a break during a tour of the city.

*Palau de la Musica Catalan/Palacio de la Música Catalana

Not far E of the Plaça de Catalunya in Carrer Alta de Sant Pere (Calle Alta de San Pedro) is the Palau de la Musica Catalan (palace of music). This great building, designed by the architect Domenech i Muntaner is a fine example of Spanish art nouveau ("Modernismo") which has always retained a distinct individuality. The lavish and excellently maintained decor, especially of the concert hall, is one of the finest examples of that period.

University

Leading W from the southern corner of the Plaça de Catalunya, the shopping street Carrer de Pelai (Spanish: Calle de Pelayo) leads to the Plaça de la Universitat (Spanish: Plaza de la Universidad). The University was founded in 1450 and the present building was erected in 1863–73.

Rambla de Catalunya/Rambla de Cataluña

The NW continuation of the Ramblas is formed by the Rambla de Catalunya which runs from the Plaça de Catalunya as far as the Avinguda de la Diagonal.

Passeig de Grácia/Paseo de Gracia

Running NW parallel to the Rambla de Catalunya is the Passeig de Grácia a magnificent highway 61.5 m/67 yds wide 1200 m/¾ mile long with fine rows of plane trees and elegant shops. Carrer de Aragón (Spanish: Calle de Aragón), branches off on the right; on the left-hand side stands the Church of Nuestra Señora de la Concepción which was moved from the old town in 1869 together with a cloister dating from the 14th c. (considerably damaged during the Civil War in 1936).

Casa Milá

Farther along on the right of the Passeig de Grácia stands the Casa Milá (1910), designed by Antoni Gaudi; its sweeping shapes and plant-like iron balcony railings are strongly influenced by Art Nouveau.

Avinguda de la Diagonal/Avenida de la Diagonal

The N end of the Passeig de Grácia opens into the Plaça de Joan Carles I (Spanish: Plaza de Juan Carlos I) and here the visitor crosses the 10 km/6 mile long Avinguda de la Diagonal (Spanish: Avenida de la Diagonal) which runs almost exactly diagonally across the rectangular grid of streets of the new part of the town in an east-west direction. Near its western end lies the stadium of F.C. Barcelona (125,000 seats); also in the neighbourhood are the buildings of the university city (Zona Universitaria).

Old Town

* Barri Gòtic/Barrio Gótico

NE of the Ramblas extends the Barri Gòtic (Spanish: Barrio Gótico = Gothic quarter), the most important remains of the medieval old town. Most of the narrow maze of streets is a pedestrian zone; there are many shops (fashions, jewellery, souvenirs, ceramics, textiles, leather goods) and also small inns.

Old Town

Casa de Ciutat

By following Carrer Ferran Jaume I NE from the Rambla dels Caputxins (see page 53) we soon reach the Plaça de Sant Jaume (Spanish: Plaza de San Jaime). Here on the right (on the SE side) stands the Casa de Ciutat (town hall), originally dating from the 14th c. and still having its Gothic lateral façade (the main front dates from 1847). In the interior can be seen the great council chamber (Salón de Ciento; 14th c.) and the Salón de las Crónicas which was painted by Josep Maria Sert.

Palau de la Generalitat

Opposite the town hall stands the former Casa de la Diputación, the seat of the medieval provincial assembly in the 15th c. It is now used as offices for the Generalitat de Catalunya (provincial government). Notable are the magnificent Gothic patio (inner courtyard) and on the first floor the Chapel of St George, also Gothic. To the rear of the building can be seen the charming orangery. On the N is the Audiencia, the former lawcourt. Carrer del Bisbe Irurita (Spanish: Calle del Obispo Irurita) which leads from here to the Cathedral is spanned by a delicate Gothic building.

** Cathedral

Open
Daily 7.30 a.m.–1.30 p.m. and 4–7.30 p.m.

On Monte Tabor, the highest point in the old city (alt: 12 m/40 ft), stands the Cathedral of Santa Cruz or Santa Eulalia. It was begun in the year 1298 on the site of an old

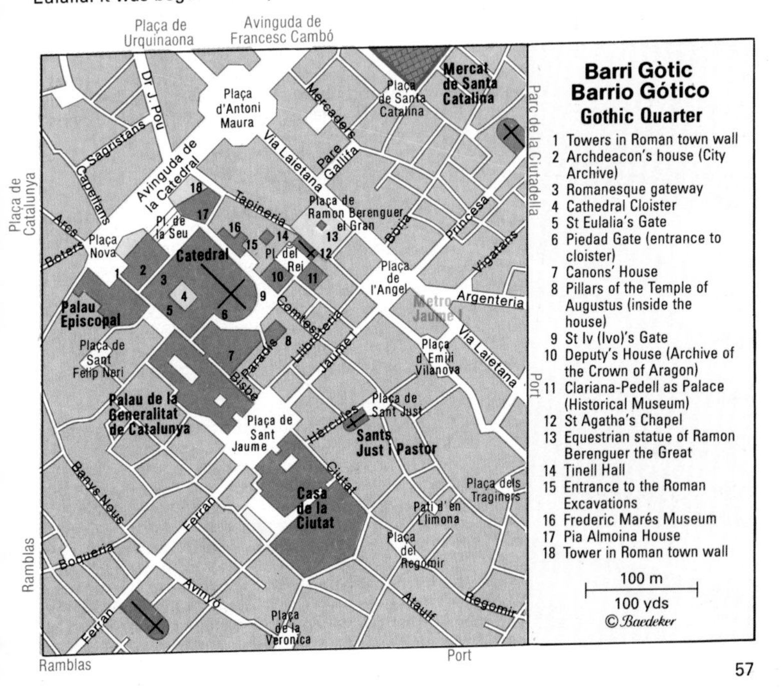

Columbus Column by the harbour

Cathedral in the Old Town

Romanesque building of which only a few stone reliefs remain on the NE portico; the building was finished in 1448 except for the main façade and the dome, which were added in 1898 and 1913 respectively.
The layout of the building is unusual; the apse and the altar are in the SW and the main façade faces NW.

Cloister

If, as described above, the visitor comes from the Plaça de Sant Jaume he will first reach the beautiful cloister (Claustro) with its magnolias and palms; it is entered through the Portal de Santa Eulalia and dates from 1380 to 1451. All along it are numerous chapels with altars dedicated to various saints. In the SW corner is the Capilla de Santa Lucia which was founded in 1270; the adjoining Chapter House (Sala Capitular) houses the Cathedral Museum (Museu de la Catedral) with paintings by Spanish artists of the 14th and 15th c.

Interior

The high Gothic interior (82.3 m/273 ft long, 37.2 m/122 ft wide, 25.5 m/84 ft high) is divided into three aisles. The nave and the side aisles of the cathedral are almost of the same height. High up in the clerestory is a row of little windows. Along the side aisles run dwarf galleries, below which are chapels, most of them from the 16th/17th c., with very elaborate Baroque altars. The finest of them is the Capilla del Santisimo Sacremento (also Capilla del Santo Cristo de Lepanto), which can be found to the left of the high altar and is the former Chapter House. Inside can be seen the alabaster tomb of Bishop Olegarius (d. 1136) and also the so-called "Christus von Lepanto", believed to be the figurehead from the flagship of Don Juan of Austria (see Marine

Museum, page 44) which was captured in the successful battle against the Turks in 1571. In the chapel just before the left transept is a Black Madonna which is similar to the figure of the Virgin of Montserrat (see entry).
The magnificent stained glass dates partly from the 15th c. Notable are the walled-in 15th c. choir stalls and the beautiful pulpit of 1403. In the Capilla Mayor is a late Gothic retable of the 16th c. From the Capilla Mayor stairs lead down to the crypt which is illuminated by numerous candles. Here stands the alabaster sarcophagus of Saint Eulalia, an Italian work dating from about 1330.
The Treasury (Catalan: Tresor, Spanish: Tesoro) in the Sacristy is well worth seeing.
From the SW tower of the cathedral (210 steps; entrance from the interior) there is a very fine view of the city, its hinterland and the sea.

Casa del Arcediano

To the W of the main front of the cathedral stands the Casa del Arcediano, built in the 15th c. with a magnificent inner courtyard. The building houses the state archives (Catalan: Arxiu Històric de la Ciutat, Spanish: Archivo Histórico de la Ciudad).

Palau Episcopal

Directly opposite, on the far side of Carrer del Bisbe Irurita, stands the Episcopal Palace (Palau Episcopal) which was first mentioned as long ago as 926 and which has been rebuilt several times.

Museu Frederic Marés/Museo Federigo Marés

Location
Carrer dels Comtes de Barcelona 10

Open
Tues.–Sat. 9 a.m.–2 p.m., 4–7 p.m., Sun. and public holidays 9 a.m.–2 p.m.
closed on Mon.

Entrance fee

Immediately to the E of the Cathedral, on the far side of Carrer dels Comtes de Barcelona (Spanish: Calle de los Condes de Barcelona), there stands in a little square the Museu Frederic Marés, founded in 1946. The building was formerly the residence of the Dukes of Barcelona and the Kings of Catalonia and Aragón. The rich collection of sculpture includes pieces from classical, Romanesque, Gothic and Baroque ages as well as items from the 19th c., most of them from Spain. A second collection exhibits accessories, luxury objects and jewellery. There are also smaller specialised collections on the cultural history of tobacco and photography and devotional objects from the Monastery of Montserrat (see entry).
By following Carrer dels Comtes de Barcelona SE we come to the little Plaça del Rei (Spanish: Plaza del Rey) which lies a short way off the road. The square was once the central feature of the palace of which in the NW corner stands the mighty five-storied Mirador (observation tower).

Museu d'Históría/Museo de Históría

Location
Plaça del Rei

Open
Tues.–Sat. 9 a.m.–2 p.m., 3.30–8.30 p.m., Sun. and public holidays 9 a.m.–2 p.m., closed on Mon.

In the Plaça del Rei stands the Casa Padellàs, originally built in the 15th c. on a nearby site and re-erected here in 1931; it is a typical town residence of the late Middle Ages. When shafts were being dug for the foundations in its new location considerable remains of the former Roman town were found, and this was the impetus for earmarking the building for the establishment of the Historical Museum.

Entrance fee

Also forming part of the Historical Museum are the deconsecrated Iglesia Santa Agata, which stands a little higher up, and a large hall of the former Royal Palace (see Museu Marés above), the Salón de Tinell, built in 1370. It was here that Columbus was received by the Reyes Católicos after his return from his first voyage to America.
The Casa Padellàs houses the majority of the exhibits, among which can be seen finds from pre-Roman and Arab times, from the Middle Ages, from the time of Catalan sea power as well as items on popular themes.
Of interest in the Church of Santa Agata are the painted wooden ceiling, a huge Gothic altar, two Gothic tombs in an elevated position and some ecclesiastical vestments. In the former sacristy can be seen the great iron movement of a tower clock dating from 1576. The old windows in the choir and in the clerestory show various coats of arms. In the great vaulted hall (Saló del Tinell) diagonally opposite, which was part of the former Royal Palace, temporary art exhibitions take place.
The Plaça del Angel lies a short distance to the E; nearby off the main road (Via Laietana) which runs SE, can be seen remains of the old city wall on the right.

**Picasso Museum

Location
Carrer Montcada 15–17

Open
Tues.–Sat. 9.30 a.m.–1.30 p.m., 4–8.30 p.m., Sun. and public holidays 9.30 a.m.–1.30 p.m., closed on Mon. morning

Entrance fee

From the Plaça del Angel we follow Carrer de la Princesa and then Carrer Montcada which branches off on the right. Here at No. 15 stands the Palau Berenguer de Aguilar, a stately late-Gothic palace which now houses the Museu Picasso. The collections include, in chronological order, pictures, drawings and etchings from all the artistic periods of Pablo Picasso. Parts of the collection are being rearranged. Comprehensive diagrams explain the interrelation of the various periods.
Particular attention should be given to the famous bullfighting sequence (copies and original plaques) which was inspired by the literary model "La Tauromaquia o Arte de Torear" by José Delgado (alias Pipe Hillo; 1754–1801) a famous toreador, as well as the amusing cycle of the faun. Also of note are the paraphrases (1957) with preliminary studies of "La Meninas" by Velázquez.

Museu Textil i d'Indumentária

On the opposite side of the road (Nos. 12–14), in a 13th c. palace, can be found the Textile Museum (Catalan: Museu Textil i d'Indumentária; Spanish: Museo de Indumentaria; Open Tues.–Sat. 9 a.m.–2 p.m. and 4.30–7 p.m.). The exhibits include items of cultural interest from the 4th c. A.D. and from the North African-Coptic, Spanish-Moorish and Christian near-East culture.

*Santa Maria del Mar

Location
Plaça Santa Maria

Only a short distance S stands the Church of Santa Maria del Mar (1329–83) a three-aisled Gothic building without transepts. Apart from the Cathedral this is the most important church in the city. It was built over a late Roman necropolis where, so legend tells us, Saint Eulalia was buried. Over the richly ornamented main doorway there is a great rose window; the light interior gives a harmonious impres-

A print in the Picasso Museum

sion of space. Most of the stained glass windows date from the 15th–17th c.; in a chapel near the left side door can be seen a Black Madonna. The keystones of the vaulting are interesting (above the high altar is the Coronation of Mary). On the high altar can be seen a Gothic statue of the Madonna and in front of it a model of an old trading ship. Below the sanctuary is the entrance to the crypt.

Montjuïc/Monjuich

On the S side of the city and falling steeply down to the sea, rises Montjuïc (213 m/700 ft) which is crowned by a fortress.

Access

From the harbour (see page 42) the visitor can reach the Parc de Miramar on the NE flank of the hill and about half way to the top, by a cable car (Transbordador Aeri/Funicular Aéreo). From the Avinguda del Parallel which joins the port to the Plaça de Espanya (see page 67) a funicular, the first part of which is underground (in operation noon–2.50 p.m. and 4.30–9.15 p.m.) goes up to Montjuïc (near the upper station is a large swimming pool); a cable car forms the continuation to the fortress. As we travel up on the cable car the view, especially towards the harbour basin and the cableway spanning it, becomes better and better.

*Castell de Montjuïc/Castillo de Montjuich

On top of the hill stands the fortress where the cableway terminates (here there is a restaurant with a view). From each of the four corner towers there are magnificent views of the metropolis. On the W side can be seen an elaborate memorial to Francisco Franco. In the whole area of the fortress are a number of large calibre guns which can cover the entire harbour area. A walk on the flat roof of the Citadel is well worth-while offering a 360° panorama of the sea, the port, the city and the mountains.

Military Museum

The Military Museum (open Tues.–Sat. 10 a.m.–2 p.m., 4–8 p.m., Sun. and public holidays 10 a.m.–8 p.m.) is situated inside the Citadel which is normally open until 9 p.m. In the courtyard can be seen guns of the 19th and early 20th c. Fifteen exhibition rooms are in the former casemate. In them can be seen firearms, swords and other weapons, equipment from all over the world and in addition models of fortresses, dioramas with tin soldiers, personal and modern handguns, etc.

*Parc de Atraccions/Parque de Atracciones

Open
Mon.–Fri. 6.15 p.m.–12.15 a.m., Sat. until 1.15 a.m. Sun. and public holidays noon–12.15 a.m. (The amusements do not operate between 2.45 and 4.45 p.m.)
Performances in the theatre at 7.15 and 10.15 p.m.

Montjïuc is known chiefly for the amusement park on its NE flank. Near the entrance are extensive car parks. The park is basically a large permanent fair with a giant wheel, various rides (ghost train, auto scooter) and a variety theatre. There is a similar amusement park at Tibidabo (see page 72).
Farther downhill from the Parc de Atraccions we reach the Mirador del Alcalde (magnificent view of the inner city and the port) with its fountains; the paving here is very original and consists of concrete tubes, the tops and bottoms of bottles, chains, etc., arranged in an ornamental way. Farther down lies the Miramar observation point in the park-like Plaça de la Armada. Here is the terminus of the cableway which crosses the harbour to the outer breakwater (Transbordador Aeri; see page 48).
On the NW slope extends a large park with the palace of the International Exhibition of 1929 which has been converted into museums.

Fundació Joan Miró

Not far from the Plaça de Neptu (Spanish: Plaza de Neptuno) can be seen the original modern group of buildings of the Fundació Joan Miró. The foundation which bears his name (open Mon.–Sat. 11 a.m.–8 p.m., Sun. and public holidays 11 a.m.–2.30 p.m.) puts on temporary exhibitions of the work of the famous Catalan painter as well as works of contemporary art. Primarily it is not a museum but a centre where people can get to know art and artists. In this connection there is also the "Premi Internacional de Diboux Joan Miró" (international prize for graphic art) which is awarded each year by the foundation.

**Museu d'Art de Catalunya/Museo de Arte de Cataluña

Location
Mirador del Palau

Open
Tues.–Sun. 9 a.m.–2 p.m.

Entrance fee

Some distance from the Plaça d'Espanya (see page 67) at the top of a broad flight of steps in the open-air stands the gigantic architecturally somewhat overladen Palau Nacional (Spanish: Palacio Nacional) which is crowned by a dome; here the Museum of Catalonian Art has been housed since 1934. With its excellent collections from all periods of

"Christ in Majesty"

An archangel

Catalan art, the museum counts as one of the most important sights of Barcelona.

Romanesque art

Especially impressive and of international importance is the Department of Romanesque art (11th–13th c.) in 33 rooms. Here beautiful frescoes from many churches in the Catalonian Pyrenees can be seen. In this connection the vaulting and apses of the original locations have been exactly copied in the museum and the wall paintings affixed to them; a photograph, plan and outline sketches of each of the churches are included. Of particular interest is the room with the apses of the churches of Burgal and Santa Maria d'Aneu placed opposite one another; here high up on the walls are two general maps with the places where the panels and wall paintings were found. Also of the greatest interest are the frescoes from Tahull (the nave of the church of Santa Maria there has been completely reproduced). Also to be seen are liturgical vessels, altar panels, capitals and sculptured figures.

Gothic art

The Department of Gothic Art (14th and 15th c.; in 24 rooms) is not entirely chronological but systematically arranged. The collections are not only confined to Catalonia but also include works from other Spanish regions. On view are sculpture in wood and stone, painted panels, altar panels including, in room 52, a huge 14th c. altar of Mary which was created by members of the Serra family of painters who, it has been established, were in Barcelona between 1357 and 1405.

Renaissance and Baroque

This department (16th–18th c.) contains six rooms. It also includes exhibits from other parts of Spain and the Spanish Netherlands.

*Museu de Ceràmica/Museo de Carámica

Location and times of opening
as Museu d'Art de Catalunya

Entrance fee

The Museum of Ceramics can also be found in the Palau Nacional and is reached through the Museu d'Art de Catalunya (room 20). It is situated on the first floor; the entrance is marked. Room 1 contains Arabic and Catalonia ceramics of the 12th–17th c. Room 2 contains medieval earthenware and room 3 ceramics with glazing to give a metallic effect and a quantity of azulejos tiles with a blue design or ornamental decoration. In rooms 4 and 5 can be found polychromatic ceramics from Seville, some of them with folkloric themes and scenes. In room 6 (Aragón ware) blue decoration is again most prominent; in Room 7 (Catalonian work) of especial interest are two great pictures of 1710 which are made up of painted tiles: "La Chocolateria", a representation of a banquet in a middle class home and "La Corrida de Toros", depicting a bull fight. On smaller painted tiles can be seen some original representations of domestic and wild animals, craft work, etc. In room 8 (also Catalonian work) is an amusing shield of a one-way street showing the two-wheeled horse carriage and text which indicates that the road can only be used in the direction in which this carriage is travelling; contravention will be punished by a fine of three libras. Rooms 9 and 10 house ceramics of the 17th and 19th c. and room 11 is devoted to modern works.

Jardi Botànic/Jardin Botánico

Open
Daily 9 a.m.–1.30 p.m. and 4–6 p.m.

Entrance fee

Behind the Palau Nacional and forming part of the park of Montjuïc extends the Botanic Garden (Catalan: Jardi Botànic; Spanish: Jardin Botánico) with its beautiful flora. It was laid out immediately after the International Exhibition of 1929 in an area which includes an abandoned quarry, and because of this layout it provides various microclimatic zones which provide good growing conditions even for exotic plants. Otherwise the plants are arranged primarily from a geographical point of view. The garden is one of the most important places of its kind in Spain. Adjoining the garden is the Institut Botànic (Botanic Institute) which is only available to specialists.
Passing the institute building and some sports grounds we reach the Poble Espanyol (see page 66).

Museo Etnològic/Museo Etnológico

Location
Passeig de Santa Madrona

Open
Tues.–Sat. 9 a.m.–8.30 p.m., Mon. 2–8.30 p.m., Sun. and public holidays 9 a.m.–2 p.m.

Entrance fee

The Museo Etnològic (Ethnological Museum), set up from 1973 in the new building on a hexagonal plan, shows clothing, old utensils, furniture and applied art, especially from Africa, America, Asia and Oceania. It is proposed to furnish a further department. Because of restricted space the exhibits are from time to time changed.
The Spanish and Catalan Department of the museum is to be found in the Poble Espanyol (see page 65).

Museu Arqueològic/Museo Arqueológico

The Archaeological Museum (official Museu Arqueològic de Barcelona) can be found in one of the former pavilions of the International Exhibition of 1929. The emphasis of the collection is on exhibits from Spain itself. They are divided into the subject groups of pre-history, culture of the Balearic Islands, finds from Greek and Roman town Ampurias (see Empuries), and classical archaeology. In the vestibule can be seen a collection of Etruscan antiquities. The museum has also specialist laboratories at its disposal.

Location
Passeig de Santa Madrona

Open
Tues.–Sat. 9.30 a.m.–1 p.m., 4–7 p.m., Sat. and public holidays 9.30 a.m.–2 p.m.

Entrance fee

**Poble Espanyol/Pueblo Español

The "Spanish village" (Catalan: Poble Espanyol; Spanish: Pueblo Español) is situated in the western part of the park which extends along Montjuïc. It was erected for the

Location
Avinguda Marques de Comillas

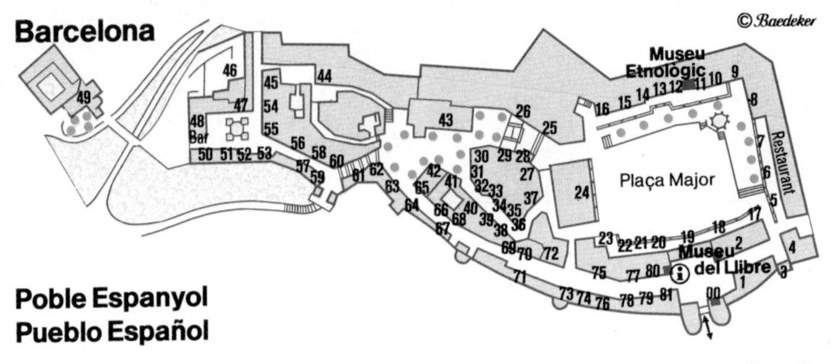

Original locations of the buildings, replicas of which are in the "Spanish Village" (Poble Espanyol/Pueblo Español)

1 Miájadas (Cáceres)
2 Cáceres
3 Plasencia (Cáceres)
4 Cáceres
5, 6 Sigüenza (Guadalajara)
7 Navalcarnero (Madrid)
8 Santillana del Mar (Santander)
9 Borja (Zaragoza)
10 Riaza (Segovia)
11 Santillana del Mar (Santander)
12 Alquezar (Huesca)
13, 14 Burgo de Osma (Soria)
15 Aranda de Duero (Burgos)
16 Casbas (Huesca) und Sigüenza (Guadalajara)
17, 18 La Fresneda (Teruel)
19 Sangüesa (Navarra)
20 Graus (Huesca)
21 Jérica (Valencia)
22 Montblanch (Tarragona)
23 Sigüenza (Guadalajara)
24 Vallderrobles (Teruel)
25 Cambados (Pontevedra)
26 San Esteban de Lorenzana (Lugo)
27 Cangas de Oñís (Oviedo)
28 Pontevedra
29 Betanzos (La Coruña)
30 Maluenda (Teruel)
31-33 Albarracín (Teruel)
34, 35 Fraga (Huesca)
36 Calaceite (Teruel)
37 Catí (Castellón)
38 Peñafiel (Valladolid)
39 Fraga (Huesca)
40 Borja (Zaragoza)
41 Albarracín (Teruel)
42 Corella (Navarra)
43 Utebo (Zaragoza)
44 Écija (Sevilla)
45 Murcia
46 Palma de Mallorca
47 La Jana (Castellón)
48 Tárrega (Lérida)
49 Cataluña
50 Cornudella (Tarragona)
51 La Garriga (Barcelona)
52, 53 Santa Pau (Gerona)
54 Baeza (Jaén)
55 Besalú (Gerona)
56 Rupit (Barcelona)
57 Isona (Lérida)
58 Camprodón (Gerona)
59 Rupit (Barcelona)
60 Montblanch (Tarragona)
61 Belianes (Lérida)
62 Santa Pau (Gerona)
63, 64 Vergara (Guipúzcoa)
65 Corella (Navarra)
66, 67 Estella (Navarra)
68 Roncal (Navarra)
69 Molinos de Duero (Soria)
70 Sos del Rey Católico (Zaragoza)
71 Vinuesa (Soria)
72, 73 Tora (Zamora)
74 Segovia
75 Toro (Zamora)
76 Santillana del Mar (Santander)
77 Ayllón (Segovia)
78 Toro (Zamora)
79 Sigüenza (Guadalajara)
80 Torija (Guadalajara)
81 Cáceres

A picturesque corner . . .

. . . in the Poble Espanyol

Open
Daily 9 a.m.–8 p.m.

Entrance fee

International Exhibition of 1929 to contain copies of characteristic buildings of Spanish provinces. Well-known artists including Maurice Utrillo were involved in the choice and realisation of the layout and in the planning. The houses are grouped as in most Spanish country towns around the Plaça Mayor, the rectangular main square, near the massive entrance gate. At the entrance can be found the information bureau, a branch of a bank and book and tobacco shops as well as a little book museum.

In the main square there is a restaurant and the Spanish and Catalan Department of the Ethnological Museum (Museu Etnològic/Museo Etnológico; see page 64). From time to time open-air performances are also put on here.
W of the main square the Poble Espanyol continues along several picturesque little streets and alleys offering views of beautiful interior courtyards. It is remarkable how very many craft industries have been established in the buildings and in which works of popular art and applied art are produced and sold. These include objects in glass, ceramics, enamel, textiles, leather work, graphics, etc., in a colourful variety and a large selection at reasonable prices; in most cases the workshops can be inspected.
From the Poble Espanyol the Avinguda del Marquès de Comillas leads downhill back to the inner city.

Exhibition Grounds

The area between the Palau Nacional and the Plaça Espanya is occupied by the extensive halls and open spaces of

Resurrected Bauhaus art: Mies van der Rohe Pavilion

the exhibition grounds (officially "Fira de Barcelona"). Between the foot of the steps and the Plaça Espanya runs the Avinguda de la Reina Maria Cristina, a major boulevard with fountains, which at night are often illuminated.
The Olympic stadium for 1992 is being built nearby.

*Pavillon Mies van der Rohe

Shortly before the Avinguda de la Reina Maria Cristina coming from the Poble Espanyol reaches the exhibition grounds it passes the Pavillon Mies van der Rohe. Ludwig Mies van der Rohe, born in Aachen in 1886, was the last director of the Bauhaus in Dessau and he designed the German Pavilion for the International Exhibition in Barcelona (1929); for the centenary of his birth this authentic copy of the original pavilion was dedicated. The effect of the building is produced by the strong clear lines and by a aesthetic effect of the materials used (glass, steel, natural stone). Adjoining is a document centre which works closely with the Mies van der Rohe archives of the Museum of Modern Art in New York.

Plaça de Espanya/Plaza de España

The busy circular Plaça de Espanya (Spanish: Plaza de España) is the principal traffic junction in the W of the town. Here the broad Avinguda de la Gran Via, which traverses in a straight line the entire area of the city, crosses the Avinguda de la Parallel which skirts the foot of Montjuïc. In the centre of the square stands the lavish fountain monument "España Ofrecida a Dios" ("Spain dedicated to God"); adjoining on the N is the Arenas de Barcelona (bullring).

Plaça de Espanya

Building of the Church of . . .

. . . the Sagrada Familia goes on

Sights in the North

*Templo de la Sagrada Familia

Location
Carrer de Mallorca

Entrance fee

In the northern part of the town, beyond the Avinguda de la Diagonal, rises the striking Templo de la Sagrada Familia (Temple of the Holy Family) which is visible from afar. It is an incomplete monumental church building in neo-Catalan style. The design is considered to be the major work of the Catalan architect Antoni Gaudi (1852–1926) who in 1883 took over the building, which had already been started in the previous year, and who completely changed the design according to his own ideas. The costs of this "Church of the Poor", as Gaudi often called it, are still being met by donations and public subscription.

The church is planned to have a total length of 110 m/360 ft and a height of 45 m/148 ft with the main dome 160 m/525 ft high. So far, only the four-towered east doorway (the "nativity door") the outer walls of the apse, the crypt, in which Antoni Gaudi was buried in 1926, and parts of the west doorway and the walls of the nave have been completed. Building progresses at irregular intervals and it is not known when this gigantic project will be finished.

Artistically the Templo de la Sagrada Familia is an extremely individual mixture of stylistic elements and new ideas. The ground plan, the division of space and the lines of the building are principally Gothic and also neo-Gothic

Templo de la Sagrada Familia

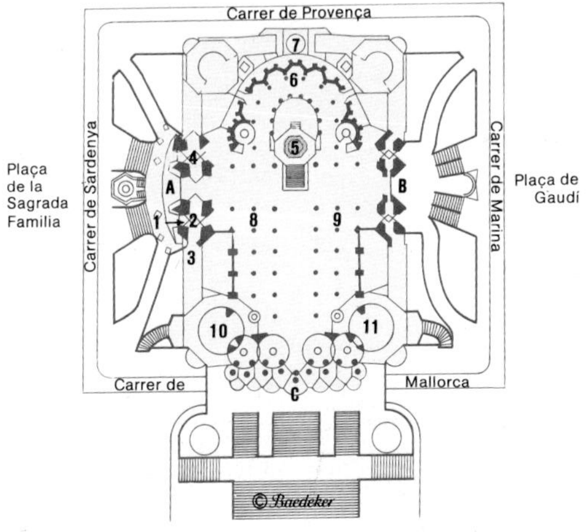

A Doorway of the Passion
B Christmas Doorway
(over the above the towers of the façade)
C Doorway of Glory

1 Entrance
2 Vestibule
3 Gaudi-Multivision
4 Sales kiosk
5 Altar (crypt below)
6 Apse
7 Lady Chapel
8 Gaudi Museum
9 Model Workshop
10 Baptistry
11 Chapel of the Sacrament

which was widespread in the middle of the 19th c. But these elements are combined with flowing plant motifs which were introduced in the time of Art Nouveau.
At the entrance to the church site there is an audio-visual explanation concerning the history of the building. Within the enclosing walls are two tower cranes; semi-finished masonry lies ready to be incorporated and from this the design can be seen from close at hand. Where the nave adjoins the apse there is an altar protected by a canopy; below this the main crypt is situated but normally this is closed. However, visitors are permitted to go into the two side crypts; in the right-hand one can be seen a large model of the finished church (scale 1:25) and here also is the model workshop, which, because of the enormous amount of ornamental features, has a special importance. On the walls are cross-sections of other important churches compared with the Sagrada Familia. The left-hand crypt houses the Museu Gaudi and here in model form there is a huge section through the nave and documents about other buildings by Gaudi, his workshop, detailed models, cartoons and façade ornamentation.
The towers of the right-hand doorway can be ascended, but because of the open nature of the circular staircase, this is not pleasant for anyone without a head for heights. From the towers there is a good view of the inside of the church and its surroundings; the mosaic decoration on the cupola of the tower is best viewed from here.

A modernistic work in the Parc Güell ▶

**Parc Güell/Parque Güell

Location
Carrer Olot

NW of the Templo de la Sagrada Familia in the district of Vallcarca on the edge of the city there extends on the side of a hill the Parc Güell (laid out 1900–14). This was also created by Antoni Gaudi who lived here. On the SE wall of the park (Carrer Olot) can be seen coloured majolica medallions bearing the name of the park. Hard by the entrance is a gatehouse in flowing forms with a decorated tower and almost entirely covered with coloured majolica. Nearby is a little bar. Here begins the twin symmetrical series of steps which lead up to a pillared hall. The steps are separated by a fountain, the principal element of which is a coloured animal looking something like a salamander. The pillared hall picks up elements of Greek-Doric style. The outermost row of pillars are distinctively sloped inwards in order to cushion the sideways thrust of the roof vaulting. Between the capitals of the gloomy archaic columns there is rich polychrome decoration of ceramic and glass mosaic.
On the roof of the pillared hall a broad level area was created, the enclosing wall of which is formed as a long wave-like bench; the curved lines create almost enclosed individual areas of communication. Here especially the visitor can admire the original decoration of ceramic fragments in many colours which completely cover the bench. From the terrace an extensive view of the city and the sea can be enjoyed.
In the park there can be seen other things designed by Gaudi; colonnades, grottoes, viaducts, etc. His former residence is furnished as a museum.

**Tibidabo

NW of the city centre rises Tibidabo, a 532 m/1746 ft high hill which is one of the most popular venues for excursions in the whole area. Its name comes from the Bible, "Tibi dabo montem" meaning "I will give you a mountain".

Access

From the Plaça de Catalunya (see page 55) we go by the railway which runs underground (Ferrocarril de la Generalitat) to the terminus at Avinguda del Tibidabo. From here, there is an old-timer tram, known, because of the dark blue painted cars, in Catalan as "Tramvia Blau" (Spanish: "Tranvia Azul") uphill to the funicular (lower station 223.5 m/734 ft above sea level; model of Tibidabo; restaurant). The funicular is the last stage to the top of Tibidabo. From the city there is also an 8 km/5 miles long winding road up the mountain.

Museu de la Ciència/Museo de la Ciéncia

Near the Tramvia Blau can be found in Carrer Teodor Roviralta No. 55 the Science Museum (Museu de la Ciència), an endowment of the Catalonian Social Bank (La Caixa). It houses permanent exhibitions on the subjects of optics, mechanics and space research; associated with it are a meteorological station, a planetarium and an observatory. The Science Museum is open from Monday to Saturday from 10 a.m. to 8 p.m.
Above the upper station of the funicular there stands on the summit of Tibidabo the mighty Church of "Sagrado Cora-

zón de Jesus" (Church of the Sacred Heart); this building was completed in 1961 in an historicised style but is only of limited value from the point of view of the history of art. On tho roof is a large statue of Christ and behind the church a house for spiritual exercises. Nearby are the Barcelona radio transmitter (1924) and the television transmitter of Catalunya Radio (1963).
Close to the entrance to the amusement park and near the upper station of the funicular is a little mirador (observation platform) from which there is a magnificent view of the whole of Barcelona and, in good weather, as far as the Balearic Islands.
Inland can be seen Montserrat, Montseny and, in the north, the Pyrenees.

Amusement Park

The major public attraction of Tibidabo is the Parc de Atracciones, an amusement park laid out in several terraces on the steep side of the mountain. It has various rides (big dipper, suspension railway, auto-scooter, go-cart track) and other amusements, as well as games of skill, several restaurants, etc. The park is especially attractive for families with children, preferably as a half-day excursion from Barcelona. The park is open from 10.30 a.m. to 9.15 p.m. on weekdays, until 9.45 p.m.on Saturdays, Sundays and public holidays. Visitors under five years of age or over 60 are admitted free, but the various rides, etc., have to be paid for separately.

Pedralbes

At the S foot of Tibidabo lies Pedralbes and here in the Gothic church (1326) can be seen the alabaster tomb of Queen Elisenda de Montcada (d. 1364), the consort of

Amusement park on Tibidabo

James II. In the three-storied adjoining cloister is the Capilla de San Miguel, with notable Gothic wall paintings (1346) by Ferrer Bassa.

Bellcaire

See Torroella de Montgrí

Begur/Bagur G8

Country: Spain
Province: Girona
Altitude: 220 m/722 ft
Population: 2000

Location

Begur (Spanish: Bagur) is situated a short distance inland from the Costa Daurada approximately in the latitude of Girona.

The Town

The focal point of Begur is its old fortress which stands on a conical hill and until 1810 served military purposes. The impressive panorama extends as far as Estartit and the Islas Medas, behind which in the distance the northern limit of the Golf de Roses can be discerned. The Parish Church of Begur dates from the 18th c. and still has parts of the vaulting of its predecessor.

Playa de Fornells

Location
2 km/1 mile S from Begur

The Playa de Fornells and Aiguablava are the most important beaches of the town of Begur which is situated a little way inland. At the Playa de Fornells stands the luxurious Hotel Aiguablava and a number of fine villas. There is a little pleasure boat harbour with the Club Nàutico; however, bathing is extremely limited for the coast is entirely rocky and the only way into the water is down concrete ramps. Visitors who prefer a sandy beach should stay in Aiguablava.

Aiguablava

Aiguablava adjoins the Playa de Fornells and the beach is reached by a private roadway. The somewhat small but busy beach is framed by steep cliffs and surrounded by pine woods. The area includes several rocky bays with surprisingly clear and clean water. There is also a Parador Nacional here, one of the luxurious and tasteful hotels so typical of Spain.

Begur, crowned by its castle

Playa de Fornells: the little harbour

Besalú E5

Country: Spain
Province: Girona
Altitude: 151 m/496 ft
Population: 2000

Location

Besalú on the Riu Fluvià lies in the extreme N of Catalonia only 50 km/31 miles from the Franco-Spanish border as the crow flies. The river here is joined by the Riera de Capellada and 35 km/22 miles farther on flows into the Mediterranean.

**The Town

Besalú, a short way off the main road, is the old capital of the county of Garrotxa and is the centre of a small country parish. The heart of Besalú has retained its ancient character, with narrow streets and old sacred and secular buildings. On the hill above the town rise the dominating ruins of the Church of Santa Maria.
In summer concerts of classical music take place here.

Plaça Major/Plaza Mayor

The harmonious Plaça Major, the chief square and central point of the old part of the township is lined with shady arcaded walks. On the W side stands the Town Hall and the Oficina Municipal de Turisme (tourist bureau). At the end of Carrer Tallaferro can be seen a recently restored stately building with arbours on the ground floor and Romanesque twin windows on the first floor.

Santa Maria

Carrer Tallaferro climbs to the remains of the former Collegiate Church of Santa Maria (the area is not always open to the public and visitors should enquire at the Oficina de Turisme). Of this high Romanesque building (12th/13th c.) little more than the arch of the choir remains, since it was deconsecrated in 1836 and gradually taken down. The Gothic statue of the Madonna which was formerly in the church can now be seen in the Museum of Girona. The ducal palace which also once stood in this area has almost completely disappeared.

Sant Vincenç/San Vicente

From the main square it is only a few steps to the late Romanesque Parish Church of Sant Vincenç in Carrer Major; the tower was considerably restored in the 16th century. The apse of the church faces the street; in the SE wall of the nave is a remarkable Romanesque doorway (Port de Sant Rafael) with round arches and capitals ornamented with figures. The portal in the main façade is less impressive; above it can be seen a window which is partly Romanesque and partly Gothic. When services are not being held the interior of the church can only be seen by prior arrangement with the Oficina de Turisme. To the left of the high altar is the Gothic tomb of Pere de Rovira who brought the relics of St Vincent to Besalú.

Sant Pere/San Pedro

In the Plaça de Sant Pere, SW of the main square, stands another Romanesque church. The massive three-aisled

Besalú: a medieval picture ▶

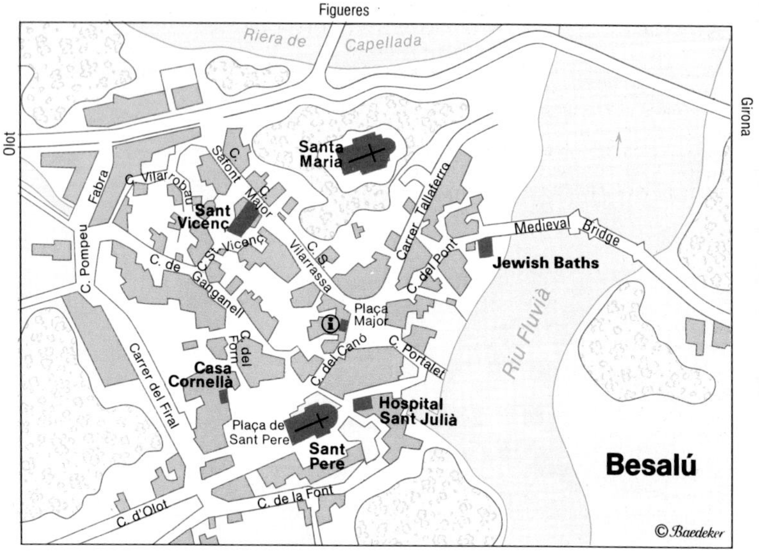

building with transepts and a choir ambulatory is dedicated to St Peter and was once part of the Benedictine monastery founded in 977. Today it is considered one of the most important Romanesque churches of Catalonia. On the smooth almost plain façade the central window high up is particularly striking (field-glasses useful); the pillars, which bear capitals with richly figured ornamentation, are flanked by sculpted lions. The tower was altered in the 17th/18th c.

Casa Cornellà

In the Plaça de Sant Pere, opposite the church mentioned above rises the Casa Cornellà, a stately palace the origins of which go back to Romanesque times. The inner courtyard with its two-storied arcades is charming; the palace contains a small collection of local exhibits.

Hospital de Sant Julià

East of the church of Sant Pere stands the Hospital de Sant Julià (12th c.) a one-storey building. There are beautiful figured capitals in the round arch of the doorway.

Jewish Bath

From the main square Carrer del Pont leads to the medieval bridge over the Riu Fluvià. In the street on the right a little way away can be seen the Mikwe (signpost 'Miqwe'; visits only by arrangement with the Oficina de Turisme), the former Jewish ritual bath. This is also a relic of the Romanesque age since there was a strong Israelite community in Besalú. Later the rectangular basin, to which a few steps lead down, was used from time to time as a dye works before it was filled with mud and debris by flooding of the nearby river. Not until 1964 was the bath restored. From the forecourt there is a good view of the bridge and the river.

Medieval Bridge

The Riu Fluvià is spanned by a great bridge which was restored in 1315. It is in the form of an obtuse angle and on the town side is protected by a gate and in the middle by a tower, both with a portcullis. Its five irregular arches and its characteristic silhouette have made it the landmark of Besalú. There is a good view of the medieval structure from the nearby modern road bridge.
An excursion from Besalú via Castellfollit de la Roca (see entry) to the little town of Olat (see entry), situated in an old volcanic landscape, is recommended.

La Bisbal

G7

Country: Spain
Province: Girona
Altitude: 39 m/128 ft
Population: 7500

Location

La Bisbal lies half way between the provincial capital of Girona and the Mediterranean coast on the southern flank of the estuarine plain of the Riu Ter.

The Town

La Bisbal has greatly expanded from its medieval heart. It is a well-known centre of ceramics and the location of the Escola de Ceramica (Technical School of Ceramics). In every part of the town there are shops with products of the local ceramic manufactory on sale. In addition to objects made exclusively for the souvenir trade, which are often of doubtful taste, there can be found a good selection of simple aesthetic ware, pottery articles of everyday use which are functionally pleasing and reasonably priced. In the inner part of the town the bed of the Daró river is spanned by a twin-arched medieval bridge. The Romanesque castle in the centre of the town, once the seat of the Bishops of La Bisbal, has a defence tower built to a square plan.
A little way outside the town to the S stands the Monastery of Santa Llúcia (Spanish: Santa Lucia).
N of La Bisbal in the plain lies the archaeological site of an Iberian settlement, Poblado Iberico (see Ullastret).

Cruilles

Location
3 km/2 miles W of La Bisbal

The village of Cruilles still has to a large extent the appearance of an unspoiled medieval township. There are only a few remains of the former fortress; the early Romanesque parish church with the Museu Parroquial nearby with its triple-vaulted choir is worth inspection. About ½ km/¼ mile outside the village in Sant Miquel de Cruilles can be seen an old Romanesque monastery.

Blanes

H5

Country: Spain
Province: Girona
Altitude: sea level
Population: 19,000

Location

Blanes, the most southerly resort of Girona and of the Costa Brava, lies immediately to the N of the estuary of the Riu Tordera which here forms the boundary of the province of Barcelona and also of the Costa Daurada (Spanish: Costa Dorada).

The Town

Blanes, today one of the well-known resorts of the Costa Brava, developed from a fishing port which is still of considerable economic importance. The town is renowned for its lace manufactory.
There are many facilities for sports in Blanes.
In the area of the Old Town the sandy beach to the NE of the pleasure and fishing harbour is bounded on the SW by the exposed rocky cliff called Sa Palomera. This cliff can be climbed and from its top there is a good view of the coast in the near vicinity. The Oficina de Turisme (tourist office) is on the coastal road; farther to the SW extend the newer parts of the town and the complex of hotels.

Blanes: a bird's eye view of the resort

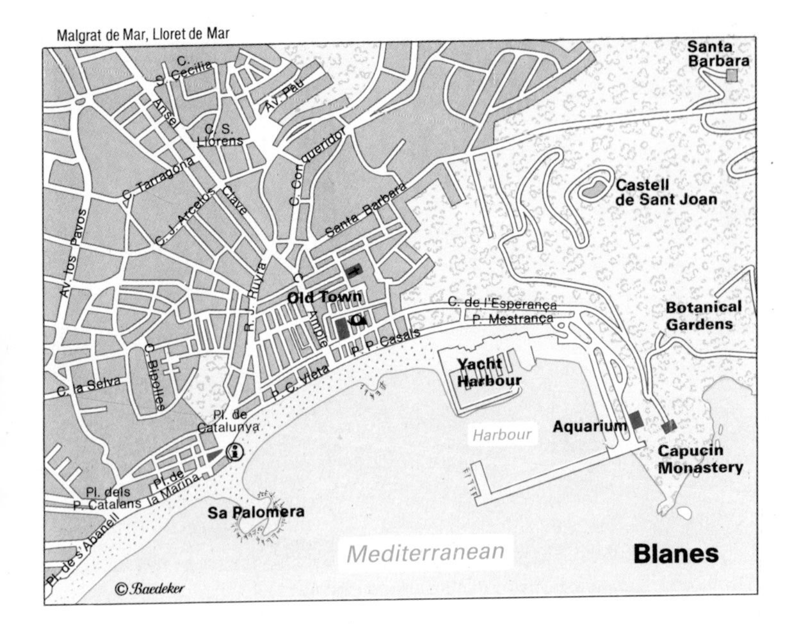

Old Town

The sea and the Old Town are separated by the promenade along the shore, from which the most important streets run at right-angles. On Carrer Ample ("wide street") can be seen a notable Gothic fountain; farther inland the centre of the town is bounded by an ancient town gate, the Portal de Santa Maria.

The Parish Church stands high above the maze of houses; it is predominantly Gothic and has three aisles of almost equal height. The interior is somewhat gloomy; over the main doorway can be seen a rose window.

Harbour Area

The shore promenade (Passeig Maritim/Paseo Maritimo), with its seats shaded by conifers and its rose bushes, is an attractive place; the tourist market takes place here. Half way along the Passeig stands a memorial to Joaquim Ruyra (1858–1939). At the northern end can be seen a monument consisting of three old rust-eaten anchors; this has been dedicated by the fishermen of Blanes to all friends of the sea.

Nowadays the harbour is used for commercial fishing only to a limited extent. Near the harbour are the Llotja del Peix (fishing exchange) and the aquarium (with a research station) which was opened in 1961.

Marimurtra: a poem by Goethe in Catalan and Castilian

*Marimurtra (Botanical Garden)

Open
Daily 9 a.m.–6 p.m.

Entrance fee

In the NE of Blanes, not far beyond the harbour, lies the renowned Botanical Garden of Marimurtra (regular bus service from the town centre). It was laid out by a German merchant Karl Faust (d. 1952; his bust can be seen in the pergola near the entrance) and contains more than 3000 botanical species, predominantly from the Mediterranean area. The magnificence of the flowers in the extensive beds on the hillside is overwhelming. Visitors are given a brochure at the entrance with the individual beds numbered in accordance with the numbering on the ground. The severe winter of 1984/85 has led to considerable damage to the stock of plants. The Botanical Garden occupies the greater part of the tongue of land and in many places there are charming views of the steep coastline. Far below on a picturesque bay stands a little round temple and from here a flight of steps leads up to a waterlily pool where there is a ceramic plaque on which is inscribed Goethe's well-known poem "Song of Mignon" in German as well as in Catalan and Spanish translations.

*Castell de Sant Joan/Castillo de San Juan

NE of the little town on a hill 166 m/380 ft high are the scanty remains of the Castell de Sant Joan, a fortress built in the 11th c. It can be reached on foot or by car (making first for the Botanical Garden and then above the harbour turning sharp left and climbing up between fine residential properties). Outside the remains of the walls stands a little single-aisle chapel of Gothic date. Inside on the left hangs the model of a two-masted sailing ship and on the right there is a copy of the Madonna statue of Montserrat (see entry). The decoration of the altar wall is modern. The view from the top of the hill is exceptionally fine, to the S can be seen Blanes and its beaches, to the N the hills near the coast and higher up the Ermita de Santa Bàrbara.

Cabo de Creus

See Cadaqués

Cadaqués

E8

Country: Spain
Province: Girona
Altitude: sea level
Population: 1600

Location

The former fishing town of Cadaqués is situated in the far N of the Costa Brava on a large hilly peninsula which juts out into the sea as the Cap de Creus and is bounded on the N by the Golf de Roses.

Cadaqués: a white town by a blue sea

At the beginning of the 20th c. the little town was a favourite resort of painters and writers especially from the S of France and Spain, including André Breton, Paul Eluard, the naturalised Frenchman Max Ernst and others. The famous Surrealist Salvador Dali, Catalan by birth, had his country house in nearby Port Lligat.
The International Music Festival, which takes place annually in summer in the Parish Church is renowned.

**The Town

The old centre of Cadaqués, with its white houses and narrow streets often only suitable for pedestrians, lies on the side of a hill at the top of which stands the church. A local group of artists has taken on the responsibility for maintaining and looking after the exceptional picturesque townscape. The little mussel-shaped bay of the harbour with its crystal clear water is not very suitable for bathing. The more important beaches are to be found farther N towards the Cap de Creus otherwise indented rocky coasts hold sway. There are many opportunities for water sports, there is a sailing school where boats can be hired and a school for water-skiing. Excellent diving can be had along this rocky coast.
In the casino art exhibitions on various themes are mounted.

Santa Maria

The Parish Church of Santa Maria was rebuilt in the 17th c., after the former church had been completely destroyed in one of the numerous attacks by pirates. The interior has a notable Baroque altar (1727) by Pau Costa and a Baroque organ. The church is the venue of an international music festival.

Museu Perrot-Moore

Near the harbour can be found the Museu Perrot-Moore (open daily 5–9 p.m.; entrance fee), containing a good collection of paintings from the 15th c. onwards, including works by German, Dutch and Italian masters of the 16th and 17th c. and of the classic modernists (Impressionism, Cubism, Surrealism).

Port Lligat

Location
2 km/1 miles from Cadaqués

Salvador Dali has spent the greater part of his life in Port Lligat; his country house (not open to the public) is an extremely unconventional building. Recently the artist has avoided being in residence.
The Dali Museum in Figures (see entry) should be visited.

*Cap de Creus/Cabo de Creus

Location
4 km/2½ miles from Cadaqués

The Cap de Creus, the exposed most easterly point of the Iberian peninsula, can be reached on foot or by boat. The 80 m/263 ft high spur, the Cape Aphrodision of ancient Greece, has a lighthouse.

Caldes de Malavella, where the Romans bathed

Cala Fornells

See Begur

Caldes de Malavella/Caldas de Malavella G–H5

Country: Spain
Province: Girona
Altitude: 94 m/309 ft
Population: 3000

Location

Caldes de Malavella (Spanish: Caldas de Malavella) lies on the Riera de Caldes and on the edge of the extensive hilly country which extends a good 15 km/9 miles to the S of Girona.

The Town

Caldes de Malavella is a small provincial spa with mineral and thermal springs up to 35 °C/95 °F which were known and used by the Romans. In various parts of the town there are springs which are generally available to the public. Several firms are engaged in marketing table water, including "Vichy Catalan", but apart from this the spa and baths have lost their importance. In the centre of the town stands the red plastered "Casa Rosa" (now a local museum and a youth centre) with a peculiar tiled entrance dating from the time of Art Nouveau.

Roman Baths

The scanty remains of the Roman Baths are situated on the property of a firm producing mineral water; a walled basin and other foundation elements and two archways can be seen.

Spa Facilities

The spa establishment is situated outside the town on the through road. The spring water is used especially for diseases of the digestive and respiratory tracts and cardiac complaints, as well as for metabolic disorders and rheumatism.

Caldes d'Estrac/Caldetas de Estrach

See Arenys de Mar

Caldes de Montbui/Caldas de Montbuy J1–2

Country: Spain
Province: Barcelona
Altitude: 180 m/590 ft
Population: 10,000

Location

Caldes de Montbui (Spanish: Caldas de Montbuy) lies on a hill above the Riu Caldes about 25 km/16 miles N of Barcelona.

The Town

Caldes de Montbui claims to possess one of the largest thermal springs in Europe. The water emerges at a temperature of 70 °C/158 °F; it is principally used to treat rheumatism as well as circulatory and respiratory conditions. One of the springs is in the rebuilt Roman bath; there is also a little archaeological museum in the former 14th c. hospital. Among the houses of the old town is an old synagogue. The Parish Church of Santa Maria is a building in high Baroque; in the interior can be seen a remarkable Romanesque crucifix (11th–12th c.).

Calella (Province: Girona)

See Palafrugell

Calella de la Costa

J4–5

Country: Spain
Province: Barcelona
Altitude: sea level
Population: 10,000

Location

Calella de la Costa, not to be confused with Calella near Palafrugell (see entry) in the Province of Girona, lies near the northern end of the Costa Daurada (Spanish: Costa Dorada) about 25 km/30 miles N of Barcelona.

The Town

The townscape of today is characterised by gigantic hotels and apartment complexes which have developed along the broad sandy beach. The former quiet village has become a holiday estate with a great deal of activity; the infrastructure provides everything which the seaside holidaymaker requires. There are schools for sailing, windsurfing and water-skiing (in each of which apparatus and equipment can be rented), a sports centre (bowling, table tennis, minigolf), tennis courts, facilities for riding, bicycle rental and an area for the favourite local game of frontón (also known as pelota); bars and a nightclub complete the facilities. By far the largest number of visitors come from Western Germany and the place has been named somewhat maliciously "Calella de los Alemanes". The ancient centre of the town with predominantly two-storied houses and a striking church of mixed architectural styles has relatively little of interest. A weekly market takes place in the main square.

Pineda

Barely 4 km/2½ miles NE lies the coastal village of Pineda which recent building has almost joined to Calella. Like Calella Pineda is geared to seaside holidays but on the whole is quieter than its neighbouring resort.
On the other side of the road on a little hill stands the Ermita de Gracia, a small white chapel which can be seen from a long way away.

Calella de Palafrugell

See Palafrugell

Calonge

G7

Country: Spain
Province: Girona
Altitude: 38 m/125 ft
Population: 5000

Location

Calonge is situated 3 km/2 miles inland from the coast SE of Girona.

The Town

Calonge is still a relatively quiet little town which is dominated by its old castle standing on a hill in the centre. The four-towered building dating from the 12th and 15th c. is not open to the public; immediately to the left of the entrance to the castle courtyard can be found the Archaeological Museum (Museu arqueològic; open June and Sept. daily 5–8 p.m., July and Aug. daily 6–9 p.m., closed in winter; entrance fee). Nearby stands the church with its plain Baroque façade; above the entrance is a relief of St Martin. The little parish museum (cult articles, early medieval architectural remains) is only open on Sunday mornings. On the nearby slopes around Calonge there are extensive housing developments. The nearest beaches are at Sant Antoni de Calonge and Palamós (see entry).

Camprodón

E3

Country: Spain
Province: Girona
Altitude: 950 m/3118 ft
Population: 2000

Location

Camprodón lies on the southern slopes of the Collado de Ares/Col d'Arès across which runs the Spanish-French border (customs formalities normally between 8 a.m. and 8 p.m.). The town, skirted by the main road, lies some 15 km/9 miles from the summit of the pass.

The Town

This township in the valley of the Riu Ter has a charming old-fashioned centre with narrow streets and houses built close together; it is advisable to leave your car on the outskirts. Camprodón is especially popular with French visitors.

In the little main square, with its shady plain trees, stands the parish church (beautiful high altar) dedicated to Saints Viktor and Palladios; beyond it to the right and somewhat higher up stands the church of the former monastery which had been built in the 11th c. on the foundations of a church 100 years older. Also of interest is the 12th c. Church of St Pere (St Peter's) and the arched bridge which was built across the river in the 17th c.

Molló/Mollo

Location
5 km/3 miles N of Camprodón

The village of Molló lies in a gently undulating verdant landscape. A little way from the village stands a charming little 12th c. Romanesque church of which there is a good view from the road over the pass.

Canet de Mar

See Arenys de Mar

Castellfollit de la Roca/Castellfullit de la Roca E4

Country: Spain
Province: Girona
Altitude: 296 m/971 ft
Population: 1200

Location

Castellfollit (Spanish: Castellfullit) lies far inland in the valley of the Riu Fluvià (between Besalú and Olot) and approximately in the latitude of the Golf de Roses.

*The Town

The best view of this fantastic town can be had from the road coming from Besalú before reaching Castellfollit. The old part of the township with its narrow little streets was built on a basalt spur which falls almost vertically to the river. Near the extreme point of the rocks stands the old church. The town museum (archaeology, ethnology, art and natural science) was opened in 1986.

Castellfollit de la Roca; impregnable from the valley

Castelló d'Empúries/Castelló de Ampurias E7

Country: Spain
Province: Girona
Altitude: 18 m/59 ft
Population: 2000

Location

Castelló d'Empúries (Spanish: Castelló de Ampurias) is situated not far inland from the Golf de Roses in the estuarine plain of the rivers Muga and Fluvià.

Sights

The large Church of Santa Maria, dating from the 13th–15th c., exhibits partly the architectural forms of the Romanesque period. The reason for this was the intention of the Counts of Ampurdán to make the place once more into a bishopric, a status which it had not held since the 7th c. Of interest is the Gothic doorway with a statue of the Apostles (some modern copies) the upper part of which is badly damaged and is incomplete; in the Tympanum is a representation of the Adoration of the Magi. The tower has beautiful Romanesque pillared arcades. In the three-aisled interior can be seen a Gothic retable (screen at rear of altar). Also of interest are the former Marine Exchange (Liotja de Mar), the old ducal palace (now the town hall) and the remains of the town wall with its gates and the seven-arched bridge over the Riu Muga.

Céret D5

Country: France
Département: Pyrénées-Orientales
Altitude: 171 m/561 ft
Population: 7000

Location

Céret is situated in the lower valley of the River Tech about 30 km/18 miles SW of Perpignan.

General

The picturesque township of Céret lies in fertile countryside where early vegetables are grown. At the beginning of the 20th c. it was known as the stronghold of Cubist art which was represented especially here by the Spanish-Catalan sculpture and graphic artist Manolo (actually Manuel Martinez Hugué; 1872–1945). He was also responsible for the monument to the composer Déodat de Séverac (1873–1921) in the main square of the old town of Céret.
The town is headquarters of a Catalan culture centre.

The Town

In the charming centre of the town are a number of huge ancient plane trees which contribute a great deal to the pleasant atmosphere. On the N side of the main square stands the Palais de Justice, the Town Hall and the Office de Tourisme; on the N is the Musée d'Art Moderne (Museum of Modern Art; closed on Tues.), in which works by such well-known artists of the early modernistic period such as

Maillol, Matisse, Dali, Miró and Manolo can be seen.
By following Rue Jaurès from the square to the S not far to the right of the church we come to the Place Pablo Picasso where stands the Porte d'Espagne, a remnant of the former town walls. Nearby is a monument to Picasso which was designed according to one of his own drawings.
Not far NW outside the town a 14th c. bridge ("Pont du Diable", devil's bridge) spans the Tech in an arch 45 m/50 ft wide.
Farther upstream we come to Amélie-les-Bains (see entry) and the Col d'Arès/Collado de Ares, over which runs the Franco-Spanish border (customs formalities normally between 8 a.m. and 8 p.m.).

Costa Brava

Country: Spain
Province: Girona

General

The Costa Brava ("wild coast") is the 200 km/125 mile long northernmost part of the Spanish Mediterranean coast, between the French border and the estuary of the Riu Tordera near Blanes which here forms the boundary between the provinces of Girona and Barcelona.

**Landscape

Because of its impressive scenery and its comparatively short distance from the countries of central Europe the Costa Brava is one of the most popular holiday areas in Spain. The exceptionally strongly indented coastline is for the most part rocky and many of the steep promontories cannot be reached by car but only by boat. Between these cliffs, however, lie picturesque fishing villages and little towns with sandy bays and newly constructed holiday complexes (called Urbanizaciones).
The visitor who is disinclined to undertake the long drive along the coast, which because of its curves is somewhat tiring, can reach the best places on the Costa Brava by making use of the generally good side roads diverging from the national road N11 which runs parallel to the motorway A17.

Note for caravan and motor caravan drivers

Most places in the hilly area or in the narrow valley estuaries usually have in their older parts very narrow and winding streets. These should therefore be avoided by drivers with trailers or of motor caravans which are larger than a minibus; if this advice is ignored there will certainly come a moment when the vehicle becomes hopelessly blocked.
The places in the Costa Brava can be found in this book under the corresponding named headings or can be found by consulting the index at the end of the book.

Costa Daurada/Costa Dorada

Country: Spain
Province: Barcelona and Tarragona

Location

The Costa Daurada (Spanish: Costa Dorada; "golden

coast") also known as the Costa de la Maresma ("marshland coast") includes practically the entire coastal areas of the provinces of Barcelona and Tarragona. It adjoins on the S the Costa Brava and extends approximately 260 km/ 160 miles along the Mediterranean. Its southern end is formed by the estuarine area of the River Ebre (Spanish: Ebro). The part of the Costa Daurada with which this book is concerned is its most northerly section between the estuary of the Riu Tordera and the Catalan capital Barcelona.

Landscape

The Costa Daurada between the Riu Tordera and Barcelona forms a strong contrast to the Costa Brava which adjoins it on the N. The area is considerably flatter and in places marshy, the coastline runs almost in a straight line. The broad beaches of predominantly fine sand which extend for miles quickly led to a rise in tourism but there were no natural barriers to the quick extension of resorts and therefore today the consequences of a long period of a building boom are evident; in many places unimaginative anonymous hotel blocks spoil the region. However, it is here that some of the best-known seaside resorts of the Spanish Mediterranean coast are to be found.
One feature characterises all the coastal resorts in this area; the old village centres are separated from the sea by the busy national road N2 and the railway line.
Places on the Costa Daurada can be found in this book under the appropriate heading or looked up in the index at the end of the book.

Côte Vermeille

Country: France
Département: Pyrénées-Orientales

Location

The Côte Vermeille ("purple coast") extends between Collioure (SE of Perpignan) and the French-Spanish border at the Col des Balitres. The adjoining flat and sandy strip of coast to the N is part of the holiday area of Languedoc-Roussillon (see Perpignan).

*Landscape

The Côte Vermeille is rocky and strongly indented; in the bays lie a number of picturesque little towns which are popular as seaside resorts. Since there are no bypasses these places in the main season have to suffer from considerable through traffic. The road (charming views) and the railway follow the coast in numerous curves and at various heights. Apart from vineyards there is very little vegetation.

Vineyards

Extensive cultivation of vines on the steep cliffs goes on up to an altitude of 300 m/985 ft above sea level; the wines are marketed under the name (appellation contrõlée) of "Banyuls" and are some of the best in this region. They include red wine and the so-called "vins doux naturels" (pure sweet wine). The appellation "naturally pure" is, however, misleading since both the characteristic flavour and also the high sugar content are achieved by adding concentrated alcohol to the fermenting must and thus interrupting fermentation before all the sugar is converted.

From Collioure to the Col des Balitres (about 30 km/19 miles)

*Collioure

Collioure, which was once the port of Perpignan, is a picturesque seaside resort; its little harbour and old castle attracted artists such as Matisse, Derain, Braque, Picasso and Dufy. The place was known to the Phoenicians as a port. The castle was once the seat of the kings of Mallorca and the queens of Aragón; some of the rooms can be inspected.
The fortress-church which dominates the northern part of the bay with its massive round tower, a former lighthouse, was built in 1691; inside can be seen beautiful altars and the church treasure.
From the church a causeway runs along the beach to the former island of Saint-Vincent, on which stands a little chapel. Another causeway leads to the lighthouse.

Port-Vendres

Port-Vendres, commercial, fishing and pleasure port, as well as a watering place lies on a very well protected bay. In the 17th c. Sébastien Vauban, the most important defence architect in France developed Port-Vendres into a naval harbour; the Fort du Fanal is a relic of that time. The fishing port is the leading one of Roussillon. To the E of the town Cap Béar projects seaward. A very narrow and winding road leads to the lighthouse (beautiful view to the S).

Collioure, a jewel of the Côte Vermeille

Banyuls-sur-Mer

Banyuls has given its name to the whole area where vines are cultivated. It is also popular as a seaside resort and has a large and well constructed pleasure harbour. The town is protected from biting winds by the high ground around it so that exotic plants such as carobs, eucalyptus and palms thrive. Banyuls is the headquarters of an oceanographic station and has an aquarium with Mediterranean fauna. On the Ile Grosse, which is joined to the mainland by a causeway, stands a war memorial by Aristide Maillol (1861–1944) who was born in Banyuls. His former little estate, in the garden of which he is buried, lies barely 5 km/3 miles to the SW.

Cerbère

Cerbère is the French frontier post before the crossing into Spain. The townscape is characterised by the huge railway complex, the construction of which was necessary because the main lines of Spanish railways have a broader gauge than those of other European countries. This entails either a change of train or a change of bogies. Not far to the SE rises Cap Cerbère with deeply fissured black rocks (car park; good view of the Spanish coast to the S).

Col des Balitre

The Franco-Spanish frontier crosses the summit of the pass called Col des Balitres (173 m/568 ft).

El . . .

See main name

Elne

C6

Country: France
Département: Pyrénées-Orientales
Altitude: 52 m/170 ft
Population: 6000

Location

Elne occupies a hill in the coastal plain of Roussillon, about 15 km/9 miles SE of Perpignan

The Town

The old-fashioned little town, the chief place of Roussillon in the 5th/6th c., nestles around the Cathedral of Ste Eulalie which occupies an elevated site. The Romanesque building dates from the 11th c.; a Gothic extension was begun but was never finished, and the foundations for a ring of chapels outside the apse can still be seen. The cloister, partly Romanesque and partly Gothic, (open June–Sept. daily 10–11.45 a.m. and 2–6.45 p.m.; in winter only to 4.45 or 5.45 p.m.) was added in the 12th and 14th c. and is notable for richly figured capitals on the groups of pillars. In a little cathedral chapel there is a museum with archaeological finds of the Iberian and Roman eras. Outside the apse of the cathedral lies a small terrace, from which there is a good view of the foothills of the Pyrenees.

The square in front of the church is the starting point for a walk (circuit des remparts) through the upper town and along the walls which surround it. On the SW corner of these walls there is an observation point with an orienteering table.

Empúria Brava/Ampuriabrava E7

Country: Spain
Province: Girona
Altitude: sea level

Location

Empúria Brava (Spanish: Ampuriabrava) lies in the northern part of the Costa Brava, near the place where the Riu Muga flows into the Golf de Roses.

The Town

Empúria Brava is a lagoon estate, laid out on a drawing-board pattern. where the planners have been entirely governed by the demands of modern tourism. Hotels are greatly outnumbered by private houses and small apartment blocks which for the most part are quite tastefully designed and few are more than two storeys high. The buildings are grouped around an extensive network of artificial canals which are linked to a harbour where boats can

Empúria Brava: moorings by the houses

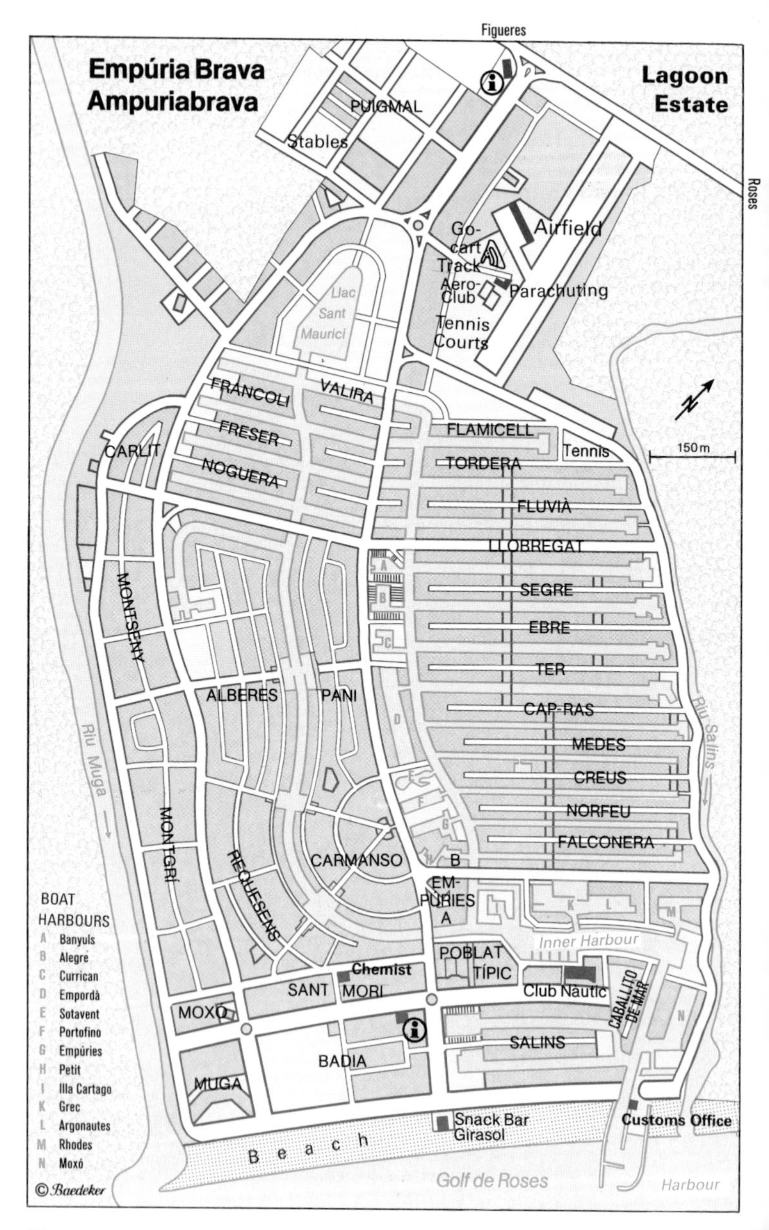

Empúria Brava
Ampuriabrava
Lagoon Estate
Figueres
Roses
PUIGMAL
Stables
Go-cart Track
Airfield
Aero-Club
Parachuting
Tennis Courts
Llac Sant Maurici
FRANCOLI
VALIRA
FRESER
NOGUERA
CARLIT
FLAMICELL
TORDERA
Tennis
150 m
FLUVIÀ
LLOBREGAT
SEGRE
EBRE
TER
CAP-RAS
MEDES
CREUS
NORFEU
FALCONERA
MONTSENY
ALBERES
PANI
MONTGRÍ
REQUESENS
CARMANSO
EMPÚRIES
Riu Muga
Riu Salins
Inner Harbour
POBLAT TÍPIC
Chemist
SANT MORI
Club Nàutic
CABALLITO DE MAR
MOXÓ
SALINS
BADIA
MUGA
Snack Bar Girasol
Customs Office
Beach
Golf de Roses
Harbour
BOAT HARBOURS
A Banyuls
B Alegre
C Currican
D Empordà
E Sotavent
F Portofino
G Empúries
H Petit
I Illa Cartago
K Grec
L Argonautes
M Rhodes
N Moxó
© Baedeker

be moored. Here can be found the Club Nàutic, a somewhat unconventional complex of buildings dominated by a tower and including a swimming pool with a diving platform.
A small airfield has been laid out a little way inland.

Aiguamolls de l'Empordà Nature Park

On both sides of the lagoon estate in the flat countryside near the coast extends the Parc Natural dels Aiguamolls de l'Empordà which covers an area of 4784 hectares/11,821 acres. In this largely marshy area through which flows the Riu Fluvia, a great many species of animals and plants have been preserved. Here can be seen birds of prey, flamingoes, various kinds of waterfowl and waders (field-glasses!); in the fresh, brackish and sea water live great numbers of flat fish, carp, eels and amphibians.
In those areas which are marked as completely protected visitors may not leave the paths nor may anything be taken away; dogs must be kept on the lead. Some protection against flies and midges is strongly advised. The information centre for the nature park can be found off the road from Empúria Brava to Sant Pescador; a natural history museum was opened in 1987.

Empúries/Ampurias — F7

Country: Spain
Province: Girona
Altitude: sea level

Location

The excavation site of the ancient town of Emporion, now Empúries (Catalan)/Ampurias (Spanish), lies near the southern end of the Golf de Roses where rise the slopes of the Empordà (Spanish Ampurdán). This fairly modern settlement bears the name of Sant Marti de Empúries (Spanish San Martin de Ampurias).

History

In the 6th c. B.C. Greeks founded this settlement which at that time lay on an island near the mouth of the River Fluviá. The river has meanwhile moved farther N owing to silting. The older part of the Greek town which has been called Palaiapolis by the archaeologists was at that time presumably called Kypsela. Considerable inroads of Greek colonists from the NE made necessary the foundation of a new settlement farther to the S on the mainland; this was called Emporion (= market) and today is known as Neapolis (= new town) and forms the largest part of the excavation area. Between the two settlements lay the harbour which has since been completely enclosed by the land. It is presumed that close by there was also an Iberian place called Indika. When in the 3rd c. B.C. the Romans took over the territories in the Mediterranean ruled by the Greeks, they also conquered this colony. Here during the Second Punic War the first Roman troops landed under the command of Scipio the Elder (Scipio Africanus major) in order to secure a defensive position against Hannibal. A little later in the year 195 B.C. the elder Cato used the settlement as a stronghold for the subjugation of the Iberians. About the middle of the 1st c. B.C. Caesar finally established a colony here for the veterans of his army. In the 1st and 2nd c. A.D. Emporiae, as the community was called by the Romans, attained its zenith. In the 3rd c. attacks by the Frankish/Alemannic armies led to decline and destruction. In early Christian times Empúries was the see of a Bishop. The nearby town of La Escala was founded in the 17th c. when the remains of Emporion came in useful as building material. The Spanish archaeologist Emilio Gandia y Ortega (1866–1939) carried out the first excavations on the site; his bronze bust can be seen in the lower town on the former agora.

**The Ruins

Open
Tues.–Sun. 10 a.m.–2 p.m. and 3–7 p.m.;
winter 10 a.m.–1 p.m. and 3–5 p.m.

Entrance fee

The excavated part of the site which is now open to visitors is divided into the Greek lower town and the Roman upper town. Empúries has an extremely picturesque position near the sea with extensive views of the promontories to the N and to the S. Pines and cypresses contribute to its park-like appearance. The remains of the most important ancient buildings are numbered or have written descriptions; and the way round is clearly marked. There are parking places within the excavation site.

The lower town

The Greek lower town is entered through the remains of a mighty gate in the former town wall; then we reach a small square and to the left the remains of a temple dedicated to

Empúries: the lower town, once securely held by the Greeks

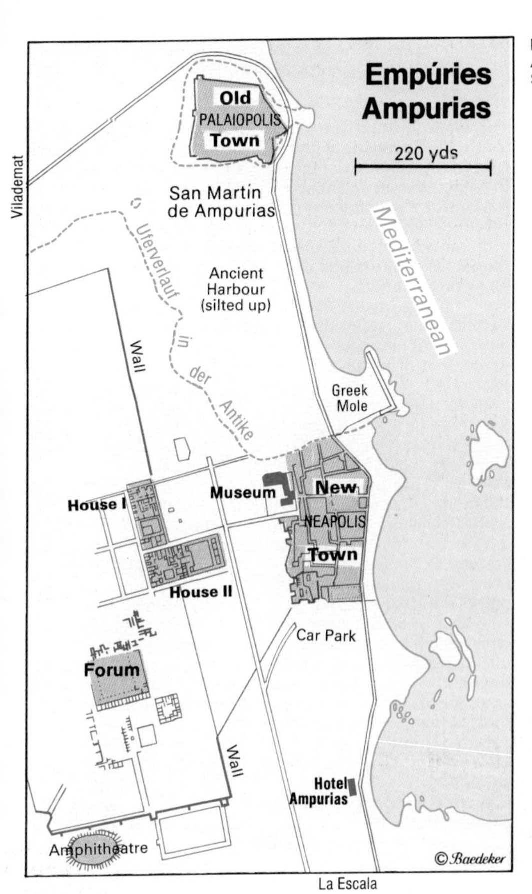

Plan of the Archaeological Site

the healing god Asklepios; the original of the statue (3rd c. B.C.) found in the temple is of pentelic marble and can be seen in the Archaeological Museum of Barcelona (see entry); here it has been replaced by a copy. Immediately adjoining are the foundations of another temple possibly dedicated to the goddess Hygieia, the consort of Asklepios. In various places can be seen large cisterns hacked out of the soft rock; these once provided the town with water. Now we return to the square again and on the far side we see the remains of the large temple which was dedicated to the god Serapis (a synthesis of Zeus and Asklepios). In the museum (see below) is a model reconstruction. From here we follow the broad main road to the agora (market place). Nearby is the early Christian basilica; in this area can be seen a number of sarcophagi, not yet been completely excavated, of the former Spanish-Visigoth necropolis.

Continuing along the path we come to the remains of some mosaic floors with geometrical ornamentation, some bearing inscriptions.

Museum

The walk through the lower town ends at the museum (officially Museo Monográfico), the successor of a monastic church which had existed into the 19th c. The collections are to a large extent arranged chronologically. As well as illustrations of the archaeological working processes and tools, ceramics including black and red figured Attic work, sculpture, remains of mosaics and jewellery there are also some model reconstructions illustrating life in an ancient Greek and Roman town.

Upper Town

Behind the museum the ground rises gently to the Roman town higher up which has an extent of 300 x 700 m/382 x 766 yards, and of which until now only a small part has been excavated. A number of buildings have been restored; the boundary between the original building and the restoration is marked by brick straps in the walls. The plateau at the top of the hill on which the town is situated provides an excellent view, including the castle of Torroella.
First we cross the area of house No. 1, the so-called Casa Villaneuva. It was reconstructed according to the principles of the Roman architect and building theorist Vitruvius (1st c. B.C.) as a model and this can be seen in the museum (see above). *In situ* are the remains of floor mosaics. The house is comfortably and spaciously laid out with many rooms, a bathroom, store rooms, cisterns and a garden. Somewhat smaller but comparable in its furnishings is house No. 2 which is the next stop on the tour. Then we reach the former forum (market place), the focus of public life in Roman towns. It forms a square with a side of 70 m/75 ft and is situated exactly in the axis of Cardo Maximus, the main road of the Roman town, coming from the S. This area has suffered greatly from thefts. To the S of the forum on the Cardo Maximus can be seen the foundations of a number of shops.
The main road goes on to the civic town gate which is situated in the southern surrounding wall (1st c. A.D.; the ruts caused by cart wheels can clearly be seen on the threshold.
Immediately outside the wall to the right of the gate lies the not particularly large amphitheatre; only a very few remains of this have been preserved.
To the left of the town wall was the palaestra, the site of sporting exercises, but practically nothing of this can be seen today.

L'Escala/La Escala

Location
2 km/1 mile S of Empúries

L'Escala (Spanish: La Escala) is a traditional fishing port and is popular in summer for holidays. However, near the village the beach is rocky with only a few stretches of coarse pebbles. The better beaches lie to the S. In the middle of the village is a very small harbour bay which has limited space for boats; there are a number of fish restaurants near the beach.

L'Estartit/Estartit

F8

Country: Spain
Province: Girona
Altitude: sea level

Location

L'Estartit (Spanish: Estartit), part of the parish of Torroella de Montgri (see entry), is situated not far N of the estuary of the Riu Ter at the edge of the Empordà (Spanish: Ampurdán).

The Town

Estartit, the port of the parish of Torroella which lies inland, is largely devoted to tourism and has relatively little atmosphere; a tall rocky bluff on which are a number of radio and television transmission stations dominates the horizon. The coast, with sandy beaches and rocky sections, is considered the finest of the Empordà.

Among the attractions of the place are diving excursions and trips in glass-bottomed boats. Estartit is a diving centre (school, compressor station) and has a large and well-equipped pleasure harbour.

The beaches in the immediate vicinity are long, wide and sandy and it is here that most of the tower blocks are to be found. Farther N the mountains reach right down to the sea; the coast is very rocky and with its grottoes is especially suitable for snorkelling and diving.

Estartit: the harbour . . .

. . . and snorkelling

Illes Medes/Islas Medas

The rocky Illes Medes (Spanish: Islas Medas) lie a bare 1 km off the coast. In this area the sea is a protected natural area; pleasure divers must note that fishing, including private fishing as well as taking away any marine creatures, is strictly forbidden.

Figueres/Figueras E6

Country: Spain
Province: Girona
Altitude: 30 m/98 ft
Population: 28,000

Location

Figueres (Spanish: Figueras) is situated about 35 km/ 22 miles N of the provincial capital of Girona, some 15 km/ 9 miles NW of the Golf de Roses.

**Museu Salvador Dali

Open
Daily 9 a.m.–9 p.m.

Entrance fee

Photography not permitted

The Museu Salvador Dali can be recognised from a long way away by its honeycomb of plexiglass domes which top the classical building of the former theatre (1850) in which the museum is accommodated. The Dali Museum is not only the main attraction of Figueres but one of the most important sights in the whole of Catalonia and, apart from the Prado in Madrid, the most visited museum in Spain. Nowhere else can be seen such a concentration of the work of the great Surrealist who was born in Figueres. The exhibition rooms are grouped on several floors corresponding to the former circles of the theatre from which the roof has been removed. In the windows and on the window ledges can be seen a great number of figurines in artificial material in every imaginable pose.
No one can fail to be fascinated by the multitude of exhibits. There has been no artistic movement which was not defamiliarised and parodied, no technique which was not handled like a virtuoso, no material which was not used in an unexpected way. We mention here only a few individual items which are particularly striking. On the first floor is a great ceiling painting based on Baroque patterns which increases the perspective effect of its model and makes it grotesque. Of two hovering figures that are viewed from below we see almost nothing but the huge soles of the feet while the bodies are lost in the depth of the room. In one of the upper rooms the sense of seeing is led astray by other means; in a darkened room there hang two empty picture frames illuminated by spot lights, a gigantic nose and mouth made of artificial material as well as strands of wool and tow. From a balcony the entire ensemble can be observed through a diminishing lens and here we can appreciate how everything makes sense and we see a female face. On the top floor there is a series of stereo pictures similar to those in a peep-show.
In the former auditorium, which is now the inner courtyard,

Art or a joke? or both? Museu Dali ►

PENSAMENT
REBROTA SEMPRE I
SOBREVIU ALS SEUS IL·LUSOS ENTERRADORS"

stands a column made of old motor tyres, on it the sculpture of a man and right at the top a gaily painted boat hung with gigantic blue beads. At the foot of the column is a black vintage car. On its bonnet a luxurious female figure. The former stage is shut off by a tall glass wall behind which, in a space which almost suggests a ritual chamber, hangs a monumental painting; opposite this is a second painting beneath a red canopy which resembles an altar. Even the external façade and the monument in front of the entrance have been derationalised by Dali.

Sant Pere/San Pedro

Very near the museum stands the Gothic church of Sant Pere (Spanish: San Pedro) with a small Romanesque side chapel. The destruction caused in the Spanish Civil War was rectified in 1941–48.

Museu del Empordà/Museo del Ampurdán

Open
Tues.–Sun. 10 a.m.–2 p.m. and 5–7 p.m.;
closed Mon.

Entrance fee

In the Ramblas, a broad main series of boulevards shaded by plain trees in the inner town, can be found in house No. 2 the Museu del Empordà (Spanish: Museo del Ampurdán) illustrating the history of the Catalonian countryside of Empordà (Spanish: Ampurdán) which extends to the S of the town. On the ground floor can be seen works of contemporary painters of the region. On the first floor the exhibits include ancient glass, bronze, jewellery and utensils, amphora with black figures and terracotta items, etc. Most of the earlier finds come from the excavations of the Iberian settlement in Ullastret (see entry) and from Ampurias (see

Vilabertran: shady arcades in the cloister

Empúries); there is also Romanesque and Gothic Art, Baroque costumes and model ships. On the second floor are a number of panels mostly of Renaissance and Baroque date, with some from the 19th c. and all primarily of regional importance.

Museu de Juguets/Museo de Juguetes

Near where the extension of the Ramblas forms a square there can be found, in the Hotel Paris (house No. 10), the Museu de Juguets (toy museum); In the square is a monument to Narcis Monturiol (1819–85) who is considered to be the inventor of the first practical underwater craft.

Fortress

NW of the inner town stands the pentagonal Fort San Ferran (Spanish: San Fernando) which was built in its present form in 1743. In its time it was alleged to be the second largest fortification in Europe. Formally it is believed that there was a Capuchin monastery here. Visitors are not permitted inside the fort.

Vilabertran

Location
2 km/1 mile N of Figueres

The former monastic church of Vilabertran, dedicated to St Mary, is a beautiful three-aisled 11th. c Romanesque building; in the N transept can be seen a Gothic border. The cloister also dates largely from the Romanesque era. A classic side chapel adjoins the church which houses a very fine 15th c. Gothic crucifix.

Girona/Gerona G5–6

Country: Spain
Province: Girona
Altitude: 68 m/223 ft
Population: 88,000

Location

Girona (Spanish: Gerona) the capital of the Catalonian province of the same name, is situated about 35 km/22 miles inland from the Costa Brava on the Riu Ter which is here joined by its tributaries the Onyar, the Güell and the Galligans.

History

Girona was founded by the Iberians and probably at the time of the first colonisation by the Greeks. There are still remains of the Iberian walls to be seen. In the Roman era the town was called Gerunda and during the Arab domination, from whom it was temporarily recovered by Charles the Great in 785, it was known as Djerunda. The fact that Girona has a strategically favourable position on the most important of the long-distance roads crossing the Pyrenees was the reason that it was often fought for and became to be known as the "town of a thousand sieges". From the late 10th c. Girona was an independent duchy and then for a time was subject to the dukes of Barcelona. In the uprising

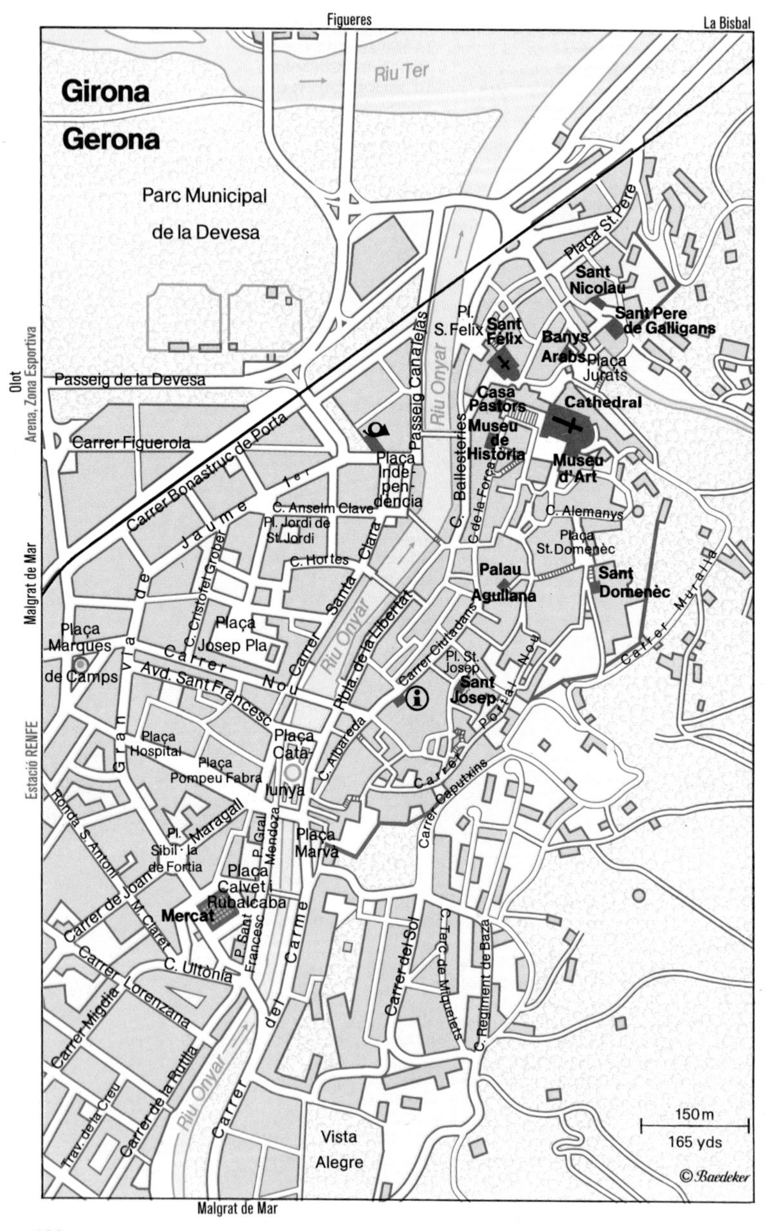

Figueres
La Bisbal
Girona
Gerona
Riu Ter
Parc Municipal
de la Devesa
Olot
Arena, Zona Esportiva
Passeig de la Devesa
Carrer Figuerola
Carrer Bonastruc de Porta
Jaume I
Gran Via de
Malgrat de Mar
Estació RENFE
Plaça Marques de Camps
C. Anselm Clavé
Pl. Jordi de St. Jordi
C. Hortes
Plaça Independència
Passeig Canalejas
Riu Onyar
Pl. S. Feliu
Sant Fèlix
Banys Arabs
Plaça St. Pere
Sant Nicolau
Sant Pere de Galligans
Plaça Jurats
Cathedral
Casa Pastors
Museu de Historia
Museu d'Art
C. Ballesteries
C. de la Força
C. Alemanys
Plaça St. Domenèc
Palau Agullana
Sant Domenèc
Carrer Muralla
C. Cristòfol Grober
Plaça Josep Pla
Carrer Nou
Avd. Sant Francesc
Carrer Santa Clara
Rbla. de la Libertat
Carrer Ciutadans
Pl. St. Josep
Sant Josep
Portal Nou
Plaça Hospital
Plaça Pompeu Fabra
Plaça Catalunya
C. Albareda
Carrer Caputxins
Ronda S. Antoni
Pl. Sibil·la de Fortia
Maragall
P. Gral Mendoza
Plaça Marvà
Plaça Calvet i Rubalcaba
Carrer de Joan M. Claret
Mercat
P. Sant Francesc
Carrer del Carme
C. Ultònia
Carrer Lorenzana
Carrer Migdia
Carrer de la Rutlla
Trav. de la Creu
Carrer del Sol
C. Terç de Miquelets
C. Regiment de Baza
Vista Alegre
150 m
165 yds
© Baedeker
Malgrat de Mar

against Napoleon the town resisted a French force in 1809 for seven months before it capitulated and the troops had to be allowed to enter the town. French occupation lasted until 1814. For its resistance against the besiegers the town received the title of honour "Inmortal Gerona".

New Town

The New Town lies on the left bank of the Riu Onyar. Near the river in the Plaça de la Independència, which is surrounded by arcades, stands a monument commemorating the resistance of the population against Napoleon's troops. Farther to the N and extending to the Riu Ter is the Parc Municipal de la Devesa (40 ha/99 acres) with plane trees and sports grounds.

Old Town

The old-world Old Town lies on the slopes along the right bank of the Onyar. Between the railway bridge in the N and the Plaça Catalunya which was laid out over the bed of the river, there is a colourful row of old houses with many pedestrian bridges; the best light is in the afternoon. The riverside is dominated by the Church of Sant Fèlix (Spanish: San Feliú) and the cathedral. Parallel to the bank runs the Rambla de la Libertat (pedestrian precinct), the principal thoroughfare of the Old Town with arcaded walks, shops and street cafés.

Girona: the Old Town by the river

Sant Fèlix/San Feliú

Near the N end of the Old Town (most easily reached from the Plaça Independència across the Pont d'en Gómez) stands the former Collegiate Church of Sant Fèlix (11th–18th c.). This is a three-aisled Gothic building with very low side aisles which have late Romanesque galleries and sculptured capitals. The choir was finished in 1318, the west front dates from the 17th c.; the high belfry, originally Gothic, was considerably damaged by lightning in 1581 and because of the reconstruction which followed it no longer has its original form.
The entrance to the church is through the doorway in the right-hand wall of the nave. It has no transepts but in the left-hand wall of the nave there is a vaulted Baroque chapel (Capilla de San Narciso) dedicated to St Narcissus, Bishop of Gerona in the time of Diocletian. In the choir can be seen a carved Gothic altar which can be illuminated by using the coin-operated switch to the right of the entrance. Near the altar can be seen a number of sarcophagi dating from the 2nd to the 6th centuries A.D.
Following the right-hand wall of the nave of St Felix's Church, we come to the so-called Portal de Sobreportes, a sturdy city gate flanked by two towers; nearby stands the classical Church of Sant Lluc (St Luke). Behind the gateway lies the little Plaça de la Catedral, most of which is taken up by the mighty Baroque flight of 90 steps (1690) which lead up to the cathedral.

Casa Pastors

The mansion of the Pastors family, opposite the foot of the steps, received its present form in the 18th c.

Museu de Història/Museo de História

Carrer de la Força leads S from the cathedral square and here in the building of a former Capuchin monastery is the Museu de Història (museum of civic history; open Tues.–Sat. 10 a.m.–2 p.m. and 5–7 p.m.; closed Sun. p.m. and Mon.). The principal exhibits concern the pre-history of the region and the age of industrialisation (19th/20th c.)
The part of the Old Town extending from here to the S was until the 15th c. the Jewish quarter of Girona.

*Cathedral

The Gothic cathedral which dominates the townscape was begun in 1312 and completed towards the end of the 16th c. The massive Baroque main doorway (18th c.) faces the flight of steps leading down to the square; its ornamentation is modern. Outside the south wall of the nave with its Gothic doorway (lacking its original ornamental figures) extends a small square (Plaça dels Apostols).
The interior of the cathedral consists of a single aisle; the nave is 50 m/164 ft long, 23 m/75 ft wide and 34 m/116 ft high, making it one of the largest vaulted Gothic buildings in existence. The apse, however, is considerably lower and with the choir ambulatory and encircling chapels is of classical form. The high altar, beneath a baldaquin (canopy), has a gilded reredos, a fine example of 14th c. silversmith's work. Behind it is a stone bishop's seat, ornamented with a garlanded frieze; this is reputed to have been the throne of Charlemagne.

Tapestry of the Creation

Iconography

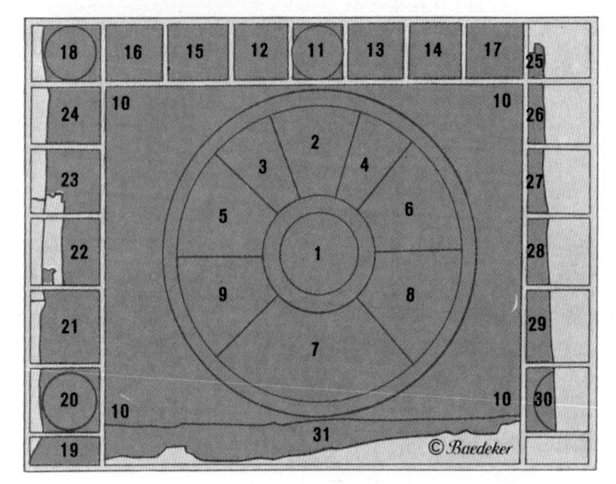

1 Christ as Pantocreator (Ruler of All)
2 The Spirit of God moves over the Waters
3 Angel of Darkness
4 Angel of Light
5 Creation of the Firmament
6 God divides the Waters
7 Creation of the Birds and Fishes
8 Adam names the Animals
9 Creation of Eve from the rib of Adam
10 The four Winds
11 Allegory of the Year with the Wheel of Time
12 Autumn: a man harvesting grapes
13 Winter: a woman by her stove
14 Spring: a man digging in his field
15 Summer: a man with a threshing flail
16 Samson with the jawbone of an ass
17 Abel sacrifices a lamb
18 Allegory of Geon, a river of Paradise
19 February: equipment for hunting and fishing
20 Day of the Sun
21 March: frog, snake and stork
22 April: flowers, trees and a man ploughing
23 May: blossom on trees and a horse
24 June: men fishing
25 A second river of Paradise (fragment)
26 July: a peasant mowing
27 August: a cornfield (fragment)
28 September: threshing corn (fragment)
29 October: harvesting grapes (fragment)
30 Day of the Moon (fragment)
31 Legend of the discovery of the Cross in Jerusalem by St Helena (fragment)

**Cathedral Museum

On the left of the nave is the entrance to the Cathedral Museum (open Tues.–Sat 10 a.m.–1 p.m. and 4.30–7 p.m.; closed Sun. p.m. and Mon.; entrance fee). Explanatory leaflets (some in foreign languages) can be borrowed from the ticket office. Among the notable exhibits there are, in the first room, a Romanesque Madonna (11th–12th c.) which is very similar to the miracle-working image of Montserrat (see entry) and an illuminated handwritten document of the Apocalypse (975). In the second room can be seen a late-Gothic cross (1503–07; No. 20) inlaid with pearl and enamel, as well as another (No. 25), dating from the 14th c. with inlaid work. In Room 3, in a showcase on the wall is a 14th c. book cover in silver; in the central display case can be seen a remarkable collection of 15th c. sculptures, as well as the Emperor Charles V's bible (No. 38) which is 14th c. Italian work. Two altar frontals (Nos. 41 and 42) are notable; one, dating from the 14th c. is embroidered with gold and silk, the other (13th c.) has 21 scenes from the life of Christ.

Tapestry
(explanation, see page 109)

Room 4 is reserved for what is by far the crowning glory of the museum, the magnificent coloured tapestry depicting the history of the Creation. This silk embroidery was done in the 11th c. and follows early Christian precursors; this can be seen from the representationn of a clean-shaven Christ as Creator of the World in the centre of the cycle, surrounded by the biblical quotation in Latin "And God said 'let there be light', and there was light".

*Cloister

The Romanesque cloister on a trapeziform plan dates from the 12th c.; it is reached from the museum down a number

Capital in the cathedral cloister: "Noah in the Ark"

of steps. Unfortunately some of the figured capitals of the pillared arcades are rather damaged, but they are impressive because of the complexity of the representation; the Biblical scenes also include details of everyday life. Below the vaulted roof can be seen a number of gravestones. Above the cloister rises a Romanesque stump of a tower, the structure of which is determined by single and twin arched window openings. A stairway leads up to the first floor of the cloister and here can be seen a fine collection of richly embroidered ecclesiastical vestments; from a balcony there is a pretty view to the N of the gardens, of the little Romanesque Church of Sant Pere de Galligans (see page 112) and of a remnant of the old town walls.
Behind the choir of the church there is a little garden (Jardins de la Francesa) from which one enjoys a good view of the apse and of the Romanesque tower stump at the end of the nave.
Farther to the E can be seen the remains of a defence tower called the "Gironella" and of the old town walls.

Museu d'Art/Museo de Arte

The Museu d'Art joins the nave of the cathedral on the right (open Tues.–Sat. 10 a.m.–1 p.m. and 4.30–7 p.m.; closed Sun. afternoons and Mon.); it houses exhibits from the pre-Romanesque era to the beginning of the 12th c.

Passeig Arqueològic/Paseo Arqueológico

Banys Arabs/Baños Arebes

From the cathedral a marked archaeological walk takes in the most important sites of the Old Town. After passing the

Sant Pere de Galligans, now a museum

town gate (see page 108) in the reverse direction we come on the left to the Arab baths (Banys Arabs; open Tues.–Sat. 10 a.m.–1 p.m. and 4.30–7 p.m; closed Sun. afternoons and Mon.) which possibly had their origins in a Jewish Mikwe (ritual bath); their late Romanesque vaulting has been restored in more recent times.

Sant Pere de Galligans/San Pedro de Galligans

The Romanesque Church of Sant Pere de Galligans is situated a little way downhill and on the other side of the stream bearing the same name. This fortified 12th c. building, once part of a Benedictine Monastery, has been deconsecrated and now houses in the cloisters the Museu Arqueològic (Spanish: Museo Arqueológico). Notable are the decorative rosettes and the banding in the round-arched doorway. In the beautiful three-aisled interior temporary art exhibitions take place.

Sant Nicolau/San Nicolas

Close by Sant Pere stands the considerably smaller but equally Romanesque Church of Sant Nicolau (12th c.). This also has been deconsecrated and is used for exhibitions.

Southern Part of the Old Town

Sant Domènec/Santo Domingo

SE of the cathedral and a little higher up in the Plaça de Sant Domènec stands the monastery of the same name. It was built in the 13th c. and reconstructed in the 14th, 17th and 18th c. The church and the monastery buildings are in Gothic style.
In the same square stands the main façade of the former university which in the 16th and 17th c. was of considerable importance in the educational life of the country.

Palau Agullana/Palacio Aguillana

In the maze of streets to the SW of Sant Domènec stands the former town palace of the Agullana family which extends across an alley of steps with a flying buttress.

San Josep/San José

Still farther to the S in the Plaça San Josep we come to the former monastery of the same name which was built in the 16th c. and belonged to the barefoot Carmelites; it now houses the State Archives.

Sarrià de Ter/Sarri de Ter

Location
4 km/2½ miles N of Girona

The industrial township of Sarrià de Ter (Spanish: Sarri de Ter) lies in the valley of the Riu Ter. In the part of the parish called Sarrià de Dalt, to the W of the motorway, stand the ruins of a castle belonging to the Montagut family.

Medinyà/Mediñ

Location
9 km/5½ miles N of Girona

The pretty village of Medinyà (Spanish: Mediñ), lying off the main road, is dominated by its well-maintained 12th c. castle.

Granollers

J2

Country: Spain
Province: Barcelona
Altitude: 148 m/486 ft
Population: 36,000

Location

Granollers lies in the valley of the Riu Congost about 25 km/15 miles N of Barcelona.

The Town

The district capital Granollers is a lively commercial and industrial centre at the junction of important lines of communication. In the centre there can still be seen a number of old houses; the 14th c. church and the former corn exchange (Llotje; 16th c.) are noteworthy. The archaeological museum is worth a visit.
A considerable part of Granollers was destroyed during the Carlist wars so that not many old buildings remain.

La Jonquera/La Junquera

D6

Country: Spain
Province: Girona
Altitude: 112 m/368 ft
Population: 2,500

Location

The Spanish frontier town of La Jonquera (Spanish: La Junquera) is situated barely 7 km/4 miles S of the Col du Perthus across which runs the Franco-Spanish frontier.

The Town

La Jonquera occupies the site of a very ancient settlement Dolmen ("stone tables" = megalithic graves); prehistoric cult remains can be seen in the surroundings.

Requesens

14 km/9 miles NE on a hill from which there are good views are the remains of the Church of Santa Maria de Requesens which was built in pre-Romanesque days.

Col du Perthus

The A17 motorway and the national road N11 climb up N of La Jonquera to the Col du Perthus. Over the summit of the pass (290 m/950 ft) runs the frontier between France and Spain. It is supposed that in 218 B.C. Hannibal used this, one of the lower Pyrenees passes, on his way to Italy.

L' . . . , La . . .

See main name

Llança: moorings in the harbour

Llançà/Llansá D7

Country: Spain
Province: Girona
Altitude: 6 m/20 ft
Population: 3000

Location

Llançà (Spanish: Llansá) lies in the extreme N of the Costa Brava some 10 km/6 miles from the Franco-Spanish frontier.

The Town

The centre which is surrounded by a wall is situated a little way from the coast at the foot of the extensive karstic hillsides which have little vegetation. The Baroque Church of Sant Vincenç dates from the 18th c.; a fine fortified tower stands in the main square. The former Romanesque Hermitage of Sant Silvestre (11th c.) is noteworthy.

Port de Llançà/Puerto de Llansá

The more lively part of the town and the more important from the tourist point of view is the port, Port de Llançà. There is a short sandy beach along the harbour bay, overlooked by a little promontory (El Castellar) which can be climbed on foot. From the top the heavily indented coast can be seen, especially towards the S. The harbour is of limited size and is mainly occupied by small motor boats.

Lloret de Mar: activity on the beach

Statue of a fishwife

To the N there are other pretty little coves as well as a holiday colony. By crossing a small pass (fine views) we arrive in Colera (see Port-Bou).
Almost exactly to the S of Llançà in hilly country stands the old Benedictine Monastery of Sant Pere de Rodes (see entry).

Lloret de Mar — H6

Country: Spain
Province: Girona
Altitude: sea level
Population: 8000

Location

Lloret de Mar in the extreme S of the Costa Brava is the last resort before the boundary with the Costa Daurada, i.e. between the provinces of Girona and Barcelona.

The Town of Lloret de Mar

Lloret de Mar is one of the best known resorts on the north Spanish Mediterranean coast. The former little fishing town developed some time ago into a hotel and tourist settlement of great style where the beach, amusements and night-life predominate. Flanking the long and fairly wide beach with its coarse sand (very crowded in the holiday season) runs a promenade shaded with palm trees; on the rocky cape which borders the beach to the SW stands the bronze sculpture of a fishwife looking out to sea.

Water World

Outside the town to the W the leisure centre "Water World" has been laid out, a complex with a swimming pool with artificial waves, water chutes, mini-golf, children's playground, restaurants, etc. It can be reached by a free bus from Lloret; the park is open daily from 10 a.m.

Malgrat de Mar **J5**

Country: Spain
Province: Barcelona
Altitude: sea level
Population: 10,000

Location

Malgrat de Mar is the last resort at the northern end of the Costa Daurada near the estuary of the Riu Tordera.

The Town

Malgrat, once a small industrial town, now gets its living principally from tourism and the infrastructure is correspondingly varied. There are go-cart tracks, places where bicycles and motorcycles can be hired, pedal cars, tennis courts, many shops, restaurants, bars and discotheques. All the hotels are in a single line parallel to the beach and the railway.
In the narrow and rather winding old town stands a church with a stump of a Gothic tower and a late Baroque façade. There is an old watch tower on a hill above the little town.

*Marineland

Open
Sealion and dolphin displays daily at 10.30 a.m., 12.30, 3.30, 5.30 and 7 p.m.
Parrot displays daily at 11.30 a.m., 2.30, 4.30 and 6.30 p.m.

Entrance fee

The route to Marineland from Malgrat is signposted via Palafolls and not easy to find. Visitors should first follow the road near the coast towards Blanes and turn left before they come to the tunnel under the railway and the bridge over the Riu Tordera. Marineland is not only a large aquarium but also a complete leisure centre. The main attraction is the sealion and dolphin display which takes place several times a day. The sealions are impressive with their balancing act; the highly intelligent and lively dolphins perform a series of astonishing feats, leaping many metres out of the water towards balls or titbits, pulling a little boat through their pool and performing other tricks.
The parrots which have their own area have learned to ride bicycles and to roller-skate.
Apart from these performances there is a little zoo, a basin containing pearl mussels (for a small fee a girl diver will retrieve a mussel from the bottom and with luck you may even find a pearl in it); there is a pool with rowing boats, a restaurant, a picnic place and a children's playground.

Marineland Malgrat: dolphins performing ▶

1 Children's Playground
2 Cafeteria
3 Picnic Area
4 Parrot Circus
5 Dolphin and Sealion Show
6 Penguins
7 Mini-Indianapolis
8 Marineland Express
9 Pearls from Polynesia
10 Swimming Pool
11 Souvenirs

Palafolls

Location
3 km/2 miles N of Malgrat de Mar

Palafolls lies a little way inland. The Church of Sant Genis, which was originally Romanesque, was somewhat unfortunately restored in the 19th c.

Mataró

J3

Country: Spain
Province: Barcelona
Altitude: 26 m/585 ft
Population: 100,000

Location

Mataró lies on the Costa Daurada about 30 km/90 miles E of Barcelona.

The Town

Mataró is a rather sober commercial and industrial town. In 1848 the first Spanish railway ran from here to Barcelona. The more elevated part of the town has been in existence since Roman days. The developments near the beach are of considerably more recent date. The Baroque Church of Santa Maria (18th c.) with paintings by Sert and Viladomat is worth a visit.

Vilassar de Mar/Vilasar de Mar

Location
6 km/4 miles SW of Mataró

The little township of Vilassar de Mar (Spanish: Vilasar de Mar) is another popular resort; in the upper town can be seen a number of medieval watch-towers.

Montseny (Serra de Montseny/Sierra de Montseny) H3

Country: Spain
Province: Barcelona and Girona
Altitude: up to 1712 m/5618 ft

Location

The Montseny massif is barely 50 km/31 miles NE of Barcelona and 30 km/19 miles inland from the Costa Daurada. The Riu Tordera rises in this mountainous region.

*Landscape of Montseny

The Serra de Montseny (Spanish: Sierra de Montseny) is a range of medium height almost completely covered by forest. The highest point is Turó del Home, 1712 m/5618 ft, the highest mountain in the Catalonian coastal range. Important sources of income are forestry and agriculture; tourism also plays a considerable role, for the area includes a nature park which is extremely popular with walkers.

Santa Fe

From Sant Celoni in the valley of the Riu Tordera an extremely winding but exceptionally scenic route with fine views leads to Santa Fe del Montseny (alt. 1100 m/3610 ft), the most important place in the area of the nature park. The village has developed around a former abbey and now provides a good base for mountain walkers. To the W rises the Turó del Home, on the summit of which (magnificent panorama) a meteorological station has been erected.

Montserrat

Country: Spain
Province: Barcelona
Altitude: up to 1241 m/4073 ft

Location

Montserrat, famous for its monastery, rises some 50 km/31 miles NW of Barcelona. It is outside the area covered on the map at the back of this guide.

Access

The visitor wishing to drive from Barcelona (see entry) to Montserrat is advised to leave the town centre on the Avinguda de la Diagonal in a SW direction and soon this road merges with the motorway to Martorell. From Martorell follow the main road which goes via Olesa to Monistrol. A short way beyond Olesa a bridge across the valley leads to the cableway (large sign "Aeri"; officially Funicular Aeri del Montserrat) the upper station of which is situated right by the monastery on the mountain. There is also a direct rail

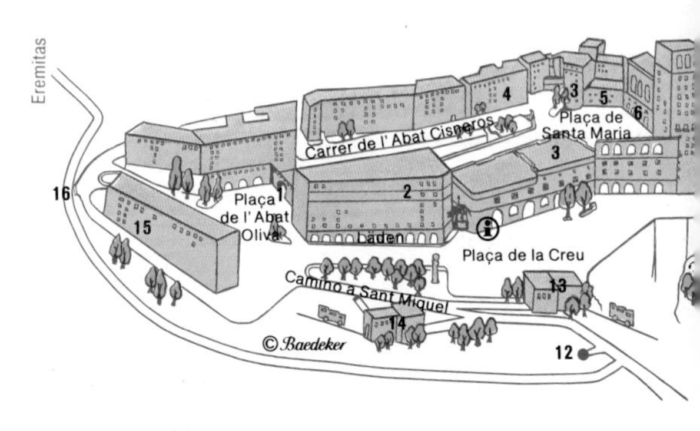

1 Main Entrance to the Monastery area
2 Audiovisual Information
3 Museum in two buildings
4 Hotel
5 Gothic Cloister
6 Gateway Building
7 Basilica
8 Song School (Escolania)

line from Barcelona to the cableway leaving from the station beneath the Plaça de Espanya.

The road up Montserrat (8 km/5 miles; at times very steep but well engineered) branches off the main road in Monistrol and winds up the mountain offering fine views of the surrounding country. The road ends at the monastery where there is a large car park.

Visitors coming from the region N of the Catalonian capital are well advised to avoid the conurbation of Barcelona. The best route is to take the motorway A7, parallel to but at some distance from the coast, as far as Cerdanyola and then follow the branch to Terrasa and finally the road to Monistrol where we take the diversion indicated above.

History

At one time Montserrat was falsely taken to be Montsalvatsch in the Wolfram von Eschenbach legend of the Holy Grail (it is more probable that this was the little pilgrimage place of Salvatierra on the S flank of the Pyrenees). According to the legend the monastery was founded in 880 in honour of a wonder-working statue of the virgin; the first recognised mention of the place is in 888. In 976 it was handed over to the order of Benedictine monks, and in 1025 it was considerably extended by monks from the Catalonian towns of Ripoll and Vic. Pope Benedict XIII raised it in 1409 to the status of an independent abbey; towards the end of the century a monastic printing press was set up. A former monk of Montserrat went in 1493 with Columbus's fleet to the New World and he is supposed to have named the little island of Montserrat in the Antilles (now a British Crown Colony) after the monastery. In 1522 Ignatius of Loyola, the founder of the Jesuit order, spent some time in the monastery. Napoleon's troops invaded Spain at the beginning of the 19th c.; the huge treasure of the monastery disappeared during the War of Liberation (from 1808) and

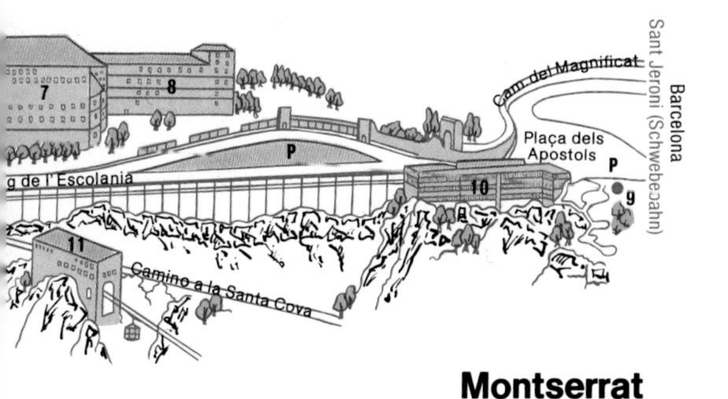

Montserrat

9 Monument to Ramon Llull
10 Restaurant
11 Cableway (Aeri)
12 Monument to Pablo Casals
13 Funicular to the Holy Grotto (Cova Santa/Cueva Santa)
14 Funicular to Sant Joan (San Juan)
15 Gendarmerie (Guarda Civil)
16 Via Crucis (Way of the Cross)

the convent was destroyed in 1811 by the French. Other painful losses occurred as a result of closure during the Carlist wars (1835–60). The monastery still has its associated school ("Escolania") of sacred music, founded in the 15th c., the youthful members of which sing the Ave Maria, the Salve and at Vespers. The principal festivals of Montserrat are on 27 April and 8 September.

**Scenery

Montserrat (legendary mountain), the Montsagrat (sacred mountain) of the Catalans, is one of the greatest sights in the whole of Spain both for its scenery and for its famous monastery. It is a huge conglomerate massif 10 km/6 miles long and 5 km/3 miles broad which rises high above the right bank of the Riu Llobregat in an almost isolated position with steep slopes on all sides falling from the Catalonian plateau; its fantastic rock formations which were caused by an erosion make it appear from a distance like an enormous castle. The highest summit of the massif is Sant Jeroni (Spanish: San Jerónimo) 1241 m/4073 ft. From the SE a huge cleft, known as Vall Malalt (Spanish: Valle Malo = evil valley) cuts through the mountain; the monastery stands at its beginning on an outcrop at a height of 725 m/2379 ft. The NE slope is covered by pine woods, the sides and the top by evergreen bushes; the renowned flora of the mountain (some 1500 species) was largely destroyed in 1986 by a fire.

*Monastery

The monastery with the basilica and the associated buildings forms a small town in itself. The road ends at the large

car park. Here the visitor has access to an extensive observation terrace on which stands a modern monument to the poet and mystic Ramón Llull (Latinised Raimundus Lullus; 1232–1316) who was born in Palma de Mallorca. The eight steps of the monument resemble a circular stairway and are called the "steps of knowledge" (stone, fire, plants, animals, man, heaven, angel, God); nearby can be seen a circular memorial to the dead.
The inside of the actual monastery complex is reached across the Plaça de la Creu (Spanish: Plaza de la Cruz = square of the cross), named after the sculptor of a cross, dating from 1927 on the left-hand side. The square is flanked by a restaurant, souvenir shops, a post office, telephone boxes and an exchange office. Audio-visual information about Montserrat is available every 30 minutes at the bottom of the steps. On the Plaça de l'Abat Oliba, near the main entrance to the monastery, farmers' wives from the surrounding villages sell their produce.

Museu de Montserrat/
Museo de Montserrat

Now we enter a broad square the Plaça de Santa Maria. To the right of the wide central avenue which leads to the basilica is the entrance to the modern part of the museum beneath the square (admission tickets are valid for both departments). It contains works by Catalan painters of the 19th and 20th c. and is principally of regional importance. The old department is diagonally to the left outside the main façade of the church. It includes a small Egyptian collection (several copies of well-known large sculptures, copper work, seals, a human mummy and two sarcophagi); here also are finds from the New Stone Age, Roman and Byzantine ceramics and ornaments, coins, ancient glass ware, Jewish cult objects (tallit = prayer room, schofare = rams' horns for ritual use, and tora = rolls).
Farther to the left below the rock is the Hostal Abad Cisneros (hotel).

Basilica

At the end of the square rises the gateway dating from 1942 to 1968 which marks the limit of the church area; its lower part has five arches and the upper part three. The reliefs in the three upper arches portray (from the left) St Benedict, the Assumption (according to the dogma of Pope Pius XII) and St George, patron saint of Catalonia. From time to time pilgrim groups from Catalonia dance the Sardana, an old folk dance here. To the left of the façade can be seen remains of the former Gothic cloister (15th c.)
Between the gateway and the actual church there is a fairly narrow inner courtyard with a statue (1927) of St Benedict near which is the door to the cloister (not open to the public). The decorative graffiti on the side of the façade are modern. In the gateway is also the baptistry which is entered from the inner courtyard. The entrance is ornamented with 20th c. reliefs.

*Statue of the Madonna (Montserrat)

The basilica in which the revered statue of the Madonna can be seen dates from the 16th c. but was largely altered and restored in the 19th and 20th c. The façade shows Renaissance forms but the figure of Christ and the Apostles were only put up in 1900.

Montserrat: reputed to be the mountain of the Holy Grail ▶

There are two entrances into the church; through the main doorway you enter the nave while the right-side doorway is a direct entrance leading to the statue of the Madonna (one way only).
The nave is 68 m/74 yds long, 21 m/23 yds wide and 33 m/67 ft high. It is faintly lit by numerous votive candles. The interior decoration is modern (19th–20th c.).
The figure of the Madonna of Montserrat, called by the Catalans Santa Imatge, by the Spanish Santa Imagen, is one of the most important pilgrimage figures in the whole of Spain. As is often the case in Spanish churches it is placed high up above the high altar and is reached by a staircase in the transept. Here the stairs are framed in beaten silver ornamentation. The coloured wooden sculpture dates from the 12th or 13th c.; the face and hands have become blackened with age which is why the statue is called "la Moreneta" by the Catalans. According to legend it was carved by St Luke who came to Spain through the efforts of St Peter.
The visitor leaves the church through the left-hand transept. Outside on the rock wall there are many votive gifts including wax limbs as a thank offering for healing, and sacrificial candles as well as the sacred spring (Catalan: Mistica Font del Aiguda de la Vida) and near it a coloured majolica statue of the Mother of God.

Way of the Cross

In the Plaça de l'Abat Oliva there starts the Via Crucis (Way of the Cross). The fourteen large statue groups which date from between 1904 and 1919 were renewed after the Civil War. At the end of the Stations of the Cross is a chapel

Monument to Raimundes Lulles . . .

. . . and to Pau Casals

(Virgen de la Soledad); at the fourteenth station a path leads to the Ermita Sant Miquel (Spanish: San Miguel; 19th c.); the building which preceded it was already there in the 10th c.

Cova Santa/Cueva Santa

From the Plaça de la Creu at the upper station of the cableway (see page 119), which runs from the valley road near Olesa, the path leads to Cova Santa (Spanish: Cueva Santa = holy cave) with a chapel built in the 17th c. It is said that during the Moorish occupation the statue of Mary of Montserrat was hidden in the grotto and rediscovered by shepherds.

Sant Joan/San Juan

Near the Plaça de la Creu there is also the valley station of the cableway leading to Sant Joan (Spanish: San Juan). Close by the path is a monument to the Catalan cellist Pau (Pablo) Casals (1876–1973).
Sant Joan is one of thirteen hermitages which once existed in the area of Montserrat. From the upper station there is a fine view of the monastery. The path to Sant Jeroni (Spanish: San Jerónimo; see below) is worth taking.

**Sant Jeroni/San Jerónimo

A cableway 680 m/744 yds long with a difference in height of 535 m/1755 ft (the oldest in Spain) leads from the road near Manresa up to the Capilla de Sant Jeroni from where it is a 5-minute walk to the summit of Sant Jeroni which at 1241 m/4073 ft is the highest point of the massif.

Olot — E3–4

Country: Spain
Province: Girona
Altitude: 443 m/1454 ft
Population: 23,000

Location

Olot lies deep in the mountainous interior of Catalonia about 50 km/31 miles W of the Golf de Roses and 60 km/37 miles NW of Girona.

The Town

Olot, an industrial town and chief place of the Garrotxa region, lies in the valley of the Riu Fluvia and at the intersection of important cross-country roads. Since it was destroyed by earthquakes in 1427–28 there are almost no medieval buildings left. Although Olot is not particularly attractive, the museums are well worth a visit.

Museu Comarcal de la Garrotxa

In Carrer del Hospici stands the Museu Comarcal de la Garrotxa (regional museum of Garrotxa). It contains works of local sculptors and a small collection of fossils.

Museu d'Art Modern

The Museu d'Art Modern (Museum of Modern Art) in the town park houses pictures by Catalan masters of the 19th and 20th c., including works of the landscape school of Olot.

Museu de la Casa Trinxeria

The Museu de la Casa Trinxeria at 29 Carrer de Sant Esteve exhibits furniture and interior decoration of the 17th–19th c. as well as pictures and ceramics.

Museu Parroquial

A small museum was set up in the Chapter House of the Parish Church of Sant Esteve (18th c.; Baroque altar); it includes ecclesiastical art (liturgical vessels, painting, altar panels) of the 15th–19th c.

A Museum of Natural Science is at present under construction.

*Zona Volcànica

The Garrotxa is an ancient volcanic area; most of the craters and cones lie to the SW of the town. Experts consider these formations, which are protected areas, to be among some of the most interesting evidence of former volcanic activity in the whole of the Iberian Peninsula. The red volcanic rock is also of economic importance for it is used as building material and for the production of cement; however, the extensive quarrying is a threat to the landscape. The most impressive cone, 350 m/1149 ft in diameter, is the crater of Santa Margarida NW of the town. The relatively damp climate favours luxuriant vegetation.
There are a great many neat little Romanesque churches scattered about the countryside.

Palafrugell G7–8

Country: Spain
Province: Girona
Altitude: 87 m/286 ft
Population: 14,000

Location

Palafrugell is situated about 5 km/3 miles inland from the coast E of Girona.

The Town

Palafrugell is the commercial and shopping centre for the nearby resorts which to a large extent have been incorporated administratively in the town. The most important old building is the Gothic Church of Sant Marti (Spanish: San Martin) the façade of which was added in Baroque style.

Calella de Palafrugell G8

Location
4 km/2½ miles SE of Palafrugell

Calella (not to be confused with Calella de la Costa, see entry, in the province of Barcelona) is the most southerly of the resorts forming part of Palafrugell; it lies in a gently undulating landscape with narrow cool streets and white houses. The emphasis is more on small holiday homes than on hotels; the harbour area of this pleasant little place is

Calella de Palafrugell

almost exclusively a pedestrian zone with bars, restaurants and little shops. The beach is of coarse sand, narrow and not particularly long. At intervals spurs of rock reach far out into the water. There is a slipway for small boats. The hinterland is covered with pine woods.

Cap Roig/Cabo Roig

To the S of Calella Cap Roig (Spanish: Cabo Roig; pronounced "roach") rises out of the sea. At the landward end can be found a beautiful botanic garden (open in summer 8 a.m.–9 p.m.) which extends almost to the sea; the entrance is formed by an historicised fort.

Llafranc/Llafranch G8

Location
4 km/2½ miles SE of Palafrugell

Immediately to the N Calella is adjoined by a similar resort of Llafranc (Spanish: Llafranch) which nestles around a little bay. Both places are linked by the very picturesque Avinguda del Mar.
On the steep edge of the coast a short distance above Llafranc stands the Ermita de San Sebastián (see below). Because the road to it is very steep it is suggested that the visitor should use the somewhat longer approach from Tamariu.

Tamariu G8

Location
6 km/4 miles E of Palafrugell

Tamariu is a small and clearly one of the older holiday places in a defile between pine-covered hills. The beach is very small and of coarse sand; the bay which is protected

on all sides forms a harbour for many small pleasure boats; to the right and left reddish conglomerate rocks rise up in the sea. The place impresses by the fact that it is not entirely modern and lacks a certain sophistication.
Near to Tamariu there are several beautiful grottos in the rocky coast, including the Cova del Bisbe and the Cova d'en Gisbert, which can only be reached by boat.

*Ermita de San Sebastián

S of Tamariu close to Llafranc, the Ermita de San Sebastián stands on the steep coast. The approach (first towards Palafrugell and then left at a fork) is narrow and fairly winding. There are magnificent views of the coastal bays. On the edge of this steep coastline, 165 m/542 ft above the sea, stands the Ermita. From the shady terrace of the restaurant which belongs to the former hermitage (now an inn) there are excellent views; from here a footpath leads down the rocky coast and sharp left to the little grotto chapel of Divina Pastora, ending a few steps farther on in an exposed viewpoint with magnificent panoramas of the steep coastline. From the Ermita a footpath high above the sea on the edge of the cliff leads to the N and to Tamariu.
A few steps to the S below the Ermita stands a lighthouse and from the base there is a marvellous view of the bays of Llafranch and Calella below.

Palamós G7

Country: Spain
Province: Girona
Altitude: sea level
Population: 12,000

Location

Palamós lies in the southern third of the Costa Brava about half way between Palafrugell and Sant Feliu de Guíxols.

The Town

Palamós, a popular resort and fishing port, has a pretty situation on an outcrop of the Sierra de las Gabarras and on its broad curved bay is a beach of fairly fine sand, the western part of which is separated by some artificial breakwaters. Here the principal hotel blocks and tall apartment buildings can be found.
The old town and the port area lie at the E end of the bay, along which runs a broad promenade shaded with palms and plane trees. The commercial part of the harbour (fishing, export of cork) is not generally accessible; behind it right by the protective mole is the pleasure harbour (with Club Nàutic).
The Church of Santa Maria (predominantly Gothic, 14th–18th c.) stands in the old town. A curiosity is the completely dusty little museum in the Plaça del Forn (No. 5). Its principal exhibits are mussels and snails from all parts of the world (altogether about 5000 species) as well as old pictures (predominantly of the 18th and 19th c.) and a somewhat haphazard collection of coins.
There are fine bathing beaches on the bay to the N of Palamós including the Playa de la Fosca (a good sandy beach) and the Playa del Castell.

Fishing boats at Palamós

Pals

G7

Country: Spain
Province: Girona
Altitude: 56 m/184 ft
Population: 1700

Location

Pals is situated about 6 km/4 miles inland from the Costa Brava in the latitude of Girona.

*The Town

Pals gives an impression of a still predominantly medieval community even though already certain signs of increased commercialisation are to be noticed. The old heart of the place with its clean houses of ochre-coloured natural stone is accessible only to pedestrians. It is situated above the main road. The town walls, which are partly restored, date from the Middle Ages. At the highest point in the village, in a square shaded by robinia trees, stands the parish church (Romanesque and Gothic). The township is dominated by an isolated round tower (Torre del Homenatge) which has an iron bellcage. In the middle of the town a number of residential estates have been cleverly and tastefully modernised and are now private houses. Outside the walls on the northern side we come to the Mirador Josep Pla (named after the Catalan writer) which offers a charming panorama from E to W.

Pals: new houses in an old town

Church near Peratallada

Peratallada

Location
9 km/5½ miles W of Pals

*The Village

Peratallada is old-fashioned and has been kept almost in its original state. It lies in a gently undulating region which is intensively used for agriculture. Outside the village on the far side of the main road which skirts the place stands a Romanesque church with a partly Gothic bell turret and a doorway with a round arch, over which on a console can be seen a representation of a human head.
Coming from the main road Peratallada is entered over an old stone bridge and through a gateway. At this point the village is bordered by a ditch cut into soft stone. Some of the narrow streets are also carved into the natural rock and therefore are somewhat reminiscent of Roman streets. The former castle in the middle of the place can only be visited with a guide (daily 5, 6, and 7 p.m.); quite recently concerts have been put on here in summer.

Sant Julia de Boada

About 3 km/1¾ miles to the E in the little hamlet of Sant Julia de Boada stands a small pre-Romanesque church which is said to be one of the oldest churches in Catalonia.

Peralada/Perelada E7

Country: Spain
Province: Girona
Altitude: 22 m/72 ft
Population: 1300

Peralada: the castle

Location

Peralada (Spanish: Perelada) is situated in the plain of the Riu Llobregat about 6 km/4 miles NE of Figueres.

The Town

Castillo

Near the centre stands the Castillo, once the castle of the Rocaberti family, the counts of Peralada. It was built between the 14th and 17th c. and reveals both Gothic and Renaissance elements; in the 19th c. it was heavily restored and this has influenced the original nature of its style. In this battlemented castle, which also has beautiful gardens, there are today a casino, a restaurant and nearby an open-air theatre. The interior, which can be visited with a guide (10, 11 a.m., noon, 4.30, 5.30 and 6.30 p.m.; on Sundays and public holidays only in the morning), houses a museum which includes sculptures from the former monastery of Sant Pere de Rodes (see entry) and a library containing over 60,000 volumes.

Also of interest is the complex of buildings belonging to the church of the former monastery of Sant Domenec (11th c.; open daily 10 a.m.–1 p.m. and 5–8 p.m.); in the remains of the Romanesque cloister are some beautiful sculpted capitals.

The parish church has an elevated position and originally dates from Romanesque times but the interior has been fairly unfortunately converted to Baroque.

Perpignan B6

Country: France
Département: Pyrénées-Orientales
Altitude: 24 m/79 ft
Population: 114,000

Location

Perpignan (Catalan: Perpinyà), the capital of the Département Pyrénées-Orientales of the French part of Catalonia at the northern foot of the Pyrenees, lies in an estuarine plain on the right bank of the Têt about 40 km/25 miles from the Franco-Spanish border.

History

Although the area was already settled in Iberian and Roman times the earliest recorded mention of Perpignan was in the 10th c. In this period the Dukes of Roussillon had their seat here. The dukedom included at that time little more than the coastal plain between the foot of the Pyrenees and the town of Narbonne, while the rest of the area belonged to the House of Cerdagne-Besalú which was a branch of the dukedom of Barcelona. In 1172 the Cerdagne-Besalú family inherited also the dukedom of Roussillon.
At the Peace of Corbeil (1258) Louis the Holy transferred Roussillon and the Spanish march to the kingdom of Aragón and in the same century Perpignan began to enjoy its heyday. The town became the centre of the newly founded kingdom of Mallorca, which at that time included not only the Balearic Islands but also territory on the mainland (actually Roussillon, the Cerdagne and Montpellier). The kings Jaime I, Sancho and Jaime II resided here until Pedro II of Aragón conquered their kingdom.
In the year 1573 the town had opposed the crown of France and as a result it was besieged by troops of Louis XI and finally conquered. Because of its obstinate resistance the King of Aragón gave the town the title "Fidelissima Villa" ("truest town"). Until 1493 Perpignan remained under French rule but since King Charles VIII was dependent on stable internal political conditions because of his political and military ambitions in Italy, he gave Roussillon and Cerdagne, two regions which had always remained restless, back to the Catholic kings of Aragón and Castile. The latter had completed the Christian restoration of Spain (Reconquista) by reconquering the Moorish residence of Granada. Yet Catalan individuality remained. In 1640 the Catalans rose up against the central government of Madrid and proclaimed the French King Louis XIII Duke of Barcelona; he entered Perpignan in 1642 at the head of his troops and was greeted enthusiastically by the exhausted population. The Peace of the Pyrenees (1659) brought bitter disappointment to the Catalans. The main ridge of the Pyrenees was declared the boundary between France and Spain and the unity of Catalonia remained an illusion. Like many other French towns Perpignan was also provided with defensive works by the genial Vauban and these were only pulled down in 1900, in order to create space for an extension of the town.

The Old Town

The centre of the Old Town with its narrow streets is the Place de la République with the theatre.

Cathedral of Sant-Jean

"Le Castillet", an old town gate

Le Castillet

On the northern edge of the Old Town stands the former town gate of 1367 called "Le Castillet"; it is built of red brick and is the symbol of the town. The defensive building houses the Casa Pairal (open 9–11.30 a.m. and 2–5.30 p.m.; entrance fee) it includes a collection of Catalonian folk art and ethnology. From the tower of the Castillet there is a fine view.

Saint-Jean

Just E of the Castillet stands the Cathedral of Saint-Jean (seat of a bishop since 1601) – the architecture dates primarily from the 14th and 15th c. but includes parts of the previous church including the Romanesque Christus Gate and the Chapelle Notre-Dame dels Correchs. It is crowned by a stumpy tower with a characteristic wrought-iron bellcage (1743). Originally the church was intended to have three aisles but was altered in 1433 and made into a single-aisled building.
The interior which has bold proportions and is richly appointed, is well worth seeing; of particular interest are the grave of Bishop Montmort (17th c.), an organ gallery of 1604 and, in a chapel by the right-hand doorway, a marvellously carved plague cross (1307), probably Rhenish work. Almost all the altars date from the 16th and 17th c. and are in Catalan Baroque. The font is early Romanesque.

Loge de Mer

S of the Castillet and SW of the cathedral in the centre of the old town with its narrow streets stands the Loge de Mer (14th–15th c.) in the square of the same name. This was once the headquarters of the Exchange and of the Maritime Court. Its present appearance is due to comprehensive rebuilding in the 16th c. in which, however, the late Gothic

Loge de Mer: the former town exchange

style was retained. Notable are the ornamented windows in the upper storey. Diagonally opposite this building is a bronze sculpture of a woman ("Venus") by Aristide Maillol who was born in nearby Banyuls.

Town Hall

Close to the Loge de Mer stands the Hôtel de Ville (town hall) which arose in various phases of building (13th–17th c.). In the internal courtyard can be seen the fine bronze sculpture "La Pensée" by Maillol.

Musée Hyacinthe Rigaud

Still farther S we come to the Musée Hyacinthe Rigaud (open Wed.–Mon. 9.30 a.m.–noon and 2–6 p.m.; entrance fee). It is named after the painter Hyacinthe Rigaud (actually Hyacinthe Rigau y Ros; 1659–1743) the most important French portrait painter of his time. As well as a selection of his works it includes pictures by Spanish and Catalan artists of the 14th–16th c. including works by Ingres, Tintoretto, etc.

Musée d'Histoire Naturelle

Near the Musée Rigaud stands the Musée d'Histoire Naturelle (Natural History Museum). Its principal exhibits are the flora and fauna of southern France.

Place Arago

A few yards W of the Musée Rigaud lies the Place Arago with a monument to the physicist and astronomer François Arago (1786–1853).

Citadel

Away from the centre of the old town in the S of Perpignan rises the huge Citadel. It was constructed in the 17th and 18th c. in the form of a star. First we go through an archway into the external walls (pretty view of the town) and then cross the inner walls. Part of the Citadel is still used for military purposes and therefore not open to the public.

Palais des Rois de Majorque

The heart of the Citadel and at the same time an important example of French medioval architecture is the former Palace of the Kings of Mallorca (open Wed.–Mon. 9.30 a.m.–noon and 2–6 p.m.; entrance fee). It was built in 1276 as a residence for King Jaime I of Mallorca and the buildings are grouped around a fine inner courtyard which is enclosed by Gothic arcades. The dominating central part of the façade of the main building is a two-storied late Gothic chapel (remains of wall painting, beautiful capitals on the doorway of the upper floor); a circular staircase leads to the top of the defence tower (excellent view).

La Salanque/Côte des Perpignanais

B–C7

Location
NE to SE of Perpignan

The most extensive flat beach of fine sand on the Mediterranean coast is known as La Salanque and is situated between the Etang de Leucate in the N and the resort of Argelès-Plage in the S (the southern part is sometimes also known as the Côte des Perpignanais).

Port Leucate
Port Barcarès

Port Leucate and Port Barcarès, the most northerly places on this stretch of the coast, are situated on the narrow spit of land which separates the Etang de Leucate (also called the Etang de Salses) from the sea. They are holiday centres which were laid out a short time ago on a chess board plan. Both resorts are grouped around modern extensive pleasure ports; the rest of the infrastructure (sailing, surf and diving schools, sports grounds, shops, hotels, apartments) is exclusively geared to tourism. The freighter "Lydia" (open to inspection daily 10 a.m.–6 p.m.) was beached near Port Barcarès in 1967 to provide a special feature for the beaches. Inland on the W bank of the Etang de Leucate lies the fortified town of Salses (see entry).

Canet-Plage

Until quite recently Canet-Plage was the favourite resort of the inhabitants of Perpignan. Now it has changed into a thoroughly organised holiday and leisure centre and has forfeited its sleepy charm. Yacht harbours, sports grounds, hotels and apartments and a casino determine the nature of the place.
S of Canet-Plage stretches to Etang de Canet et de Saint-Nazaire.

Saint-Cyprien-Plage

Saint-Cyprien-Plage has also undergone an intensive modernisation process, in the course of which a marina was laid out near the old fishing harbour. The little town of Elne (see entry) lies farther inland.

Argelès-Plage

Argelès-Plage is situated close to the foot of the Pyrenees and right by the frontier of the Côte Vermeille (see entry). With an annual total of 300,000 visitors it is by far the most important and most visited resort in Roussillon. The leisure facilities are correspondingly varied (casino, pleasure harbour, etc.).

A hotel complex in La Platja d'Aro

A street in La Platja d'Aro

Castell d'Aro

La Platja d'Aro/Playa de Aro H7

Country: Spain
Province: Girona
Altitude: sea level
Population: 3000 (with Castell d'Aro)

Location

La Platja d'Aro (Spanish: Playa de Aro) lies in the southern third of the Costa Brava half way between Palamós and Sant Feliu de Guíxols.

The Town

La Platja d'Aro is one of the best-known seaside resorts in the Costa Brava. It is entirely geared to tourism; the very crowded beach (on parts of which dogs are forbidden) is a kilometre in length and formed of coarse sand. Windsurfers are directed to particular parts of the beach.
The hotel blocks are concentrated close to the beach; the lower buildings in the middle of the township (mostly a pedestrian zone) and the modest architecture are a pleasant surprise. There are many shops, including some of high quality, and provision for self-selection is good. A large car park lies at the edge of the town; it is advisable to leave your car here and to walk to the beach. The recent urbanisation extends a considerable distance inland.

Castell d'Aro/Castillo de Aro

Location
3 km/2 miles W of Platja d'Aro

Castell d'Aro (Spanish: Castillo de Aro) is the administrative centre of the parish and all in all a quiet and clean little town. It has remained almost unaffected by the bustling activity of La Platja d'Aro which is part of the community.
A shady and pleasant stepped path leads up from the main road to the little church, which although of minor interest has a Baroque doorway; in the interior the single-aisle nave is flanked by chapels. Next to the church stands the old castle (Castel de Benedormiens) in which temporary art exhibitions take place.

Poblat Ibèric/Poblado Iberico

See Ullastret

Portbou/Port-Bou D7–8

Country: Spain
Province: Girona
Altitude: sea level
Population: 2500

Location

Portbou (Spanish: Port-Bou) is the frontier town between Spain and France right on the Mediterranean coast.

The Town

Portbou has a fine situation in a bay where the blackish rocks are to a great extent exposed but there is a small beach of pebbles. Above the village stands the church which, in its present form, dates from the 19th c. and from the point of view of the history of art is only of minor importance. As in La Jonquera (see entry) large railway yards are a feature of the town. Because of the wider gauge of the Spanish railways compared with those of central Europe, passengers must change trains here, unless travelling in specially constructed carriages with adjustable bogies. The railway station and yards at Portbou were laid out in 1929 on the occasion of the International Exhibition held in Barcelona.

Col des Balitres

Location
3 km/2 miles N of Portbou

From Portbou the road winds up steeply to the Col des Balitres across which at a height of 173 km/568 ft runs the Franco-Spanish border (passport and customs control). There is a fine view from the top of the pass.

Colera

Location
5 km/3 miles S of Portbou

Travelling S from Portbou over a little pass we reach the small resort of Colera (also called San Miquel de Colera) which lies a little way off the main road. Near the village the valley is crossed by a railway viaduct.
On the right side of the well-protected bay the beach is of coarse sand and not entirely clean. Here there is a little pleasure harbour. Another and larger beach lies on the left side of the bay. Colera is a somewhat sleepy place almost without a modern touristic infrastructure. The hinterland is extensively bare and karstic.

El Port de la Selva/Puerto de la Selva — D–E8

Country: Spain
Province: Girona
Altitude: sea level
Population: 1000

Location

El Port de la Selva (Spanish: Puerto de la Selva) lies on the N side of the peninsula which juts out into the Mediterranean as an extension of the Sierra de Roda, only some 15 km/9 miles S of the Franco-Spanish frontier.

The Town

The little holiday resort of El Port de la Selva which developed from a fishing village is situated on the E side of a bay which bites deeply into the land and which is enclosed

by hills with scanty vegetation but with occasional pine woods. The beaches of fine sand extend on the S and W sides of the bay which is exposed to winds to the N and is therefore popular with windsurfers (equipment can be rented). The little town itself is less influenced by tourism than other holiday centres in the area. The pleasure-boat harbour (with a Club Nàutic and an open-air swimming pool has been recently laid out. In the vicinity are considerable remains of Stone Age settlements including a number of dolmens (stone tables) and on the Punta del Pi a necropolis with some 70 graves.
SW inland stands the former Benedictine Monastery of Sant Pere de Rodes (Spanish: San Pedro de Roda; see entry) which is now in ruins.

Ripoll

E2

Country: Spain
Province: Girona
Altitude: 682 m/2238 ft
Population: 12,000

Location

Ripoll is situated deep in the interior of Catalonia on the southern slopes of the Collado de Ares, over which runs the state boundary, and where the River Fresser flows into the Riu Ter.

The Town

Ripoll has the appearance of a middle-class industrial town. In the vicinity there are a number of coal mines.

Benedictine Monastery

In the main square in the heart of the town stands the large complex of buildings of the Benedictine Monastery of Santa Maria (Monestir de Santa Maria de Ripoll) a foundation of the Visigoth King Recared I (6th c.). The first monastic church was dedicated as early as the 9th c. but had to be enlarged 200 years later and converted into a five-aisled basilica. The monastery was the focus of a rich cultural life and even the monk, Gerbert von Aurillac (about 940–1003), later Pope Silvester II, studied sometime in Ripoll. A fire in 1835 left almost nothing of the great Romanesque church and thus the present church (1883), although based on the old plans, is obviously a newer building which, however, creates a good impression of Romanesque proportions.

**Doorway

The most important remnant of the Romanesque church is the main doorway which has been generally well maintained. It dates from the 12th c. and is now enclosed in a glazed vestibule which necessarily protects it against the destructive influences of the environment. It is notable for the great number of representations of themes of the Old and New Testaments. In the upper part can be seen scenes from the Revelation of St John (Christ enthroned flanked by Angels and symbols of the Evangelists). Below them, on the left of the gate, scenes from the Book of Kings and on the right from the Book of Exodus (migration of the people of Israel from Egypt); in the lowest part King David surrounded by musicians and mythical creatures. The figures on the doorway represent St Peter and St Paul. On the archway is the story of the martyrdom of these two saints and also the history of Jonah and the whale and in the innermost archway the story of Cain and Abel.

The Interior

The five-aisled interior of the church has a gloomy majesty; only a little light penetrates the building through the alabaster panels in the side aisles. By the entrance is a tombstone in the floor dating from 1909 enclosed by a mosaic. In the crossing on a pillar which divides the two aisles on the right can be seen a glockenspiel mounted on a wheel. The mighty choir chevet is impressive with its three subsidiary apses on both sides of the main apse. In the right transept is the grave of Berengar III (died 1131).

The Cloister

To the right of the doorway a few steps lower lies the cloister (12th–15th c.). Its figural decoration is of later date than that of the main façade and also not so important from the point of view of the history of art.

Museum

To the left of the monastery church in the former Church of Sant Pere is the museum (open 9 a.m.–1 p.m. and 3–7 p.m.; closed Mon. afternoons). It contains exhibits concerning the history and ethnology of the region including weapons, pottery and textiles.
In the main square stands a memorial stone to the heroes of 27 May 1839 when Ripoll was besieged by the Dukes of Barcelona. The associated monument (1896) represents a female figure holding a shield and on it a cockerel, the heraldic animal of Ripoll.

Roses/Rosas E8

Country: Spain
Province: Girona
Altitude: sea level
Population: 7500

Location

Roses (Spanish: Rosas) lies at the northern end of the gulf of the same name where the Riu Fluvia and a number of smaller rivers join and form an estuary in the northern part of the Costa Brava.

The Town

Roses, founded by the Greeks under the name Rhode, is a fishing port which is also popular as a holiday resort. There is a large new hotel complex to the S of the old town; the beach is long, flat and of fine sand but not very wide. Both the town and the suburb of Santa Margarida have a harbour for pleasure craft. There are also facilities for windsurfing, sailing and diving.

Citadel

Near the western edge of the town lies the site of the former Citadel which was enclosed by walls. There is not a lot left of

Roses: the Citadel, a church within the walls

the old fortifications, the most notable being the remains of a church which was associated with one of the early Christian burial places.
From the top of the Puig Rom (229 m/752 ft) to the SE there is a fine view of the town and the bay which is particularly charming at sunset.

Aqua Brava

NW of the town the aquadrome of Aqua Brava was recently laid out. The principal attraction of the leisure centre are seven large water chutes; there are also several swimming pools, a restaurant, a bar, electronic games, etc.

Santa Margarida

W of the town on the Riu Grau is the modern holiday complex of Santa Margarida which is laid out in the form of a lagoon town criss-crossed by canals with mooring places.

S'Agaró H7

Country: Spain
Province: Girona
Altitude: sea level

Location

S'Agaró, a part of Castell d'Aro (see Platja d'Aro), lies in the southern third of the Costa Brava.

**The Town

Closed to non-local vehicles

S'Agaró is a relatively new foundation. This estate of villas was only laid out in 1923. It extends on a little promontory

Artist working in the macchia, near S'Agaro

which, on the N, encloses the Bay of Sant Pau (Spanish: San Pol; a broad beach of fine sand). The Hostal de la Gavina, a first-class hotel, has a magnificent situation in a park-like landscape. By turning right outside the hotel right by the sea we can walk along the rocky coast which is divided into numerous little bays in which fine properties with beautiful gardens full of flowers are particularly attractive.

Salses

A–B6

Country: France
Département: Pyrénées-Orientales
Altitude: 12 m/39 ft
Population: 2000

Location

Salses lies on the Etang de Leucate about 16 km/10 miles N of Perpignan.

The Fort of Salses

Guided tours
(in summer)
between 9.30 a.m. and 7 p.m. every 15 minutes

Son et Lumière

Entrance fee

The Fort of Salses on the edge of the town was erected on the Via Domitiana, the old Roman road from Narbonne to Spain, and commands a defile between the Mediterranean and the mountainous hinterland, along which Hannibal had passed on his campaign against the Roman Empire. The builders of the great fortification were the Spaniards who were the Lords of Roussillon in the 15th c. French troops

Fort of Salses, built by Vauban

conquered the stronghold in 1639–40 and at the end of that century Vauban undertook some alterations. At the beginning of the branch road which leads from the main road to the fortress (signposted Château Fort) there is a little spring almost hidden and a plaque which commemorates the second International Congress of the Catalan language. The route to the fort passes a great co-operative cellar (*cave coopérative*; wine on sale) and goes underneath the railway line. The great complex with ditches and huge walls has been very well preserved. The blocks of buildings on a rectangular plan are grouped around an inner courtyard. They are reached through a gateway and across drawbridges. The fortress is dominated by a defensive tower five stories high; there is a good panorama from the top of the curtain wall which is up to 6 m/20 ft thick.

Santa Coloma de Farners/Santa Coloma de Farmés — G4–5

Country: Spain
Province: Girona
Altitude: 104 m/341 ft
Population: 6500

Location

Santa Coloma de Farners (Spanish: Santa Coloma de Farmés) is situated to the W of the motorway which joins Girona and Barcelona.

The Town

The spa of Santa Coloma de Farners has a number of buildings of pre-Romanesque and Romanesque date. The parish church was dedicated as long ago as 960; a footpath from the centre leads up to the old castle.
A Romanesque church on the plan of a Latin cross stands in the district of Sant Pere Cereal.

Sant Cugat del Vallès/San Cugat del Vallés — K1

Country: Spain
Province: Barcelona
Altitude: 180 m/591 ft
Population: 30,000

Location

Sant Cugat del Vallès (Spanish: San Cugat del Vallés) lies about 15 km/9 miles NW of Barcelona on the far side of Tibidabo.

Benedictine Monastery

Open
Mon., Wed., Fri. 10 a.m.–noon (church); daily 10 a.m.–2 p.m. and 4–7 p.m.; closed Sun. afternoons and Mon. (cloisters)

The first definite mention of the Benedictine Monastery was in the year 897; the present-day Romanesque-Gothic building dates from the 12th to 17th c. and is therefore of differing architectural styles. Most of this idyllic monastery is still surrounded by a wall. The main façade of the three-aisled church is fairly low and sturdy and possesses a Gothic

Cloister of Sant Cugat

Carvings on a capital

portal with little ornamentation. Over this can be seen a great rose window with two smaller ones on either side. The choir and the main apse together with two smaller apses are Romanesque. However, in the first is a simple Gothic window with tracery. Also in Gothic style are the stump of the crossing tower and the windows in the side aisles. The interior has a beautiful Altar of All Saints (1375) and the tomb of the Abbot Odo (14th c.). To the left of the church façade a door opens into the cloisters. The principal features of interest here are the almost one hundred figured capitals.

Sant Feliu de Guíxols/San Feliú de Guixols

H7

Country: Spain
Province: Girona
Altitude: sea level
Population: 14,000

Location

Sant Feliu de Guíxols (Spanish: San Feliú de Guixols) is situated in the southern section of the Costa Brava half way between Tossa de Mar and Palamós.

The Town

Sant Feliu, commonly known as the "capital of the Costa Brava" has an attractive situation on a bay. It is a port which is used by ships of all nationalities for the export of locally produced cork, but which is also a popular resort. Sant Feliu is a friendly little town with a pretty centre but because of the narrow beach is not very suitable for those seeking a seaside holiday.

Monastery

The remains of the former monastery stand near the entrance to the town in a large square (Plaça del Monestir). At the church is the Porta Ferrada (Spanish: Puerta de Hierro = iron gate) dating from the 11th c. which was excavated only in 1931. It is a Romanesque round-arched narthex which conceals the entrance façade to the church, now barricaded. To the left is a semi-circular defensive tower which was formerly part of the wall; to the right is the stump of a tower on a rectangular plan. The church is entered through a door in the north transept wall. Beyond the second bay the nave is spanned by a Gothic vault; the main apse is flanked by two subsidiary apses. By the north transept can be seen a copy of the statue of the Madonna in the Monastery of Montserrat (see entry).

Museum

In the monastery square stands a Baroque church portal in an isolated position (Arc de San Benet = Benedict arch) dating from 1747 and behind it is the Museu Municipal (town museum), with finds from Iberian, Greek and Roman times.

Beach
Town centre

Adjoining is the fairly small beach which is separated from the harbour only by a short breakwater. The bay is bounded on the left by the main breakwater and on the right by a

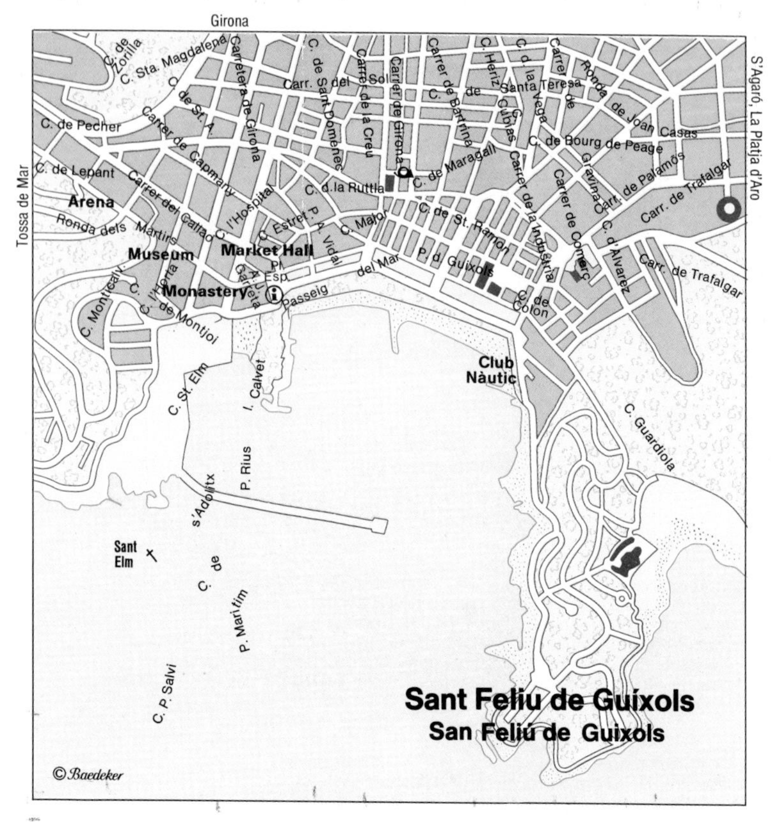

rocky cape. Along the broad promenade, planted with plane trees, are restaurants with seats in the open air. In the main square, which is only separated from the promenade by the large town hall, can be found the fruit and vegetable market and the market hall.

Mirador de Sant Elm

A road leads from the beach to the right to the observation point Mirador de Sant Elm (impressive view of the town and coast) where stands the hermitage (Ermita de Sant Elm) of the same name.

Sant Joan de les Abadesses/San Juan de las Abadesas E2

Country: Spain
Province: Girona
Altitude: 775 m/2544 ft
Population: 4000

Baroque doorway . . .

. . . and a fortified church

Location

Sant Joan de les Abadesses (Spanish: San Juan de las Abadesas) lies on the southern slope of the Collado de Ares/Col d'Arès about 10 km/6 miles from the Franco-Spanish frontier.

*Sant Joan/San Juan

In the centre of the little town stands the great church of Sant Joan (Spanish: San Juan) which formerly belonged to a monastery (Monestir de Sant Joan de les Abadesses). This had been founded in the 9th century and first belonged to the Benedictine order. The present church is the third on the site and was dedicated in 1150 when the convent had passed to the Augustinians. Extensions and alterations were undertaken in later years. The severe earthquake of 2 February 1428 which shook the entire eastern Pyrenees caused considerable damage to the church, much of which was only later put right and led to considerable non-uniformity of architectural styles. There was further damage to the church in the Spanish Civil War and when it was rebuilt the opportunity was taken to free the building from its later additions. So in the north transept a chapel was especially added to house the Baroque Pietà which until then had stood in the Presbytery.

The plan of the single-aisled Romanesque church is unusual. The chevet comprises the main apses, consisting of the choir, the choir ambulatory, the choir chapels and two subsidiary apses which were added to the transepts. It is suggested that this plan was the result of influences from

Sant Joan de les Abadesses: the Romanesque apse

Crucifixion group in Sant Joan: a world-famous work of art

the south of France. The sculpted capitals of the half pillars which bear the vault of the choir are notable. In contrast to the elaborate choir the nave is unusually small and also more sparsely appointed.

**The Descent from the Cross Group

On the high altar stands probably the most important art treasure of Sant Joan, the carved group depicting the Descent from the Cross (*c.* 1250), known as "el santissim misteri de Sant Joan de les Abadesses". It was created in the late Romanesque period and already revealed the first signs of the naissant Gothic. The group consists of Christ, Mary, the two thieves (the original of the good thief was destroyed in 1936 and is replaced by a copy), St John and St Nicodemus together with Joseph of Arimathia.

The Altar of Mary

In the south transept can be found the Gothic Altar of Mary (retaule de Santa Marie la Blanca; 1443) made of alabaster. Around the central figure of the Madonna with her child are eighteen reliefs depicting scenes from Mary's life, the childhood of Jesus and the Prophets of the Old Testament. In the interior of the church there can also be seen the 14th c. sarcophagus of the blessed Miró, canon of Sant Joan, with his recumbent effigy.

St Michael's Cloister Museum

Near the main façade of the church, in a gatehouse to the left is the doorway leading to the St Michael's Cloister (claustre de Sant Miquel) and to the museum. The cloister on a unsymmetrical plan has beautiful Gothic pillared arcades and a coffered ceiling; the basin of the fountain in the centre is an old 13th c. font. Adjoining the cloister is the former chapter house, the arches of which are still Romanesque.
The museum was opened in 1975; explanatory text in English can be borrowed from the ticket office. The exhibits come almost exclusively from the former monastery and from other churches in the town. Among them are Baroque altarpieces, finds from Romanesque times, panels, the sides of a choir stall, a number of crucifixes, wooden reliefs and embroidered vestments. Of special interest is the abbot's shroud, made of red satin with rich embroidery, depicting Christ whose soul is being taken up into Paradise by two angels.

Matthew's Doorway

To the right in the nave Matthew's doorway (Portal de Sant Mateu) leads to the abbots' apartments (open daily 11 a.m.–2 p.m. and 4–7 p.m.) which now house the monastery archives. Here can be seen a modern seated statue of the Abbot Ponç de Monells who had the church built and who holds its model in his hands. In the masonry can be seen epitaphs of three abbots' graves.

Sant Pau/San Pablo

By the main road can be seen the ruins of the church of Sant Pau which was destroyed during the Civil War. The doorway with a relief of Christ in Majesty in the typanum – unfortunately somewhat weatherbeaten – and the apse and the crossing tower have been preserved.
To the W of the town the river bed is crossed by a stone bridge which has been rebuilt according to the old design.

Sant Pere de Rodes/San Pedro de Roda E7–8

Country: Spain
Province: Girona
Altitude: 460 m/1510 ft

Location

The former monastery of Sant Pere de Rodes (Spanish: San Pedro de Roda) lies in the northern Costa Brava in the Sierra de Roda, the eastern continuation of which juts out into the Mediterranean.

**Monastery Ruins

The ruins of the former Benedictine Monastery are one of the most important examples of Romanesque architecture in Catalonia. The origins of the church date back to the 8th c., i.e. pre-Romanesque days. The school of writing of St Pere, which in the Middle Ages produced magnificent illuminated hand-written documents, was celebrated. The monastery has been deserted since the 18th c. The 11th c. church has three aisles. Near the main apse with its choir ambulatory are two side apses which issue from the transepts. The barrel vaulting is considered to be the earliest Romanesque vaulting of its kind. Of interest are the capitals ornamented with animal heads and strap work. Very little of the other ornamentation of the church has remained; the best pieces can now be seen in the Museu Marès in Barcelona (see entry) also in the Castle of Peralada (see entry). Adjoining the church on the right are the cloister and the monastery buildings; the entire complex has a defensive character. To the left of the entrance and built on to the nave stands the bell tower (beautiful acoustic arcades) and on the right the defensive tower without windows which served as the last bastion.
Above the ruins of the monastery lies the Castillo de San Salvador from which there is a magnificent panorama.

Sant Pol de Mar/San Pol de Mar J4

Country: Spain
Province: Barcelona
Altitude: sea level
Population: 2000

Location

Sant Pol de Mar (Spanish: San Pol de Mar), which is bypassed by the coastal road, lies near the northern end of the Costa Daurada between Canet and Calella de la Costa.

Description of Sant Pol de Mar

The heart of the township with its whitewashed houses and narrow, irregular streets where there are many restaurants and bars, makes a very pleasant picture. In the vicinity of the beach, which is divided from the town by the railway line, there are facilities for hiring surf boards; also a water chute, a swimming bath and tennis courts.

The little Plaça de la Vila lies near the narrow coastal road; and here is the local museum (open Sat. and Sun. 7–9 p.m.; entrance fee); on the staircase can be seen a huge battle picture made of blue painted ceramic tiles. In the same building there is also the parish library. Above the town to the N near the station stands the Church of Sant Pau, and part of a former monastery; also on a hill above the contre is the Church of Sant Jaume.

Sarrià de Ter/Sarriá de Ter

See Girona/Gerona

Serra de Montseny/Sierra de Montseny

See Montseny

Tordera H5

Country: Spain
Province: Barcelona
Altitude: 34 m/112 ft
Population: 7500

Location

Tordera lies on the river of the same name, the estuary of which forms the boundary between the Costa Daurada and the Costa Brava and also of the provinces of Barcelona and Girona; the town is about 4 km/2½ miles from the coast.

The Town

Right by the river bank on a little hill stands the Romanesque-Gothic Parish Church of Sant Bartolomeu (San Bartolomé), built of golden-brown natural stone. The façade is Baroque.

Torroella de Montgrí F7

Country: Spain
Province: Girona
Altitude: 20 m/66 ft
Population: 5500

Location

Torroella de Montgrí is situated in a plain on the N bank of the Riu Ter some 6 km/3½ miles from its mouth.

The Town

The centre of the old town is the Plaça de la Vila; and here stand the Casa Consistorial (town hall) and a little old church; all around the square are arcades with street cafés. Going N from here we first come to the Palau Solterra on the right in which there is now an art gallery. The principal church is in the northern part of the old town; it is a 15th c. Gothic building which was heavily restored in the 19th c. The main façade is rather cramped and faces a small rear courtyard; it was converted to Baroque and remains incomplete. The interior has only one aisle (without transepts) and is surrounded by a circle of chapels; on the left of the nave a small classical baptistry was added. From the little square in front of the church there is a good view of the 13th c. Castell de Montgrí which stands on a karstic massif and is approached by a fairly difficult footpath (good panorama).

Bellcaire

Location
7 km/ 4½miles NW of Torroella

Bellcaire lies deep in the SE of the countryside of Empordà (Spanish: Ampurdán) and to the N of the lower course of the Riu Ter. The Canal de Riego passes close by.
The old-fashioned village is situated off the through road. Its characteristic feature is the fortress-like church dating from the 11th–13th c. which has recently been thoroughly restored.

Tossa de Mar

He

Country: Spain
Province: Girona
Altitude: sea level
Population: 3000

Location

Tossa de Mar lies in the most southerly part of the Costa Brava some 15 km/9 miles from the estuary of the Riu Tordera which forms the boundary of the Costa Daurada.

**The Town

Tossa, one of the best-known resorts of the Costa Brava, has a picturesque situation nestling between upland ridges which are largely wooded. The silhouette of its old town (Vila Vella), high above the sea, is the perfect example of a Catalonian coastal town. Although in the outer districts there has been a great deal of building, the old town with its narrow beach gives the impression of being a place which has not got out of hand.

Upper Town

The Upper Town on a little conical hill is a protected monument. It is surrounded by a well-preserved 12th c. wall with several defence towers. In the upper part can be found the ruins of the Gothic church (remains of the nave and the south transept). In a well-restored medieval house above a little rocky bay on the southern side of the promontory is the museum (Museu Municipal de Tossa; open 10 a.m.–1 p.m. and 4 p.m.–8 p.m.; entrance fee). It contains pri-

marily modern art of the region (also works by Marc Chagall, Olga Sacharow and Oskar Zügel), as well as a mosaic which came from the old Roman settlement in the present Lower Town and also finds from the New Stone Age (fine stone work, stool tools, terra sigillata, household pottery and coins).
There are charming little inns in the strects of the Upper Town some of which have terraces. At the highest point stands a lighthouse (good view of the sea and coast).

Lower Town

The heart of the Lower Town with its narrow streets and clean white houses is also pleasant. Near the western edge the scanty remains of a Roman settlement (Vila Romana; entrance is signposted) have been excavated. Very little apart from a few foundation walls now remains.
The beaches on the predominantly rocky coast are in the surroundings of Tossa and not directly within the

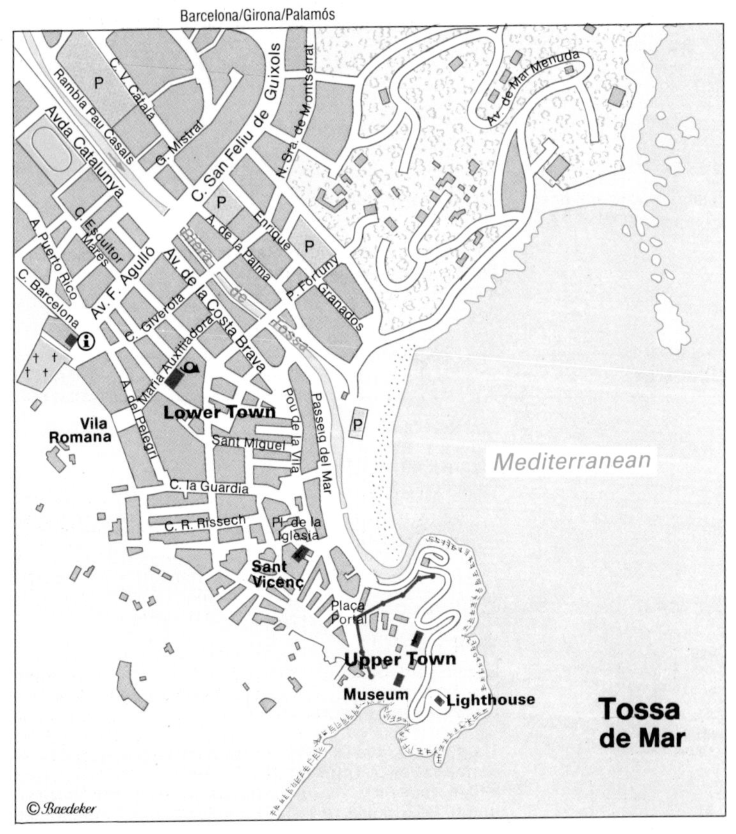

Tossa de Mar: the beach below the upper town

boundaries of the town. Marked paths lead to them and there are also excellent places for snorkellers and divers using breathing apparatus.

Ullastret

F–G7

Country: Spain
Province: Girona
Altitude: 49 m/161 ft
Population: 500

Location

The village of Ullastret is situated in the estuarine plain of the Riu Ter S of the river.

**Poblat Ibèric/Poblado Ibérico

Open
Tues.–Sun. 10.30 a.m.–
1 p.m. and 4–8 p.m.

Entrance fee

The Poblat Ibèric (Spanish: Poblado Ibérico), the excavated Iberian settlement, is famous. Motorists can drive to the site; the area is laid out like a park and planted with pines, cypresses and evergreens.

History

The settlement of Ullastret is one of the largest of its kind in northern Spain. The Puig de Sant Andreu and the Illa d'en Reixac, joined by a narrow isthmus, were already occupied in the Old Stone Age and it is on this site that the fortified town was built, probably in the 7th c. B.C. Excavations have proved that the Iberians, the ancient people of the country, were already in the 6th c. B.C. engaged in trade with Phoenicians, Etruscans and Greeks. The last named were also responsible for founding the town of Emporion (see Empúries) on the coast in the 6th c. and this is only 15 km/9 miles

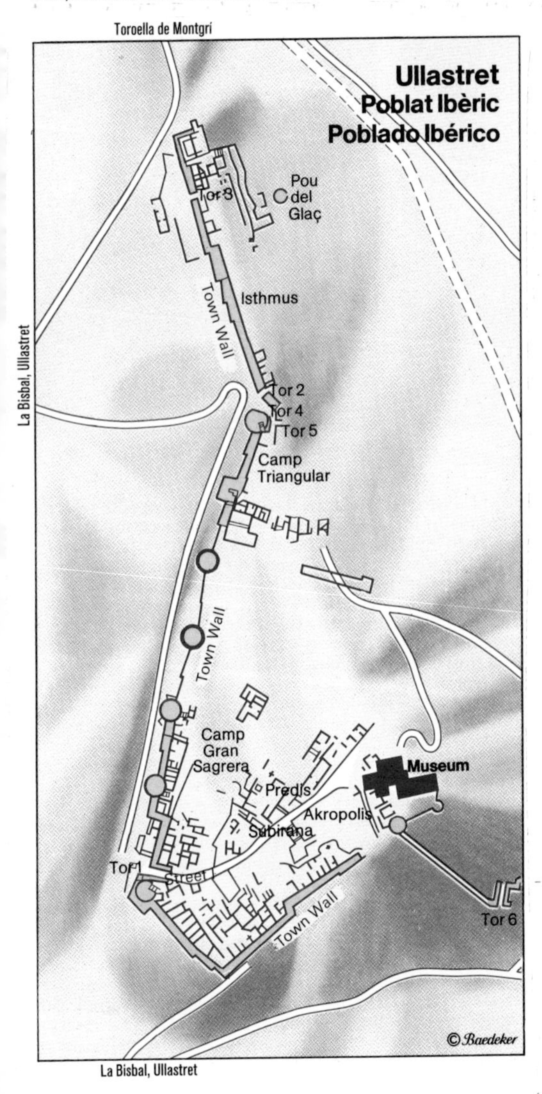

Ullastret: Town wall . . .

. . . and foundations of Iberian houses

N of Ullastret as the crow flies. It is also probable that the Iberians, principally under the influence of the Greeks, began to build in stone and to adopt the use of the potter's wheel. At the turn of the 5th and 4th c. B.C. the Iberian town with its defensive walls reached the zenith of its development and of its economic prosperity. But increasing competition from nearby Emporion caused the decline of the town in the 3rd c. B.C. and it was given up 100 years later. The town remained forgotten until the 1930s; systematic excavation began in 1947 and is still going on. Until the 19th c. a lake extended round the ruined site and although this was drained the surrounding countryside is occasionally flooded even today after especially heavy rain.

From the gate in the fence around the archaeological area (large car park outside, where the ticket office is also situated) the visitor walks or drives to the western town wall along which we now proceed. This wall is strengthened by six great round towers which were built at fairly regular intervals of about 30 m/33 yds. In all there were six gates through the wall in this area.

It is advisable to start the visit of the excavations at gate 1 (limited space for parking) which pierces the mighty defence wall. From here the broad street 1 leads to the upper town (acropolis), on the highest point of which stand the museum buildings. Street 1 is crossed by other series of roads which lead into the living areas. Most progress with the excavations has been made in the settlement part of the site bordering the town wall. At a number of places large shafts were driven vertically into the ground and these

served as store rooms and cisterns (since the town lay on an elevated site and above the water table the collection of rain water was important). To the left of street 1 in an area called "Predis subitana" are also remains of foundations and cisterns. In the area of the upper town the remains of two temples have been uncovered.
The areas to the N are not yet open to the public. In the Camp Triangular objects of the 5th and 4th c. B.C., when the town was at its most prosperous, were found. The narrow isthmus finally leads to the parts of the settlement which were situated on the Illa d'en Reixac, an island in the lake which once existed here.

Museum

The museum stands on the highest part of the acropolis hill. The exhibits comprise farming implements, weapons including Iberian examples, a number of human skulls, some of which are of people who had been executed and some revealing traces of trepanning; fossilised fauna and items connected with spinning and weaving; moulds for bronze clasps, painted ceramics (mainly Greek items imported from Attica). In the main room is a model of the excavation site; on the walls can be seen large sketch maps, with the places where coins and ceramic objects were found, as well as an archaeological map of the Province of Girona. Unfortunately comprehension is made difficult as all the explanations are only in Catalan.
From the little terrace outside the museum there is a view principally to the S over the plain which is used intensively for agriculture.

Vic/Vich

G2

Country: Spain
Province: Barcelona
Altitude: 494 m/1621 ft
Population: 28,000

Location

Vic (Spanish: Vich) lies in a wide valley some 60 km/37 miles N of Barcelona.

General

The old town of Vic, the Ausa of the Romans and a bishopric from 616, is well known to the Spaniards because it was the native town of the philosopher, mathematician and publicist Jaume Balmes (1810–48) who is considered to be the most important Spanish academic of the 19th c.

Cathedral

Open
10 a.m.–1 p.m. and 4–7 p.m.

The Sacristan will act as guide on request (donations welcome)

The cathedral, which stands on the edge of the old town, was founded in 1040, extensively renewed in 1803–21 and repaired after considerable damage during the Spanish Civil War. On the classical main front to the right of the central doorway a metal plaque gives its elevation as 486.8 m/1597 ft above sea level. The beautiful Romanesque bell tower adjoins the left-hand wall of the nave.

The interior

The cathedral is entered through a little doorway in the left-hand wall of the nave. Its plan is that of a three-aisled

hall church in the most severe solid style with Baroque ornamentation. The walls above the side chapels and the inside of the main façade and of the apse are completely covered with monumental frescoes (1926–30) by the painter Josep Maria Sert and there is no denying his Baroque models. Near the entrance, in a railed-off chapel of the left side aisle, can be seen the famous Baroque silver sarcophagus (18th c.) with the mortal remains of St Bernat Calbó a local saint.

**The Marble Altar

In the choir ambulatory the most remarkable object is a coloured and richly gilded Gothic marble altar (by Pere Oller; 15th c.) which once served as the high altar and miraculously remained undamaged when the church was destroyed during the Civil War. The central figures are Mary with her child and St Peter who can be recognised by the symbols of a papal crown and key; on both sides there are twelve reliefs of scenes from the life of Jesus and St Peter. On the predella are Apostles and Evangelists and in the centre Christ as the Man of Sorrows.

Chapter House

The chapter house, the crypt and the cloisters can only be seen when the visitor is accompanied by the sacristan. In the Gothic chapter house is a painted keystone representing St Peter.

*Cloister

The cloister is laid out in three styles, Romanesque, Gothic and Renaissance. We now enter the Gothic part (14th c.). In the middle is the monument of Jaume Balmes who was sometime the advisor to Pope Pius IX. The pope's bust can be seen in the cloister. This part of the cloister also is distinguished by lightness and clarity; there is rich ornamental tracery in the pillared arcades.

Crypt

The crypt dates from the early 11th c. and contains some elements of Visigoth and Arabic origin. The capitals and the alabaster window panes in the apse are notable.

*Museu Episcopal/Museo Episcopal

Open
10 a.m.–1 p.m.; also
4–7 p.m. on weekdays

Entrance fee

Immediately opposite the left side aisle of the cathedral stands the Episcopal Museum (Museu Episcopal). By far the most impressive department is that of Romanesque art; in the first room is a famous carved group depicting the Descent from the Cross (*c.* 1123). There are also wall paintings from Romanesque churches in the vicinity and farther afield, including a complete 12th c. church apse representing the Creation and Fall of Man; there are also a great number of excellent panels and other church apses.
The second room is devoted to Gothic; here there is a remarkably fine altar panel of alabaster with the Passion of Christ. Also worth mentioning is a large group of figures (*c.* 1467) which were part of a saint's grave in the cathedral. There follow a number of Gothic altar panels.
The Baroque department is situated one storey higher. In these rooms there are other pre- and early-Christian exhibits, Roman amphorae, terra sigillata and glass and a

◀ *Vic: cathedral cloister, with a memorial to Jaume Balmes, counsellor to Pope Pius IX*

Christ as Ruler of the World

St Martin

comprehensive collection of paraments and vestments. A large collection of painted ceramics (tiles, vessels, some with metal effect glazing, polychromatic pictures of saints and ethnic exhibits).

Roman Temple

By the side of the Baroque façade of the Church of Nuestra Señora de la Piedad in the eastern part of the old town can be seen the remains of a Roman temple of the 2nd. c. A.D. which has been considerably restored. There are remains of medieval walls and vaulting on its right side.

Plaça Major/Plaza Mayor

The heart of the old town, which is encircled by a ring road, is the main square (Plaça Major) in its northern part. At the SE corner a narrow road leads to the Casa Consistorial (town hall; also tourist information office) which was originally Gothic and which was extended in the 16th and 17th c. The interior has a gallery with portraits of famous citizens and a part of the civic archives.

Vilassar de Mar/Vilasar de Mar

See Mataró

Practical Information

Airlines

Spain

British Airways

Passeig de Grácia 58
E-08007 Barcelona
tel. (93) 2 15 21 12

Iberia

Passeig de Grácia 30
E-08007 Barcelona
tel. (93) 3 01 39 93

Plaça Marqués de Camps 8
E-17001 Girona
tel. (972) 20 58 00

Most other airlines serving Barcelona have desks at the airport.

Airports

See Getting to the Costa Brava

Bicycle and Motorcycle Rental

Exploring the interior of the region by bicycle is rewarding, even though the interior of the Côte Vermeille and the Costa Brava is largely mountainous. Bicycles can be hired at all important tourist centres, sometimes even motorised bicycles and mopeds.

Boat Excursions

Boat excursions are arranged to various places from all the resorts. Leaflets and timetables can be obtained from local tourist information offices (see Information) and from the area of the harbours. There are boat services (also car transport) from Barcelona to the Balearic Islands (Majorca, Minorca and Ibiza).

Bullfighting

Bullfights (*corridas de toros*) were held until the 16th c. as a form of weapon training as well as on the occasion of fiestas, the mounted *caballeros* with their lances being pitted against the bulls. At the beginning of the 17th c. bullfighting began to take a less hazardous form, and the present rules are attributed to Francisco Romero, born in Ronda about 1700. The building of the first large bullring (*plaza de toros*) in Madrid in 1749 finally made it a public spectacle in which only professional *toreros* take part. The building is exactly circular, with the expensive seats on the shady side (*sombra*) and the cheaper ones in the sun (*sol*). The bullfight (*lidia*) has three main parts (*suertes*). After a brief prologue during which the *capeadores* tease the bull by playing it with their brightly coloured capes (*capas*) there follows the *suerte de picar* or *suerte de varas*, in which the mounted *picadores* provoke the bull to attack them, plunge their lances (*garrochas*) into its neck and withstand the charges of the infuriated beast as best they can. When the bull has been sufficiently weakened (*castigado*) the second stage, the *suerte de banderillas* begins. The *banderilleros* run towards the bull carrying several *banderillas* and, skilfully eluding its charge at the last moment, stick them into its neck. The normal banderillas are sticks 75 cm/30 in. long with barbed points and paper streamers; the *banderillas a cuarta* are only 15 cm/6 in. long. Bulls which are too fierce or vicious are distracted by plays with a cloak (*flores*). When three pairs of banderillas have been planted in the bull's neck the *suerte suprema* or *suerte de matar* begins. The *espada* or *matador*, armed with a red cloth (*muleta*) and a sword (*estoque*), begins by teasing the bull with the cloth and seeks to manoeuvre it into a position in which he can give it the death stroke (*estocada*), after which the coup de grâce is administered by a *punterillo* with a dagger. If the bull has shown itself courageous and aggressive it will be loudly applauded. Clumsy bullfighters are hissed, booed and subjected to verbal criticism.

In Barcelona bullfights are held on almost every Sunday and public holiday from Easter to November and sometimes also on weekdays (particularly Thursdays). They take place between 4 and 6 or between 5 and 7 in the afternoons, but only in good weather. During the dog days (July–August) and from mid-October onwards only the lesser forms of bullfighting, known as *novilladas*, with less experienced bullfighters (*novilleros*) and young bulls (*novillos*), are held. In Catalonia bullfights usually take place only on great feast days and during the summer fair (*feria*).

Camping

France

In France camping plays a larger role than in other European countries. Practically every place of touristic interest has one, and quite often several camp sites (*terrains de camping*). The sites are classified with from one to four stars according to the facilities provided. During the main holiday season sites along the coast and the major holiday routes are generally full but usually a place can be found a short way inland.

Because of the large number of camp sites a detailed list here is superfluous.
Camping away from camp sites is generally not allowed.

Spain

More than two-thirds of all Spanish camp sites are situated in the autonomous region of Catalonia and here they are concentrated in the area near the coast. The equipment of the sites is considerably above the average for the country; the sites are divided officially into four categories designated L (luxury), 1, 2 and 3.
Every camp site provides safe keeping for articles of value; it is advisable to deposit with them large sums of money and valuables.
In the case of justified complaints the visitor should demand the *Hoja de Reclamaciones*, a form which the owner of the site must hand over on demand. The original of the completed form is sent to the provincial office of the Catalonian regional administration, in the case of the area of this book to Barcelona or Gerona, or to the State Secretary for Tourism (Secretarial del Estado de Turismo, Celle Maria Molina 50, Madrid 6, Spain).
Although in the more heavily frequented coastal regions camping sites practically adjoin one another, the total capacity in the season is not sufficient so that it is advisable, at least for a stay during the months of high summer, to book in good time in advance.
Spending one night in a caravan or motor caravan in lay-bys and car parks is allowed but not on the open roads. Camping away from recognised sites is frowned upon, not least because of the danger of forest and heath fires breaking out in the dry months of the year.

List of camp sites

Every year the national or regional authorities publish lists of officially recognised camp sites; these can be obtained from the French or Spanish information offices (see Information).

Warning for drivers towing caravans and motor caravan drivers

Through roads usually avoid the old centres of the mountain and coastal resorts. Drivers towing caravans and drivers of motorised caravans are advised to avoid the temptation of entering the centre of these places as often the streets are so narrow that traffic jams are likely to occur.

Car Rental

France

Avis

in Perpignan:
Boulevard du Conflent 13; tel. 68 34 26 71
Aéroport de Perpignan; tel. 68 34 26 71

europcar

in Perpignan:
Avenue Général de Gaulle 28; tel. 68 34 65 03
Aéroport de Perpignan; tel. 68 34 65 03

Hertz — in Perpignan:
Cours Escarguel 9 bis; tel. 68 51 37 40
Aéroport de Perpignan; tel. 68 52 14 33

interRent — in Perpignan:
Boulevard des Pyrénées 2; tel. 68 56 96 96

Spain

Avis — in Barcelona:
Carrer Casanova 209; tel. (93) 2 09 95 33–4
Carrer Aragón 235; tel. (93) 2 15 89 38 and 2 15 84 30
Plaça Pio XII (Hotel Princessa Sofia); tel. (93) 2 09 95 33
Barcelona Airport, in El Prat de Llobregat; tel. (93) 3 79 40 26

in Girona:
Carretera de Barcelona 35; tel. (972) 20 69 33
Aeroport de Girona; tel. (972) 20 69 33

in La Platja d'Aro:
Galerias Neptuno 11; tel. (972) 81 73 44–45

in Lloret de Mar:
Carrer Sant Pere 70; tel. (972) 36 64 53 and 36 80 53

europcar — in Barcelona:
Carrer Consell de les Cent 363; tel. (93) 3 17 57 03
Carrer Viladomat 214; tel. (93) 2 39 84 01
Barcelona Airport; tel. (93) 3 17 69 80 and 3 17 84 30

in Girona:
Avinguda Barcelona 31 (Hotel Inmortal); tel. (972) 20 54 18

Hertz — in Barcelona:
in Sants Station; tel. (93) 3 22 97 59
Carrer Tuset 10; tel. (93) 2 17 80 76 and 2 17 32 48
Barcelona Airport; tel. (93) 2 41 13 81 and 3 70 57 52
in Girona:
in the Main Station; (972) 21 01 08
Aeroport de Girona; (972) 20 20 03

in La Platja d'Aro:
Carretera de Palamós 6; (972) 81 72 47

interRent — in Barcelona:
Carrer Balmes 141; tel. (93) 2 17 44 42 and 2 17 31 94
Barcelona Airport; tel. (93) 3 02 28 32 and 3 02 45 78

In addition there are smaller local rental firms which often work closely with the large hotels and can give their guests special rates. Vehicle rental is subject to the very high Spanish turnover tax (33%) even when the booking is made from abroad. Credit cards are generally accepted.

Consulates

See Diplomatic and Consular Offices

Currency

France

Currency

The unit of currency is the French franc (F) of 100 centimes. There are bank notes for 10, 20, 50 100 and 500 F and coins of 5, 10 and 20 centimes as well as ½, 1, 2, 5 and 10 F.

Exchange rates variable

1 F = 9.5 pence   £1 = 10.45 F
1 F = 17 cents $1 = 5.8 F

Currency regulations

There is no restriction on the import of foreign currency to France. The export of foreign currency is at present limited to 12,000 F unless a declaration was made on entry of a higher amount. Visitors are recommended to use traveller's cheques, Eurocheques, etc.

Spain

Currency

The unit of currency is the Spanish peseta (Pta). There are banknotes for 200, 500, 1000, 2000, 5000 and 10,000 Ptas and coins of 1, 5, 10, 25, 50 and 100 Ptas.

Exchange rates

100 Ptas = 49 pence   £1 = 203 Ptas
100 Ptas = 88 cents $1 = 112 Ptas

Currency regulations

There is no restriction on the import of foreign currency to Spain but visitors are recommended to declare large amounts. Spanish currency up to a limit of 100,000 Ptas may be brought in. The export of Spanish currency is permitted up to 100,000 Ptas and of foreign currency up to a amount equal to 500,000 Ptas or up to the amount declared on entry. Visitors are recommended to use traveller's cheques, Eurocheques, etc.

Credit cards

Large hotels and restaurants, car rental firms, airlines and retailers generally accept the more widely used credit cards (American Express, Diners Club, Access, Visa, etc.).

Security note

The loss of Eurocheques and/or cheque cards should be immediately reported to the issuer of the card.

Diplomatic and Consular Offices

France

United Kingdom

Embassy
35 rue du Faubourg St-Honoré
F-75008 Paris
tel. 1 42 66 91 42

There is an honorary consul at Perpignan

United States

Embassy
2 Avenue Gabriel
F-75008 Paris
tel. 1 42 96 12 02 and 1 42 61 80 75

Canada

Embassy
35 Avenue Montaigne
F-75008 Paris
tel. 1 42 25 99 55

Consular section
4 rue Ventadour
F-755001 Paris
tel. 1 40 73 15 83

Spain

United Kingdom

Consulate
Avinguda Diagonal 477
Edificio Torre de Barcelona, 13th floor
E-08036 Barcelona
tel. 3 22 21 51

United States

Consulate
Via Laietana 33
E-08003 Barcelona
tel. 3 19 95 50

Canada

There is no consulate in Barcelona.
The British consulate acts for citizens of all Commonwealth countries.

Emergencies

Emergency telephones can be found along the French and Spanish motorways. In the event of a breakdown or accident help can be obtained from the Guardia Civil or the Policia de Tráfico which patrol motorways and main roads. In Barcelona one can dial 091 for police and 080 for fire service. Elsewhere call the operator.

Events

Spain

January

Caldes de Montbui: Fiesta de Sant Antoni (patronal festival with blessing of animals), the Sunday after 17 January

Tossa: Pelegri de Tossa (pilgrimage and procession), 20/21 January; Sant Vincenç (patronal and great winter festival), 22 January

February

La Platja d'Aro: carnival

March

Vic: Mercat del Ram (palm market), with processions from the 10th day before Palm Sunday

May

Caldes de Montbui: Fiesta de Sant Sebastià (patronal festival), 1 May
Figueres: town festival, lst weekend in May
Ripoll: town festival, 11 May; on the following weekend National Wool Day

Whitsun

Caldes de Montbui: Feria Agricola (agricultural festival)

Corpus Christi

Processions in many places

June

Palafrugell: Festa Major (local festival) in Calella
Palamós: local festival
Roses: Sant Joan (patronal festival) with fireworks and dancing; Sant Pere (patronal and fishing festival) with Sardana dancing
Tossa: summer festival, 29 June
Sant Joan de les Abadesses: Sant Antoni (patronal festival), 13 June

June–September

Besalú: Concert of classical music; art exhibition

July

Calonge: local festival
Palafrugell: Festa Major (town festival)
Roses: Catalan folk dance and music festival
Tossa: Toquem a correr (folklore festival) with art exhibition
Camprodon and Ripoll: Sadana-Festival

July–August

Cadaqués: international music festival (classical music)
Calonge, Palamós, Torroella de Montgrí, Sant Feliu de Guíxols: music festivals

July–September

Palamós: international music festival

August

La Bisbal: town festival
Palamós: festival of sea songs
Pals: local festival
Peratallada: Festa Major (local festival)
La Platja d'Aro: local festival
El Port de la Selva: local festival
Roses: Festa Major (town festival) with sporting contests, regattas and folk dancing
Torroella de Montgrí: local festival
Ullastret: local festival

September

Everywhere: Dia de Catalunya (Catalonian national day) with folk dancing (Sardana, etc.)
Begur: Festa Major (town festival)
Besalú: Festa Major (local festival), last weekend in September
Cadaqués: local festival
Figueres: international music festival in Vilabertran
Olot: "Gegants, Nans i Cavallets" (dance of the giants, dwarfs and little horses), 8 September
La Platja d'Aro: local festival in Castell d'Aro
Sant Joan de les Abadesses: Festa Major (great local festival), 2nd Sunday in September
Tossa: Sardana dancing competition

October

Caldes de Montbui: Fiesta Mayor (local festival) with folkloric performances and exhibitions

November

Calonge: local festival
Peralada: local festival

December

La Platja d'Aro: "the living crib" in Castell d'Aro

Sardana

The Sardana, an old round dance, is the characteristic folk dance of the Catalans. Originally it formed part of the customary pilgrimages; today it is carried on as an independent folkloric event.

Note

During the summer season there are festivals and entertainments and sporting contests in many places which are not held on a specific date and generally are not repeated annually. Information can be obtained from local information offices, hotel reception desks, etc.

Excursions

Considering that visitors do not normally travel along the whole length of the Mediterranean coast of south-west France and northern Spain but choose a base and explore the surroundings from there, the following list gives all the main places which have been described and then gives the places in the neighbourhood which are suitable for whole or half day excursions.

The suggested excursions have been so chosen that they do not exceed a radius of about 20 km/12 miles from the base. All the places mentioned can be found in the A to Z section of this guide under a main heading and there they are fully described.

France

Amélie-les-Bains

Céret

Céret

Amélie-les-Bains
Elne

Elne

Céret
Côte Vermeille
Perpignan

Perpignan

Elne
Salses

Salses

Perpignan

Spain

Note

All place names are given in their Catalonian form. For the equivalent Castillian spelling see page 214.

Arenys de Mar

Calella de la Costa
Malgrat de Mar
Mataró
Sant Pol de Mar
Tordera

Badalona

Barcelona
Granollers
Mataró

Banyoles

Besalú
Castellfollit de la Roca
Girona
Olot

Barcelona

Badalona
Granollers
Montserrat

Begur

La Bisbal
Calonge
Empúries
Estartit
Palafrugell
Palamós
Pals
La Platja d'Aro
S'Agaró
Ullastret

Besalú

Banyoles
Castellfollit de la Roca
Figueres
Olot

La Bisbal

Begur
Calonge
Empúries
Estartit
Girona
Pals
La Platja d'Aro
S'Agaró
Sant Feliu de Guíxols
Torroella de Montgrí
Ullastret

Blanes

Arenys de Mar
Caldes de Malavella
Calella de la Costa
Lloret de Mar
Malgrat de Mar
Santa Coloma de Farners
Sant Feliu de Guíxols
Tordera
Tossa de Mar

Cadaqués

Castelló d'Empúries
Figueres
Empúria Brava
Llançà
Portbou
El Port de la Selva
Roses
Sant Pere de Rodes

Caldes de Malavella

Blanes
Calonge

	Girona Lloret de Mar Malgrat de Mar La Platja d'Aro Santa Coloma de Farners Sant Feliu de Guíxols Tordera Tossa de Mar
Caldes de Montbui	Badelona Barcelona Granollers Montseny Montserrat
Calella de la Costa	Arenys de Mar Blanes Lloret de Mar Malgrat de Mar
Calonge	Begur La Bisbal Caldes de Malavella Girona Palafrugell Palamós Pals La Platja d'Aro S'Agaró Sant Feliu de Guíxols Ullastret
Camprodón	Castellfollit de la Roca Olot Ripoll Sant Joan de les Abadesses
Castellfollit de la Roca	Banyoles Besalú Camprodón Sant Joan de les Abadesses
Castelló d'Empúries	Cadaqués Empúria Brava Empúries Figueres Llançà Portbou El Port de la Selva Roses Sant Pere de Rodes Peralada
Empúria Brava	Cadaqués Castello d'Empúries Empúries Figueres Llançà Peralada Portbou

El Port de la Selva
Roses

Empúries

Begur
La Bisbal
Cadaqués
Castelló d'Empúries
Estartit
Figueres
Palafrugell
Pals
Perelada
Sant Pere de Rodes
Torroella de Montgrí
Ullastret

L'Estartit

Begur
La Bisbal
Empúria Brava
Empúries
Torroella de Montgrí
Ullastret

Figueres

Banyoles
Besalú
Cadaqués
Castelló d'Empúries
Empúria Brava
Empúries
La Jonquera
Llançà
El Port de la Selva
Roses
Sant Pere de Rodes

Girona

Banyoles
La Bisbal
Caldes de Malavella
Santa Coloma de Farners
Ullastret

Granollers

Arenys de Mar
Badalona
Barcelona
Caldes de Montbui
Mataró
Sant Cugat del Vallès

La Jonquera

Figueres
Perelada

Llançà

Cadaqués
Castelló d'Empúries
Empúria Brava
Figueres
Perelada
El Port de la Selva
Roses
Sant Pere de Rodes

Lloret de Mar	Blanes Caldes de Malavella Calella de la Costa Malgrat S'Agaró Santa Coloma de Farners Sant Feliu de Guíxols Sant Pol de Mar Tordera
Malgrat de Mar	Arenys de Mar Blanes Calella de la Costa Lloret de Mar Tordera Tossa de Mar
Mataró	Arenys de Mar Badelona Barcelona Calella de la Costa Granollers Sant Pol de Mar
Montseny	Granollers Vic
Montserrat	Barcelona Sant Cugat del Vallès Banyoles Besalú Camprodón Castellfollit de la Roca Ripoll Sant Joan de les Abadesses
Palafrugell	Begur La Bisbal Calonge Estartit Girona Palamós Pals La Platja d'Aro S'Agaró Sant Feliu de Guíxols Ullastret
Palamós	Begur La Bisbal Calonge Palafrugell Pals La Platja d'Aro S'Agaró Sant Feliu de Guíxols Tossa de Mar Ullastret
Pals	Begur La Bisbal

Calonge
Empúries
Estartit
Girona
Palafrugell
Palamós
S'Agaró
Sant Feliu de Guíxols
Torroella de Montgrí
Ullastret

Peralada

Cadaqués
Castelló d'Empúries
Empúria Brava
Empúries
Figueres
La Jonquera
Llançà
Portbou
El Port de la Selva
Roses
Sant Pere de Rodes

La Platja d'Aro

Begur
La Bisbal
Caldes de Malavella
Calonge
Lloret de Mar
Palafrugell
Palamós
Pals
S'Agaró
Sant Feliu de Guíxols
Tossa de Mar
Ullastret

Portbou

Cadaqués
Castelló d'Empúries
Figueres
Llançà
Peralada
El Port de la Selva
Roses
Sant Pere de Rodes

El Port de la Selva

Cadaqués
Castelló d'Empúries
Empúria Brava
Figueres
Llançà
Peralada
Portbou
Roses
Sant Pere de Rodes

Ripoll

Camprodón
Olot
Sant Joan de les Abadesses

Roses

Cadaqués
Castelló d'Empúries

	Empúria Brava Figueres Llançà Peralada Portbou El Port de la Selva Sant Pere de Rodes
S'Agaró	Begur La Bisbal Caldes de Malavella Calonge Lloret de Mar Palafrugell Palamós La Platja d'Aro Sant Feliu de Guíxols Tossa de Mar
Santa Coloma de Farners	Blanes Caldes de Malavella Girona Lloret de Mar Malgrat de Mar Tordera Tossa de Mar
Sant Cugat del Vallès	Badalona Barcelona Caldes de Montbui Granollers Montserrat
Sant Feliu de Guíxols	La Bisbal Caldes de Malavella Calonge Girona Lloret de Mar Palafrugell Palamós La Platja d'Aro S'Agaró Tossa de Mar
Sant Joan de les Abadesses	Camprodón Olot Ripoll
Sant Pere de Rodes	Cadaqués Castelló d'Empúries Empúria Brava Figueres Llançà Peralada Portbou El Port de la Selva Roses
Sant Pol de Mar	Arenys de Mar Blanes Calella de la Costa

Lloret de Mar
Malgrat de Mar
Mataró
Tordera

Tordera

Arenys de Mar
Blanes
Caldes de Malavella
Calella de la Costa
Lloret de Mar
Malgrat de Mar
Santa Coloma de Farners
Sant Pol de Mar
Tossa de Mar

Torroella de Montgrí

Begur
La Bisbal
Calonge
Castelló d'Empúries
Empúria Brava
Empúries
Estartit
Girona
Palafrugell
Palamós
Pals
Ullastret

Tossa de Mar

Blanes
Caldes de Malavella
Lloret de Mar
Malgrat de Mar
Palamós
La Platja d'Aro
S'Agaró
Sant Feliu de Guíxols
Tordera

Ullastret

Begur
La Bisbal
Calonge
Empúria Brava
Estartit
Girona
Palafrugell
Palamós
Pals
La Platja d'Aro
Torroella de Montgrí

Vic

Montseny

Food and Drink

France

French cuisine is world famous as much for its quality as for its variety. Great importance is paid to a varied menu. Eating in a hurry is unknown, so that at least an hour must be

devoted to a meal. Even small inns with a not very inviting exterior often have a remarkably good culinary standard in which local specialities play a great part.
A very simple breakfast (*petit déjeuner*) consisting of coffee with or without milk, tea or chocolate, croissant or light rolls (*brioche*) is often eaten in a café. Lunch (*déjeuner*) is served in restaurants between noon and 2.30 p.m. either as a fixed menu with a starter, main dish and sweet or chosen from the bill of fare.
An evening meal (*dîner* or *souper*) is just as extensive as the midday meal but the starter is generally replaced by soup. White bread is provided free with the meal and is cut from long crusty *baguettes* or *flutes*.

Of course French wine is drunk with the meal and there are famous individual kinds. In general table wines can be recommended; if a bottle of wine is preferred the visitor should seek the waiter's advice. Beers from Alsace and Lorraine are good and becoming increasingly popular.

For more about wine – see Wine

Spain

Since visitors staying in hotels will normally take their meals there, they are likely to visit restaurants (*restaurante*) only in the larger towns and seaside resorts. The Spaniards have always taken their meals much later than is the custom in most other European countries, although with the development of the tourist trade it is now usually possible to get lunch or dinner much earlier than in the past.
Spanish meals are usually substantial (hors d'œuvre, etc., followed by a main dish, fruit and cheese). It is advisable to choose the fixed-price menu (*comida*) consisting of four or more courses; à la carte meals are more expensive. Breakfast, as eaten by the local people, is usually a very simple meal, but the larger hotels which have visitors from other countries provide a substantial breakfast with coffee, tea, fruit juice, various kinds of bread and cakes, jam and marmalade, sliced cold meats and often a hot dish as well.

Spanish cuisine is characterised by the use of olive oil (*aceite de oliva*) and of garlic (*ajo*) and various herbs such as thyme, rosemary, bay leaves, etc. Egg dishes, rice dishes and fish are tasty and appetising. There are many restaurants specialising in seafood (*mariscerías*). Buffets, inns and self-service restaurants (especially in the towns) are convenient for snacks. It was once customary to serve small snacks in bars, taverns and bodegas (originally wine cellars but now bars) and with every glass of wine one got a little tasty morsel, the so-called *tapa* ("cover", since the little plate on which it was served covered the glass). Today these snacks generally are paid for separately and it can often happen that the price will exceed that of a hot meal.

Starters (*entremeses*) including sausage (from Vic and generally air-dried), olives (especially the Manzanilla and Gordal olives), seafood such as crab or mussels (the Jacobs mussels, *viera*, and the duck mussels, *percebes*, are very good). A Catalonian speciality is blood sausage, known as *butifarrôn*.

Soups (*sopas*) include especially *gazpacho*, a cold soup made from tomatoes, cucumbers, onions, garlic and peppercorns with vinegar, oil and herbs, with the various chopped-up vegetables often presented separately.

The first main course (*plato fuerte*) often consists of *tortillas* (omelettes); they come in a number of varieties from savoury to sweet. Solid and substantial are the stews such as *cocido*, a stew which is prepared in a different way in every district from chick peas, potatoes, vegetables, meat, bacon, sausage and meat dumplings. When it is properly prepared the well-known *paella* is excellent; it is a rice dish made from chicken, meat, seafood, beans and peas.

There are very many fish dishes (*pescadosi*). The *zarsuela de mariscos* consists of various baked and well-seasoned fish; small fish dishes are also suitable as tapas, especially eel boiled in oil with garlic and paprika. Any fresh fish fried in oil is also first class.

There are a great many desserts (*postres*). Spain has excellent cheeses but also numerous recipes for sweets; *turrón* (made from honey and almonds) and marzipan originated in Moorish times. There are also lardy cakes, fine fruits and good ice cream.

Drinks

The most popular drink in the country is wine. Table wine (*vino corriente* or *vino del pais*) is often mixed with water or mineral water. More about wine production in Catalonia can be found in the entry Wine.

A popular and refreshing drink is *sangria*, made from red wine, brandy, mineral water, orange and lemon juice with small pieces of fruit and ice. Each bar-keeper has his own recipe and, according to the way in which the ingredients are mixed, the result can have a pleasant or a diabolical effect even though sangria is drunk considerably more quickly than pure wine.

Beer (*cerveza*) is becoming increasingly important in Spain. There are Spanish beers (the best known is San Miguel, followed by the Damm brand which is brewed in Barcelona) and in the holiday centres there are a great many imported beers from Germany, Belgium and the Netherlands.

Soft drinks, including the various fruit juices, are popular, as is mineral water (*con gas*, carbonated water; *sin gas*, still water). Spanish drinking water is usually heavily chlorinated which has an unfortunate effect on its taste. Better is spring water which is sold cheaply in plastic canisters generally holding 5 litres.

Spanish brandy, sometimes incorrectly labelled "cognac", enjoys considerable popularity. In order to be able to appreciate the full aroma it should be ordered in a warm glass (*vaso caliente*). Sometimes in this connection there is a little ceremony – the waiter warms the glass on a spirit stove then puts a measure of brandy into it and waves the glass once more over the flame until the rising alcohol vapour ignites and a pale blue flame emerges in the glass. Then more brandy is added and a fruity aroma is given off.

Spanish Menu (*lista de comidas*)

Cutlery and crockery

Place setting: cubierto
Spoon: cuchara
Teaspoon: cucharita
Knife: cuchillo
Fork: tenedor
Plate: plato
Glass: vaso
Cup: taza
Serviette: servilleta
Corkscrew: sacacorchos

Breakfast: desayuno
Lunch: comida
Dinner: cena

Starters (*entremeses*)

Aceitunas: olives
Ensalada: lettuce
Ostras: oysters
Anchoas: anchovies
Sardinas: sardines
Rábanos: radishes
Jamón: ham (*jamón serrano*: smoked ham)
Mantequilla: butter
Pan: bread
Panecillo: bread rolls

Soup (*sopa*)

Sopa de legumbres (*de yerbas, de verduras*): vegetable soup (*con guisantes*: pea soup; *de lentejas*: lentil soup; *con tomates*: tomato soup)
Sopa de fideos: noodle soup
Sopa de arroz: rice soup
Sopa pescado: fish soup
Caldo: meat broth
Gazpacho: cold vegetable soup

Egg dishes (*platos de huevos*)

Huevo: egg (*crudo*: raw; *fresco*: fresh; *duro*: hard-boiled; *pasado por agua*: soft-boiled)
Tortilla: omelette
Huevos revueltos: scrambled eggs
Huevos frites (*huevos al plato*): fried eggs
Huevos con tomate: eggs with tomato

Fish and seafood (*pescado y mariscos*)

Frito: fried
Asado: baked
Cocido: boiled
Ahumado: smoked
A la Plancha: cooked on a hot iron griddle

Anguilla: eel
Arenque: herring
Atún: tuna
Bacalao: dried cod
Besugo: sea bream

Carpa: carp
Esturión: sturgeon
Gado: haddock
Lenguado: sole
Merluza: hake
Robadallo: perch
Salmon: salmon
Sollo: pike
Trucha: trout

Almeja: mussels
Bogavante: lobster
Calamar: ink fish
Cangrejo: crab
Camarón: prawns
Gamba: shrimps
Langosta: crawfish
Langostino: scampi
Ostras: oysters

Meat (*carnes*)

Asado: roast
Carne estofada: pot roast
Carne salada: salt meat
Carne ahumada: smoked meat
Chuleta: cutlet
Fiambre: sliced meat
Jamón: ham
Salchichón: dried sausage
Tocino: bacon

Buey: beef
Carnero: mutton
Cerdo: pork
Cochinillo, lechón: sucking pig
Cordero: lamb
Ternera: veal
Vaca: beef

Game (*caza*)

Ciervo: venison (red deer)
Corzo: venison (roe-deer)
Jabalí: wild boar
Liebre: hare

Poultry (*aves*)

Faisán: pheasant
Ganso: goose
Pato: duck
Perdiz: partridge
Pichónn: pigeon
Pollo: chicken

Vegetables (*verduras*)

Alcachofas: artichokes
Apio: celery
Coliflor: cauliflower
Cebollas: onions
Ensalada: lettuce
Espárragos: asparagus
Espinacas: spinach
Giusantes: peas
Garbanzos: chick peas
Judias: beans

Patatas: potatoes
Patatas fritas: chips
Pepino: cucumber
Pimientos: peppers
Tomates: tomatoes
Zanahorias: carrots

Seasonings (*condimentos*)

Aceite: oil
Mostaza: mustard
Pimienta: pepper
Sal: salt
Vinagre: vinegar

Desserts (*postres*)

Bollo: sweet rolls, doughnuts
Compota: stewed fruit
Dulces: sweets
Flan: pudding
Helado: ice cream (*con nata*: with cream)
Membrillo (*dulce de membrillo*): quince paste
Queso: cheese

Fruit (*frutas*)

Almendras: almonds
Cerezas: cherries
Chumbos: cactus figs
Dátiles: dates
Fresas: strawberries
Higo: figs
Manzana: apple
Melocotón: peach
Naranjas: oranges
Nueces: nuts
Pera: pear
Piña: pineapple
Plátano: banana
Uva: grape

Drinks (*bebidas*)

Agua mineral: mineral water (*con gas*: carbonated; *sin gas*: still)
Cerveza: beer (*dorada*: pale; *negra*: dark)
Café con leche: coffee with milk
Café helado: iced coffee
Café solo: black coffee
Horchata: refreshing drink made from almonds, etc.
Jugo: juice
Té: tea
Vino: wine (*blanco*: white; *tinto*: red)

Getting to the Costa Brava

By car

Because of the distance between Britain and Spain it is advisable to allow three days for the journey making two overnight stops, although it can be done comfortably by experienced motorists in two days. The mileage can be reduced by using one of the motor-rail services which will take the visitor and his vehicle at least part of the way to Spain; information can be obtained from Sealink Car Ferry Centre, Grosvenor Gardens, London SW1 or from French Railways, 179 Piccadilly, London W1. It should be pointed out that the motorways in France and Spain are subject to tolls.

By air

Catalonia is linked to the international network of air services through the airport of Barcelona (El Prat). The Spanish National Airline Iberia and British Airways fly direct from London to Barcelona. Scheduled services between North America and Spain are provided by Iberia, TWA and Canadian Pacific Airlines either direct or via London. There are also many charter flights, some of which use the regional airport of Girona.

By train

There are through services from Paris to Barcelona usually travelling overnight; it is possible to leave London late in the morning, change in Paris and travel by the Barcelona Talgo train arriving in Barcelona at about 8.30 in the morning.

Golf Courses

Spain

Real Club de Golf "El Prat"
S of Barcelona
27 holes

Club de Golf Sant Cugat
in Sant Cugat del Vallès
18 holes

Club de Golf Pals
in Pals
18 holes

Club de Golf Llavaneres
in Sant Andreu de Llavaneres
(near Mataró)
9 holes

Club de Golf Costa Brava
near Platja d'Aro
18 holes

Club de Golf Vallromanes
in Montornès (near Granollers)
18 holes

Holiday Homes

France

Especially in the recently established holiday centres there are holiday houses and flats; information can be obtained from the travel office (see Information – local agents)

Spain

Holiday apartments (*apartamentos turisticos*), usually situated in large blocks, can be rented in the coastal region.

They are often classified similarly to the hotels and divided into three categories which are designated by key symbols, from 1 the most modest, to 3 the most luxurious. The Spanish Ministry of Transport, Tourism and Communications publishes annually a brochure of apartments; similar brochures are published by the Catalonian regional authorities (Generalitat de Catalunya; Departament de Comerç, Consum i Turisme). These publications can be obtained from Spanish tourist information offices (see Information).

Hospital

Spain

Hospital Evangélico
Allegre de Dult 87
Barcelona
tel. 2 19 71 00

Hotels

France

French hotels are generally good and are classified according to the facilities provided. Except in the larger towns rooms often have only a "grand lit", the broad French double bed; when the room is used by two people it costs little more than it does for one. The most recommended hotels are those which are recognised by the Commissariat Général du Tourisme and classified by a special sign.

Categories

Official	In this book
*****	L (luxury)
****	I
***	II
**	III
*	IV

Hotels in the places included in this guide (selection)

Amélie-les-Bains

Catalogne, II, Route du Vieux Port, 40 r.
Reine Amélie, II, Boulevard Petite-Provence 30, 69 r.
Grand Hôtel des Thermes, II, Place Maréchal Joffre, 83 r.
Castel Eméraude, III, Chemin Petite-Provence, 31 r.
Des Gorges, III, Place Arago 6, 36 r.
Martinets, III Rue Hermabessière, 30 r.
Palmarium Hotel, III, Avenue du Vallespir, 63 r.

Céret

La Terrasse au Soleil, II, Route de Fontfrède, 18 r.
Arcades, III, Place Picasso, 21 r.
Pyrénées Hotel, Rue de la République 7, 15 b.

Perpignan

Des Arcades, II, Avenue d'Espagne, 128 b.
Le Catalogne, II, Cours Lazare Escarguel 28 r.
De France, II, Quai Sadi-Carnot 16, 34 r.

De la Loge, II, Rue de la Loge, 29 r.
Maillol, II, Impasse des Cardeurs 14, 15 r.
Mondial, II, Boulevard Clemenceau 40, 40 r.
Park-Hotel, II, Boulevard J. Bourrat 18, 67 r.
Windsor, II, Boulevard Wilson 28, 57 r.
Aragon, III, Boulevard Brutus 17, 33 r.
Athena, III, Rue Queya, 38 r.
Les Baléares, III, Avenue Général Guillaut 20, 48 r.
Christina, III, Cours Lassus 50, 35 r.
De la Poste, III, Rue Fabriques Nabot 6, 39 r.
Delseny, III, Cours Lazare Escarguel 14, 173 r.
Gril Campanile, III, Avenue Levernan, 43 r.
Majorca, III, Rue Font Froide 2, 61 r.
Paris – Barcelone, III, Avenue du Général de Gaulle 1, 36 r.
Regina, III, Place Arago 4, 34 r.

Salses

Relais de Castell, III, on the old route national, 30 r.

Spain

Hotels are officially classified in various categories in Spain according to their function and standard: Hoteles (singular hotel) providing accommodation with or without meals usually with their own restaurant; Hoteles-apartamentos: apartment hotels with facilities similar to hotels but with accommodation in flats or bungalows (chalets); hostales (singular hostal): modest hotels or inns providing accommodation with or without meals; pensiones (singular pensión): pensions or guest houses with a limited number of rooms, providing full board only. Hotels, apartment hotels and hostales may also be run as residencias, providing only accommodation and usually breakfast.

Paradores

In major tourist centres there are also the so-called Paradores Nacionales de Turismo (singular Parador Nacional de Turismo), high-class hotels in old castles, mansions and convents, or sometimes they are purpose-built. These paradores are excellently run and offer every comfort and amenity as well as an excellent cuisine. They are rather more expensive than ordinary hotels in the same category but provide a unique touristic experience. Advance booking is advisable.
In the area covered by this guide there are paradores nacionales in Aiguablava (near Begur) and in Vic.

Categories

Official Hotels	In this book
*****	L (luxury)
****	I
***	II
**	III
*	IV

Luxury hotels in the following list are additionally designated by a red star.

Hostales	Pensiones
***	P I
**	P II
*	P III

Hotel lists

The Spanish Ministry of Traffic, Tourism and Communications publishes annually a list of hotels and apartments. Also, particularly for the individual autonomous regions, lists can be obtained from the Spanish Tourist Information Office (see Information).

Note

For an alphabetical list of Spanish place names with their Catalan equivalents see page 214.

Warning

Most hotels in the seaside resorts are only open in summer.

Hotels in the places described (selection)

Arenys de Mar

Raymond, II, near the beach, 33 r.
Carlos I, III, 100 r.
Titus, III, near the beach, 44 r.
Carlos V, IV, 59 r.
Soraya, P II, 33 r.

in Caldes d'Estrac:
Colon, I, near the beach, Carrer de la Pau 16, 82 r.
Jet, II, Carrer Santema 25, 35 r.
Fragata, P II, Carrer Callao 8, 22 r.

in Canet de Mar:
Carlos, IV, Plaça Sant Elm, 83 r.
Rocatel, IV, Plaça Maresme 1, 40 r.
Miramar, P II, Plaça Maresme 23, 19 r.

Badelona

Miramar (no rest.), III, 42 r.
Betulo (no rest.), P II, 24 r.

Banyoles

Victoria (no rest.), III, 21 r.
del Lago (no rest.), P II, 28 r.
Mirallac (no rest.), P II, 22 r.
L'Ast, P III, near the beach, 34 r.
Rancho Grande, P III, near the beach, 32 r.

In Porqueres:
La Masia del Lago (no rest.), P II, 14 r.

Barcelona

*Avenida Palace, L, Gran Via 605, 211 r.
*Diplomatic, L, Carrer Pau Claris, 213 r.
*Gran Hotel Sarrià Sol, L, Avinguda Sarrià 50, 314 r.
*Presidente, L, Avinguda Diagonal 570, 161 r.
*Princess Sofia, L, Plaça Papa Pio XII 4, 50 r.
*Ritz, L, Gran Via 668, 195 r.
Arenas (no rest.), I, Carrer Capità Arenas 20, 59 r.
Balmoral (no rest.), I, Via Augusta 5, 94 r.
Barcelona (no rest.), Carrer Caspe 1–13, 64 r.
Colón, I, Avinguda de la Catedral 7, 161 r.
Condes de Barcelona, I, Passeig de Gràcia 7, 100 r.
Condor (no rest.), I, Via Augusta 127, 78 r.
Cristal (no rest.), I, Carrer de la Diputació 257, 148 r.
Dante (no rest.), I, Carrer de Mallorca 181, 81 r.
Derby (no rest.), I, Carrer Loreto 21, 116 r.
Europark (no rest.), I, Carrer Aragón 325, 66 r,
Gran Derby, I, Carrer Loreto 28, 39 r.
Gran Hotel Calderón (no rest.), I, Rambla de Catalunya 26, 244 r.

Gran Hotel Cristina (no rest.), I, Avinguda Diagonal, 123 r.
Hesperia (no rest.), I, Carrer de los Vergos 20, 144 r.
Hotel Apartamentos Victoria, I, Avinguda Pedralbes 16, 79 r.
Majestic, I, Passeig de Gràcia 70, 344 r.
Manila (no rest.), I, Rambles 111, 210 r.
Muntaner, I, Carrer Muntaner 505, 70 r.
Nuñez Urgel (no rest.), I, Carrer de Urgel 232, 121 r.
Putxet, I, Carrer Putxet 68–74, 125 r.
Reckord, I, Carrer Muntaner 352, 13 r.
Regente, I, Rambla de Catalunya 76, 78 r.
Royal (no rest.), I, Rambles 117, 108 r.
Aragón (no rest.), II, Carrer Aragón 569–571, 72 r.
Astoria (no rest.), II, Carrer de Paris 203, 114 r.
Augusta, II, Carrer Lincon 32, 30 r.
Bertran, II, Carrer Bertran 150, 30 r.
Condado, II, Carrer Aribau 201, 89 r.
Les Corts (no rest.), II, Traversera de les Corts 292, 80 r.
Covadonga (no rest.), II, Avinguda Diagonal 596, 76 r.
Expo Hotel (no rest.), II, Carrer de Mallorca 1–23, 432 r.
Ficus (no rest.), II, Carrer de Mallorca 163, 78 r.
Fornos (no rest.), II, Rambles 44, 30 r.
Gala Placidia, II, Via Augusta 112, 31 r.
Gaudi, II, Carrer Nou de la Rambla 12, 71 r.
Gotico (no rest.), II, Carrer Jaume I 14, 72 r.
Gran Via, II, Gran Via de les Corts Catalanes 642, 48 r.
Habana (no rest.), II, Gran Via 647, 65 r.
Mikado, II, Plaça de la Bonanova 58, 66 r.
Mitre (no rest.), II, Carrer Bertran 9 and 15, 57 r.
Moderno, II, Carrer del Hospital 11, 57 r.
Montecarlo (no rest.), II, Rambla 124, 73 r.
Numancia (no rest.), II, Carrer Numancia 74, 140 r.
Oriente, II, Rambla 45 and 47, 142 r.
Rallye (no rest.), II, Traversera de les Corts 150, 73 r.
Regencia Colón (no rest.), II, Carrer Sagristans 13–17, 55 r.
Regina (no rest.), II, Carrer Vergara 2, 102 r.
Rialto (no rest.), II, Carrer Ferran 40 and 42, 112 r.
Rubens, II, Passeig de Nostra Senyora del Coll 10, 136 r.
Suizo, II, Plaça del Angel 12, 50 r.
Terminal (no rest.), II, Carrer Provenza 1, 75 r.
Tres Torres (no rest.), II, Carrer Calatrava 32 and 34, 56 r.
Wilson (no rest.), II, Avinguda Diagonal 568, 52 r.
Zenit (no rest.), II, Carrer Santalo 8, 61 r.
Antibes (no rest.), III, Carrer de la Diputació 394, 65 r.
Auto Hogar (no rest.), III, Avinguda Parallel 64, 156 r.
Bonanova Park (no rest.), III, Carrer Capitan Arenas 51, 60 r.
Espagña, III, Carrer Sant Pau 9 and 11, 84 r,
Mesón Castilla (no rest.), III, Carrer Valdoncella 5, 71 r.
San Agustin, III, Plaça de Sant Agustin 3, 71 r.
Torello (no rest.), III, Carrer Ample 31, 72 r.
Apolo (no rest.), IV, Rambla 33, 90 r.
Cosmos (no rest.), IV, Carrer Escudellers 19, 67 r.
Internacional (no rest.), IV, Ramblas 78, 62 r.
Nouvel (no rest.), IV, Carrer de Santa Ana 18 and 20, 76 r.
Park Hotel, IV, Avinguda Marques de Argentera 11, 96 r.
Sans (no rest.), IV, Carrer Antoni de Campmany 82, 76 r.

Ambos Mundos (no rest.), P I, Plaça Reial 10, 21 r.
El Casal (no rest.), P I, Carrer Tapineria 10, 36 r.
Continental (no rest.), P I, Rambla de Canaletes 138, 32 r,
Cuatro Naciones, P I, Rambla 40, 34 r.

Paseo de Gràcia (no rest.), P I, Passeig de Gràcia 102, 34 r.
Taber (no rest.), P I, Carrer Aragón 256, 65 r.
Urbis (no rest.), P I, Passeig de Gràcia 23, 61 r.
El Abrevadero (no rest.), P II, Vila Vila 77, 46 r.
Alhambra (no rest.), P II, Carrer Junqueras 13, 36 r.
Alicante (no rest.), P II, Ronda de la Universidad 4, 38 r.
Call (no rest.), P II, Arco San Ramon del Call 4, 30 r.
Cisneros, P II, Carrer Tordera 43, 45 r.
Comercio (no rest.), P II, Carrer Nova de Zurbano 7, 57 r.
Condal (no rest.), P II, Carrer Boqueria 23, 53 r.
Dalí (no rest.), P II, Carrer Boqueria 12, 49 r.
La Hipica (no rest.), P II, Carrer General Castaños 2, 57 r.

Begur

Aiguablava, I, at the Platja de Fornells, 85 r.
Bonaigua (no rest.), II, at the Platja de Fornells, 47 r.
Bagur, III, Carrer de Coma y Ros 8, 34 r.
Sa Riera, III in the Barri de San Riera, 41 r.

in Aiguablava:
Parador Nacional Costa Brava, I, 87 r.

La Bisbal

Bisbal Park (no rest), III, 34 r.

Blanes

Horitzo, II, Passeig Maritim Sabanell 11, 122 r,
Park Blanes, II, at the Platja S'Abanell, 131 r.
Lyon Majestic, III, Villa Mas Marot 13, 120 r.
Ruiz, III, Carrer Raval 45, 59 b.
Boix Mar, IV, Avinguda Villa de Madrid, 170 r.
Costa Brava, IV, Carrer Anselmo Clavé 48, 80 r.
Mar Ski (no rest.), IV, Passeig Maritim Sabanell 4, 64 r.
Rosa, IV, Carrer San Pedro Marin 42, 151 r.
San Antonio, IV, Passeig Maritim 63, 156 r.
Stella Maris, IV, Avinguda Villa de Madrid 18, 87 r.
Clivia, P II, Carrer Esperança 44, 45 r.
S'Arjau, P II, Passeig de Mar 89, 49 r.

Cadaquès

Llane Petit (no rest.), II, 35 r.
Playa Sol (no rest.), II, near the beach, 49 r.
Rocamar (no rest.), II, Carrer del Doctor Bartolomeus, 70 r.
Port Lligat, IV, in Port Lligat, 30 r.
S'Aguarda, P I, near the beach, 27 r.
Casa Europa (no rest.), P II, near the beach, 20 r.
Cristina, P II, near the beach, 20 r.
Marina, P II, near the beach, 21 r.
Targoneta (no rest.), P II, 62 r.
Ubaldo, P II, 26 r.

Caldes de Malavella

Balneario Prats, II, with thermal bath, 76 r.
Balneario Vichy Catalán, II, with thermal bath, 80 r.
Esteve, P II, 27 r.

Caldes de Montbui

Balneario Broquetas, II, with thermal bath, 89 r.
Balneario Termas Victoria, P II, with thermal bath, 91 r.

Calella de la Costa

Amaika, II, Carrer de Barcelona, 234 r.
Mont Rosa, II, Passeig de les Roques, 120 r.
Las Vegas, II, on the coast road (km 673.7), 94 r.
Balmes, III, 204 r.
Calella Park, III, Carrer Jubara 257, 51 r.
Catalonia, III, on the coast road, 122 r.

Estrella de Mar, III, Avinguda Turisme, 75 r.
Fragata (no rest.), III, Passeig de les Roques, 63 r.
Garbi, III, Passeig de les Roques 3, 115 r.
Oasis Park, III, Carrer Montenegre 1, 237 r.
Santa Fe, III, Avinguda Cabaspre, 196 r.
Santa Mónica, III, Avinguda Turisme 28, 216 r.
Terramar, III, Carrer de la Diputació 14, 210 r.
Vell Park, III, Carrer Sant Jaume 57, 65 r.
Victoria, III, Zona Riera Faro, 242 r.
Volga, III, Carrer Jubara 350, 181 r.
Altamar, IV, Carrer de la Eglésia 330, 64 r.
Bahia, IV, Passatge Moragas 4, 72 r.
Bon Repos, IV, Carrer Vallderoure, 147 r.
Cadi, IV, Carrer Jubara 132, 81 r.
Cala, IV, Carrer Jubara 145, 120 r.
Calella (no rest.), IV, Carrer Anselmo Clave 134, 60 r.
Centrico, IV, Carrer Creus 28, 56 r.
Cisne (no rest.), IV, Carrer Jubara 142, 67 r.
Codina, IV, Carrer Amadeo 33, 156 r.
Continental, IV, Carrer Cervantes 105, 68 r.
Corona, IV, Carrer Creus 1–17, 118 r.
Costa Bona, IV, Carrer Batlle 6, 65 r.
España, IV, Carrer Anselmo Clave 80, 110 r.
Esplay, IV, Carrer Ramón y Cajal, 198 r.
Express, IV, Carrer Riera 31 and 32, 89 r.
Goya, IV, Carrer Sant Antoni 228, 91 r.
Haro-Mar, IV, Passeig de les Roques 28, 124 r.
Internacional, IV, Carrer Gaudi 2, 120 r.
Kaktus Playa, IV, Carrer Gaudi 8, 138 r.
Mar Eden, IV, Carrer Cervantes 31, 85 r.
Miami, IV, Carrer Monturiol 41, 135 r.
Neptuno, IV, Carrer Sant Josep 82–84, 103 r.
Olympic – Vistasol, IV, Zona Riera Faro, 371 r.
Osiris, IV, Zona Valldenguli, 322 r.
Las Palmeras (no rest.), IV, Carrer de la Diputació, 111 r.
President, IV, Plaça del Parlament de Catalunya, 280 r.
Relax, IV, Carrer Montenegre, 103 r.
Las Rocas, IV, 186 r.
Solimar, IV, Carrer Costa y Fornaguera 112, 76 r.
Tropicana, IV, Carrer Bruguera 274, 107 r.
Vila, IV, Carrer Sant Josep 66, 164 r.
Ideal, P II, Carrer Sant Jaume 264, 64 r.

Calonge

Park Hotel San Jorge, I, Carretera de Palamós, 85 r.
Cap Roig, II, Carretera de Palamós, 167 r.
Condado de San Jorge, II, Carretera de Palamós, 36 r.
Los Porches (no rest.), IV, Carrer Cinc de Febrer 51, 36 r.

in Sant Antoni de Calonge:
Rosa dels Vents, II, Passeig del Mar, 58 r.
Rosamar, II, Passeig del Mar 33, 63 r.
Aubi (no rest.), III, Carrer Sant Antoni 253, 55 r.
Reymar, III, Torre Valentina, 49 r.
Prince Ben Hur (no rest.), P I, Torre Valentina, 20 r.
Del Mar, P II, near the beach, Carrer Arturo Mundet 75, 40 r.

Camprodón

Güell, Plaça de Espanya 8, 40 r.
Rigat, P II, Plaça del Doctor Robert 2, 28 r.
Sayola, P II, Carrer Josep More 4, 35 r.

Castelló d'Empúries

All Ioli, IV, in Castel Nou, 37 r.
Emporium, IV, on the road to Roses, 43 r.

Empúries

In L'Escala:
Bonaire-Juvines, II, Plaça Lluis Albert 4, 31 r.
Nieves Mar, II, Passeig Maritim 8, near the beach, 40 r.
Voramar, II, Plaça Lluis Albert 2, 40 r.
Dels Pins, III, Closa del Llop, 40 r.
La Barca (no rest.), P II, Carrer Enrique Serra 25, 26 r.
Cal Català, P II, Carrer Ave Maria 2, 31 r.

L'Estartit

Bell Aire (no rest.), Carrer Eglesia 39, near the beach, 78 r.
Club de Campo Torre Grau, III, near the beach, 10 r.
Coral, III, Plaça Eglesia 8, 59 r.
Miramar, III, Avinguda de Roma 7, 64 r.
Amer (no rest.), IV, 57 r.
Club el Catalán (no rest.), IV, 112 r
Flamingo, IV, 100 r.
Medas II, IV, 69 r.
Panorama, IV, Avinguda de Grecia, 154 r.
Pinimar, IV, on the Torroella road, 55 r.
Univers, IV, Plaça Eglesia 1, 52 r
Egara, P II, Plaça Eglesia 38, 61 r.
Nerieda, P II, Avinguda de Grecia, 60 r.

Figueres

Ampurdán, II, on the national road (km 763), 42 r.
Durán, II, Carrer Lasauca 5, 67 r.
Pirineos, II, Ronda Barcelona 1, 53 r.
President, II, Ronda Ferial 33, 75 r.
Rallye, II, Ronda Barcelona, 15 r.
Trave, III, Carretera Olot, 73 r.
Bon Retorn, P II, on the national road II (km 759), 53 r.
España, Carrer La Jonquera 26, 36 r.

Girona

Costabella (no rest.), II, Avinguda de França 61, 22 r.
Inmortal Gerona (no rest.), II, Carretera Barcelona 31, 76 r.
Ultonia (no rest.), II, Avinguda Jaume I 22, 46 r.
Europa (no rest.), III, Carrer Juli Garreta 23, 26 r.
Nord Gironi, III, Carrer Major de Sarriá, 24 r.
Brindis (no rest.), P II, Avinguda Ramón Folch 13, 18 r.
Centro, P II, Carrer Ciutadans 4, 30 r.

in Sarria de Ter:
Jocana (no rest.), III, Avinguda de França 238–240, 39 r.

Granollers

Del Valles (no rest.), III, Carretera de Masnou, 30 r.
Iris (no rest.), P I, Avinguda Sant Esteve 92, 35 r.

La Jonquera

Porta Catalana (no rest.), II, on the motorway (km 149), 81 r.
Puerta de España, II, national road II (km 22), 26 r.
Frontera, III, national road II (km 22), 28 r.
Goya (no rest.), III, national road II (km 782), 36 r.
Jonquera (no rest.), III, national road II (km 782), 28 r.
El Cazador (no rest.), P II, Carrer José Antonio 132, 20 r.

Llançà

Berna, III, Passeig Maritim 13, 38 r.
Grifeu, III, Carrer Cau de Llod, 33 r.
Grimar, III, Carretera de Portbou, 38 r.
Mendisol, III, Platja de Grifeu, 32 r.
La Goleta, P II, near the beach, 45 r.

Llansa, P II, Carretera de Portbou, 21 r.
Mara Teresa, P II, Carrer Cabrafiga, 97 r.

Lloret de Mar

Monterrey, I, Carretera de Tossa, 229 r.
Rigat Park, I, Avinguda de América, 99 r.
Roger de Flor, I, Carrer Turo de'l Estelat, 98 r.
Santa Marta, I, Platja de Santa Cristina, 78 r.
Tropic, I, Passeig Marítim, 40 r.
Acacias (no rest.), Avinguda Acacias 19, 43 r.
Alexis, II, Carrer Na Marina 59, 101 r.
Anabel, II, near the beach, Carrer Felicia Serra 10, 230 r.
Astoria Park, II, Carrer Hipolit Làzaro 18, 126 r.
Bahamas, II, near the beach, Carrer Potos 25–27, 239 r.
Capri, II, Carrer Turo de'l Estelat 26, 155 r.
La Carolina, II, Camino de las Cabras 49, 65 r.
Cluamarsol, II, near the beach, Carrer Jacinto Verdaguer 7, 87 r.
Copacabana, II, near the beach, Avinguda Mistral 40–48, 162 r.
Don Juan, II, near the beach, Carrer Virgen de Loreto, 870 r.
Don Quijote, II Avinguda América, 374 r.
Eugenia, II, Carretera de Tossa, 118 r.
Excelsior, II, Passeig Jacinto Verdaguer 16, 45 r.
Fanals, II, Carretera de Blanes, 80 r.
Felipe III, II, Carrer Constantino Ribalaigua 7, 432 r.
Frigola, II, Avinguda Ferràan Aguiló 10, 217 r.
De la Gloria, II, Plaça de Paris 1, 153 r.
Gran Garbi, II, Carrer Potosi, 132 r.
Gran Hotel Casino Royal, II, Carretera Hostalric – Tossa (km 23), 417 r.
Gran Hotel Flamingo, II, Carrer Ferràn Agulló 11, 288 r.
Ifa Hotel Lloret, II, Carrer Senia de Barral 48, 105 r.
Mercedes, II, Avinguda Mistral 32, 88 r.
Metropol, II, Plaça de la Torre 2, 86 r.
Olimpic – Lloret, II, Cami de l'Angel 50, 352 r.
La Palmera, II, Carrer del Carme 31, 115 r.
Rosamar, II, Avinguda Pau Casals 8–10, 169 r.
Santa Rosa, II, Carrer Senia de Barral, 14 r.
Surf-Mar, II, Carrer Ramón Casas 2, 81 r.
Xaine Park, II, Avinguda Ferràn Agulló 15, 183 r.
Betran Park, III, Carrer Sant Josep 39, 140 r.
Bonanza Park, III, Carrer Narcis Fors, 22, 60 r.
Clipper, III, Carretera de Tossa, 367 r.
Dex, III, near the beach, Carrer Joan Llaverias 47–49, 216 r.
Festa Brava (no rest.), III, Carretera de Blanes 23–25, 106 r.
Florida Park, III, Carrer Oliva, 99 r.
Garbi Park, III, Carrer Llaurer 1, 255 r.
Guitart, III, near the beach, Avinguda Ferràn Agulló 12, 61 r.
Hawai, III, Avinguda Roca Grossa 1, 186 r.
Helios Lloret, III, near the beach, Avinguda Ferràn Agulló 21, 234 r.
Imperial Park, III, Carretera de Blanes 78, 150 r.
Maria del Mar, III, Carrer Poniente 13, 207 r.
Montecarlo, III, Carrer Sant Jorge 11, 94 r.
Montevista, III, Avinguda Roca Grossa, 219 r.
Mundial, III, Carrer Vincenç Bou 15, 100 r.
Niza, III, near the beach, Carrer del Grau 21, 152 r.
Oasis Park P, III, Carrer Pere Codina i Mont 13, 428 r.
Ridomar, III, Avinguda de Catalunya 49–51, 70 r.
Rosamar Park, III, Avinguda La Magnolia 24–26, 306 r.

Samba, III, near the beach, Camino de Blanes, 477 r.
San Juan Park, III, Carrer Anselm Clavé 10, 76 r.
Savoy, III, Carrer Domenec Carles Fanals, 154 r.
Terra Brava, III, Avinguda América 41, 132 r.
Windsor, III, Carretera de Blanes 136, 114 r.
Acapulco, IV, Riera 71, 181 r.
Blanca Aurora, IV, Carrer Oliva 19, 108 r.
Caribe, IV, Carrer Agustin Cabañas 19, 174 r.
Garbi, IV, Plaça de Carbonell 1, 221 r.
Guitart Rosa, IV, Carrer Sant Pere 63, 152 r.
Mireia, IV, Avinguda Mistral 14, 104 r.
Pirineus, IV, Carrer Sant Pere 45–47, 254 r.
Atlántida, P II, Carrer Padre Claret 4, 104 r.

Malgrat de Mar

Monte Playa, III, Passeig Maritim, 183 r.
Cartago Nova, IV, Passeig Maritim, 214 r.
Europa, IV, Passeig Maritim, 110 r.
Guillem, IV, Passeig Llevant 12, 173 r.
Luna Park, IV, Carrer Colom, 144 r.
Maripins, IV, Passeig Maritim, 187 r.
Papi, IV, Passeig Maritim, 104 r.
Poseidón, IV, Passeig Maritim, 210 r.
Reymar, IV, Passeig Maritim, 166 r.
Rosa Nautica, IV, Passeig Maritim, 133 r.
Sorra d'Or, IV, Passeig Llevant 2, 195 r.
Sorra Daurada, IV, Passeig Maritim, 252 r.

Mataró

Castell de Mata, II, on national road II (km 655.8), 52 r.
Colon (no rest.), P I, Carrer Colom 6–8, 55 r.

Montserrat

Abad Cisneros, II, 41 r.

Olot

Montsacopa, III, Carrer Mulleras, 73 r.
La Perla, P II, Carretera de la Deu 9, 35 r.

Palafrugell

Costa Brava, IV, Carra San Sebastián 10, 30 r.

in Calella de Palafrugell:
Alga (no rest.), I, near the beach, Avinguda Costa Blanca 43, 54 r.
Garbi (no rest.), II, Carrer del Mirto, 30 r.
Port Bo, II, Carrer de Port-Bo 6, 46 r.
Gelpi (no rest.), Carrer Francesc Estrabau 4, 35 r.
Mediterráneo, III, Carrer Francesc Estrabau 34, 38 r.
San Roc, III, Bahia de San Roque, 38 r.
La Torre (no rest.), III, Passeig de la Torre 28, 28 r.
Calella (no rest.), P II, Carrer Llado 6, 33 r.

in Llafranc:
Paraiso, II, Paraje Font d'en Xeco, 55 r.
Terramar, II, Passeig de Cipsele 1, 56 r.
Casamar, III, Carrer d'el Nero 3–11, 20 r.
Llevant, III, near the beach, Carrer Francesc de Blanes 5, 20 r.
Celimar (no rest.), P II, Carrer Carudo 4, 19 r.

in Tamariu:
Hostalillo, II, Carrer Bellavista 22, 70 r.
Jano, III, Passeig del Mar 5, 49 r.
Sol d'Or, P II, Riera 18, 20 r.

Palamós

San Luis, II, Carrer Onze de Septembre 61, 29 r.
Trias, II, Passeig del Mar, 81 r.
Vostra Llar, II, Carrer Alba 6, 45 r.
Marina, III, Avinguda Onze de Septembre 48, 62 r.
El Sosiego, IV, Carrer Rutlla Alta 18, 40 r.
Vostra Llar, P I, Avinguda President Macia 12, 30 r.
Xamary, P II, Avinguda President Macia 70, 36 r.

La Platja d'Aro

Colombus, I, near the beach, Passeig de Mar, 110 r.
Aromar, II, near the beach, Passeig Maritim, 167 r.
Claramar (no rest.), II, Carrer Pinar del Mar 10, 36 r.
Cosmopolita, II, Passeig del Mar, 89 r.
Rosamar, II, 61 r.
Royal Playa (no rest.), Carretera de Palamós, 42 r.
S'Agoita, II, Carretera de Palamós, 70 r.
Acapulco, III, Carrer Mediterra 1, 64 r.
Bell Repós, III, Carrer Verge de Carme, 34 r.
Costa Brava (no rest.), III, near the beach, 59 r.
Japet, III, near the beach, Carretera de Palamós 18–20, 48 r.
Miramar (no rest.), III, Carrer Verge de Carme 12, 47 r.
Els Pins, III, Carrer Verge de Carme 35, 57 r.
Planamar (no rest.), III, 86 r.
La Terraza, III, Carretera Santa Cristina 2, 72 r.
Xaloc, III, Carrer Afueras, 40 r.
Oasis Jardin, P I, Plaça de Catalunya 4, 30 r.
Cabo Buena Esperanza, P II, Carrer Alegria 2, 50 r.

Portbou

Comodoro, IV, Carrer Méndez Nuñez 1, 16 r.
Bahia (no rest.), P II, Carrer Cerbere 1, 33 r.

in Colera:
Garbet (no rest.), P II, 23 r.
Mont-Merce (no rest.), P II, 12 r.
Tocamar, P II, 12 r.

El Port de la Selva

Porto Cristo (no rest.), III, Carrer Major 48, 54 r.

Ripoll

Solana del Ter, III, on the Barcelona road, 28 r.
Monasterio, IV, Plaça Gran 4, 40 r.
Canaulas (no rest.), P II, Pont de Olot 1, 15 r.

Roses

Almadraba Park Hotel, I, Playa Almadraba, 66 r.
Bahia, II, near the beach, Passeig Maritim 153, 52 r.
Canyelles Platja (no rest.), II, Platja Canelles, 99 r.
Coral Playa, II, Platja del Rastell, 128 r.
Goya Park, II, Urbanisació Santa Margalida, 224 r.
Marian, II, Platja Salata, 145 r.
Moderno (no rest.), II, Passeig Maritim 15, 57 r.
Montecarlo, II, Urbanisació Santa Margalida, 126 r.
Monterrey, II, near the beach, Santa Margalida, 138 r.
Nautilus, II, Platja Salata, 64 r.
San Carlos, II, Urbanisació Mas Busca, 99 r.
La Terraza (no rest.), II, 111 r.
Grecs, III, Parase Grecs, 54 r.
Maritim, III, Platja Salata, 137 r.
Univers, III, Avinguda República Argentina, 207 r.
Victoria, III, Avinguda Comercial, 221 r.
Goya, IV, Riera Ginjolers, 68 r.
Marina, IV, Avinguda de Rhodes 1, 53 r.
Mediterráneo, IV, Platja Salata, 67 r.

*S'Agaró: *Hostal de la Gavina, luxury hotel*

La Carabela, P II, Plaça Catalunya 10, 36 r.
Novel Risech, P II, Avinguda Rhodes 185, 62 r.
Sant Jordi, P II, Paratge el Rastrillo, 63 r.

S'Agaró

*Hostal de la Gavina, L, 74 r.
Caleta Park, II, 105 r.

Santa Coloma de Farners

Balneario Termas Orión, III, with thermal bath, 44 r.
Central Park, IV, 30 r.
Carmen, P II, 17 r.

Sant Feliu de Guíxols

Reina Elisenda, I, near the beach, Passeig dels Guíxols 8, 68 r.
Curhotel Hipócrates, II, near the beach, Carretera Sant Pol 229, 85 r.
Eden Roc, II, Port Calvi, 104 r.
Montjoi, II, Carrer Sant Elm, 64 r.
Murla Park Hotel, II, near the beach, Passeig dels Guíxols, 89 r.
Panorama Park, II, Travesia del Raig 1, 69 r.
Roca, II, Cami de la Caleta 70, 70 r.
Avenida (no rest.), III, Carretera de Girona 10, 28 r.
Gesoria (no rest.), III, Carrer Hospital 1, 34 r.
Jecsalis, II, Carretera de Girona 9, 64 r.
Montecarlo, III, Carrer Abad Sunyer 110, 64 r.
Les Noies, III, Rambla Portalet 10, 45 r.
Regina, III, Carrer Maragall 1, 53 r.
Del Sol, P I, Carretera de Palamós, 41 r.
Barcarola (no rest.), P II, near the beach, Carrer Picasso, 46 r.
Ronda Barcarola (no rest.), P II, Paratge Sant Pol 46 r.

Sant Joan de les Abadesses

La Bonica (no rest.), P III, Carrer Sant Pol 1, 19 r.
Ter, P III, Carrer Vista Alegre 1, 27 r.

Sant Pol de Mar

Grand Sol, II, near the beach, on the national road (km 670), 41 r.
La Costa, III, Carrer Nou 32, 17 r.

Torroella de Montgrí

Vila Vella (no rest.), IV, Porta Nova 3, 26 r.
Tres Delfines (no rest.), P II, near the beach, 30 r.

Tossa de Mar

Gran Hotel Reymar, I, Platja Mar Menuda, 131 r.
Alexandra, II, Avinguda de la Palma, 76 r.
Costa Brava, II, Carrer Virgen de Montserrat, 182 r.
Delfin, II, Carrer Costa Brava 2, 63 r.
Florida, II, Avinguda de la Palma 21, 45 r.
Mar Menuda, II, Platja de Mar Menuda, 40 r.
Osiris Tossa, II, near the beach, Carrer Lope Mateo 1, 208 r.
Park-Hotel, II, Carrer Giverola 4, 70 r.
Vora Mar (no rest.), II, Avinguda de la Palma 19, 63 r.
Alaska (no rest.), III, Avinguda de la Palma, 55 r.
Ancora (no rest.), III, Avinguda de la Palma, 4, 58 r.
Avenida, III, Avinguda de la Palma 5, 50 r.
Cataluña (no rest.), III, Avinguda Ferran Agullo, 33 r.
Continental, III, at the beach near Lloret, 63 r.
Flor Tossa, III, Avinguda Peregrí 12, 45 r.
Mar d'Or, III, Avinguda Costa Brava 10, 51 r.
Mare Nostrum, III, Avinguda de la Palma, 59 r.
Ramos, III, Avinguda Costa Brava, 72 r.
Rovira (no rest.), III, Pou de la Vila 14, 108 r.
Europark, IV, Avinguda Costa Brava 25, 59 r.
Neptuno, IV, Carrer La Guardia 52, 49 r.
Argos (no rest.), P II, Carrer José Antonio 23, 16 r.
Balmaña (no rest.), P II, on the road to Hostalric (km 38), 13 r.
Casa Blanca (no rest.), P II, Carrer Barcelona, 13 r.
Giverola (no rest.), P II, Carretera Giverola 6, 35 r.
Horta Rosell (no rest.), P II, Carrer Pola 23, 30 r.
De la Huerta, P II, Carretera de Llagostera, 57 r.
Regas, P II, Carrer Tarull 10, 16 r.
Rosamar (no rest.), P II, Avinguda Costa Brava, 19 r.
Soms, P II, Travessia Sant Josep 8, 27 r.

Vic

Parador Nacional, I, 14 km outside the town, 36 r.
Can Pamplona, II, on the road to Puigcerdá, 34 r.
Ausa, III, Plaça Major 4, 26 r.

Information

in the United Kingdom

French Government Tourist Office

178 Piccadilly
London W1V 0AL
tel. (01) 4 99 69 11

Spanish National Tourist Office

57–58 St James's Street
London SW1A 1LD
tel. (01) 4 99 09 01–6

in Canada

French Government Tourist Offices	20 Queen Street West Toronto, Ont. M5H 2W9 tel. (416) 5 93 47 17
	1840 Sherbrooke Street West Montréal, Que. H3H 2W9 tel. (514) 9 31 38 55
Spanish National Tourist Office	60 Bloor Street West, Suite 201 Toronto, Ont. M4W 3B8 tel. (416) 9 61 31 31

in the United States of America

French Government Tourist Offices	9401 Wiltshire Boulevard Beverly Hills, CA 90112 tel. (213) 2 71 66 65
	645 N. Michigan Avenue, Suite 430 Chicago, IL 60601 tel. (312) 3 37 63 01
	610 Fifth Avenue New York, NY 10021 tel. (212) 7 57 11 25
	323 Geary Street San Francisco, CA 94012 tel. (415) 9 86 41 61
Spanish National Tourist Offices	665 Fifth Avenue New York, NY 10022 tel. (212) 7 59 88 22
	845 N. Michigan Avenue Chigago, IL 60611 tel. (312) 9 44 02 15
	1 Hallidie Plaza, Suite 801 San Francisco, CA 94102 tel. (415) 3 46 81 00
	Case del Hidalgo Hypolita & St George Streets St Augustine, FL 31084 tel (904) 8 29 64 60

Information in France

Note	The old local French telephone codes have been incorporated in the telephone number so that when dialling it is not necessary to prefix the number with a local code.
Amélie-les-Bains	Office de Tourisme et du Thermalisme Place de la République F-66110 Amélie-les-Bains tel. 68 39 01 98

Céret

Syndicat d'Initiative
Avenue Georges Clemenceau 1
F-66400 Céret
tel. 68 87 00 53

Elne

Syndicat d'Initiative
F-66200 Elne
tel. 68 22 05 07

Perpignan

Office de Tourisme et Accueil de France
Quai de Lattre de Tassigny
F-66000 Perpignan
tel. 68 34 29 94

Salses

Accueil Perpignan-Roussillon
on the A9 Motorway, turn-off for Salses-le-Château
F-66600 Rivesaltes
tel. 68 38 60 75

Information in Spain

Note

For an alphabetical list of Spanish (Castilian) place names and their Catalan equivalents see p. 214.

Arenys de Mar

Oficina de Turisme del CIT
Passeig Xifré 25
E-08350 Arenys de Mar
tel. (93) 7 92 15 37

Barcelona

Patronat Municipal de Turisme
Estació de França
E-08003 Barcelona
tel. (93) 3 19 27 91

Oficina Municipal de Turisme
Plaça de Sant Jaume
E-08002 Barcelona
tel. (93) 3 19 27 91

Oficina Municipal d'Informació
Plaça de Sant Jaume
E-08002 Barcelona
tel. (93) 3 18 25 15

Oficina de Turisme
Gran Via de les Corts Catalanes 658
E-08010 Barcelona
tel. (93) 3 01 74 43

Patronato Municipal de Turismo
Paseo de Gracia 35
E-08007 Barcelona
tel. (93) 2 15 44 77

Patronat Municipal de Turisme
Estació de Sants
E-08014 Barcelona
tel. (93) 2 50 25 94

Arms of Catalonia

Patronat Municipal de Turisme
Plaça Pablo Neruda
E-08013 Barcelona
tel. (93) 2 45 76 21

Oficina de Turisme
Monumento a Colom (Rambla)
E-08001 Barcelona
tel. (93) 3 02 52 24

Barcelona Airport

Oficina de Turisme de l'Aeroport de Barcelona
Barcelona – El Prat Airport
E-08820 El Prat de Llobregat
tel. (93) 3 25 58 29

Begur

Oficina Municipal de Turisme
Plaça de l'Eglésia 1
E-17255 Begur
tel. (972) 62 24 00

Besalú

Plaça de la Libertad 1
E-17850 Besalú
tel. (972) 59 02 25

La Bisbal
Oficina Municipal de Turisme

Plaça Francesc Marcià 10,
E-17100 La Bisbal d'Empordà
tel. (972) 64 09 75

Blanes

Oficina Municipal de Turisme
Plaça Catalunya
E-17300 Blanes
tel. (972) 33 03 48

Cadaqués

Oficina de Turisme del CIT
Carrer Cotxe 2-A
E-17488 Cadaqués
tel. (972) 25 83 15

Calella de la Costa

Oficina Municipal de Turisme
Carrer Sant Jaume
E-08370 Calella de la Costa
tel. (93) 7 69 05 59

Camprodón

Oficina de Turisme del CIT
Plaça d'Espanya 1
E-17867 Camprodón
tel. (972) 74 00 10

Castelló d'Empúries

Oficina de Turisme
on the road from Besalú to Roses
E-17486 Castelló d'Empúries
tel. (972) 45 08 02

Empúries

Oficina de Turisme del CIT
Plaça de les Escoles 1
E-17130 L'Escala
tel. (972) 77 06 03

L'Estartit

Oficina Municipal de Turisme
Passeig Maritim 47
E-17258 L'Estartit
tel. (972) 75 89 10

Figueres

Oficina Municipal de Turisme
Plaça del Sol
E-17600 Figueres
tel. (972) 50 31 55

Girona

Oficina Municipal de Turisme
Estació RENFE (main station)
E-17007 Girona
tel. (972) 21 62 96

Oficina de Turisme de Girona
Carrer Ciutadans 12
E-17004 Girona
tel. (972) 20 16 94

La Jonquera

Porta Catalana
Area de Peatge de la Jonquera
(motorway toll booth on the A 7)
E-17700 La Jonquera
tel. (972) 54 06 42

Llançà

Oficina del Patronat Municipal de Turisme
Avinguda d'Europa, Edifici Ajuntament (town hall)
E-17490 Llançà
tel. (972) 38 08 56

Lloret de Mar

Serveis de Turisme
Terminal de Autobuses (bus station)
E-17310 Lloret de Mar
tel. (972) 36 47 35

Malgrat de Mar

Oficina Municipal de Turisme
Carrer Carme 30
E-08380 Malgrat de Mar
tel. (93) 7 61 00 82

Martaró

Oficina d'Informació Municipal
Carrer de la Riera
E-08301 Mataró
tel. (93) 7 96 08 08

Olot

Carrer Mulleres
E-17800 Olot
tel. (972) 26 01 41

Palafrugell

Oficina Municipal de Turisme
Carrer Carrilet 2
E-17200 Palafrugell
tel. (972) 30 02 28

Palamós

Oficina Municipal d'Infirmació Turistica
Passeig del Mar 8
E-17230 Palamós
tel. (972) 31 43 90

Pals	Oficina Municipal de Turisme Plaça d'Espanya 5 E-17256 Pals tel. (972) 30 17 09
La Platja d'Aro	Oficina Municipal de Turisme Carrer Verdaguer 11 E-17853 La Platja d'Aro tel. (972) 81 71 79
Portbou	Passeig de la Sardana Edifici Ajuntament (town hall) E-17497 Portbou tel. (972) 39 02 84
	Oficina Municipal de Turisme Estació RENFE (station) E-17497 Portbou tel. (972) 39 05 07
Ripoll	Oficina de Turisme del CIT de Ripoll Plaça Abat Oliba, s/n E-17500 Ripoll tel. (972) 70 11 09
Roses	Oficina Municipal de Turisme Avinguda de Rhode E-17480 Roses tel. (972) 25 73 31
Sant Cugat del Vallès	Oficina Municipal de Turisme Plaça de Barcelona 17 E-08190 Sant Cugat del Vallès tel. (93) 6 74 09 50
Sant Feliu de Guíxols	Oficina Municipal de Turisme Plaça d'Espanya 1 E-17220 Sant Feliu de Guíxols tel. (972) 32 03 80
Sant Joan de les Abadesses	Oficina de Turisme del CIT Rambla Comte Guifré 5 E-17860 Sant Joan de les Abadesses tel. (972) 72 00 92
Tossa de Mar	Oficina Municipal de Turisme Carretera de Lloret, Terminal E-17320 Tossa de Mar tel. (972) 34 01 08
Vic	Oficina Municipal de Turisme Plaça Major E-08500 Vic tel. (93) 8 86 20 91

Language

France

By far the greater part of tourist traffic in France is national rather than international and therefore outside the large cities English is not always well understood.

Spain

In information offices, hotels and restaurants English is generally understood, but even a slight knowledge of the Spanish language will prove beneficial, for practically everyone speaks "high Spanish" (Castillano) as well as Catalan (Català). There may be some difficulty in inland areas where there are few tourists and where people speak Catalan in a local dialect. The introduction of a Catalan word or phrase is noted with courtesy.

Important words and phrases

English	French	Spanish	Catalan
good morning	bonjour	buenos dias	bon dia
good day (after midday)		buenas tardes	bona tarda
good night	bonne nuit	buenas noches	bona nit
goodbye	au revoir	adiós/hasta la vista	adéu/passi-ho bé
yes/no	oui/non	si/no	si/no
excuse me	pardon	perdón	perdó
don't mention it/not at all	de rien/pas de quoi	de nada	de res
help yourself	servez-vous	sirvase Usted	serveixi vostè
if you please	. . . s'il vous plaît	por favor	si us plau
thank you (very much)	merci (beaucoup)	(muchas) gracias	(moltes) gràcies
allow me	permettez	con permiso	amb permis
do you speak English?	parlez-vous anglais?	¿habla usted inglés?	parla vosté ingles?
I don't understand	je ne comprends pas	no entiendo	no entenc
have you a room free?	y a-t-il une chambre libre?	¿hay una habitación libre?	tenen una habitació lliure?
single room	chambre individuelle	habitación individual	habitació individual
double room	chambre à deux	lits habitación doble	habitació doble
bath/shower	salle de bain/douche	baño/doucha	bany/dutxa
key	clé	llave	clau
what does it cost?	combien ca coûte?	¿cuánto vale?	quant costa?
the bill/check	addition	cuenta	compte
where is the road . . . ?	où est la rue . . . ?	¿donde está la calle . . . ?	on és la carrer . . . ?
street (in a town)	rue	calle	carrer
road (outside a town)	route	carretera	carretera
motorway/highway	autoroute	autopista	autopista
to the right	à droite	a la derecha	a la dreta
to the left	à gauche	a la izquierda	a l'esquerra
straight ahead	tout droit	derecho	dret

Important words and phrases – *contd*

above/up	en haut	arriba	a dalt
below/down	en bas	abajo	a baix
January	janvier	enero	gener
February	février	febrero	febrer
March	mars	marzo	març
April	avril	abril	abril
May	mai	mayo	maig
June	juin	junio	juny
July	juillet	julio	juliol
August	août	agosto	agost
September	septembre	setiembre	setembre
October	octobre	octubre	octubre
November	novembre	noviembre	novembre
December	décembre	diciembre	desembre
Monday	lundi	lunes	dilluns
Tuesday	mardi	martes	dimarts
Wednesday	mercredi	miércoles	dimercres
Thursday	jeudi	jueves	dijous
Friday	vendredi	viernes	divendres
Saturday	samedi	sábado	dissabte
Sunday	dimanche	domingo	diumenge
morning	matin	mañana	mati
midday	midi	mediod	migdia
evening	soir	tarde	vespre
night	nuit	noche	nit

Courses in Catalan

Courses in the Catalan language are arranged by the following institutions:
Universitat de Barcelona, Gran Via de les Corts Catalanes 585, E-08007 Barcelona
C.I.C. Via Augusta 205, E-08021 Barcelona
Escola Oficial d'Idiomes, Avinguda de les Drassanes, E-08001 Barcelona
Rosa Sensat, Carrer Enric Granados 46, E-08008 Barcelona
Xarxa Cultural, Carrer Ample, E-08002 Barcelona
Casa de Cultura, Carrer deo Hospital 6, E-17001 Girona

Marinas

PLACE	FEATURES	FACILITIES
Aiguablava (G)	Boat harbour	Club Nàutic; water; electricity; fuel; crane; slipway
Arenys de Mar (B)	Boat harbour	Club Nàutic; water; electricity; fuel; crane; slipway; workshop
Barcelona (B)	Boat harbour	Reial Club Maritim; water; electricity; fuel; crane; slipway; workshop; customs
	Boat harbour	Reial Club Nàutic; water; electricity; fuel; crane; slipway; workshop; customs
Blanes (G)	Boat harbour	Club de Vela; water; electricity; fuel; crane; slipway; workshop
Cala Canyellas (G)	Marina	Drassana esportiva; water; crane; provisions

Marinas – *contd*

PLACE	FEATURES	FACILITIES
Empúria Brava (G)	Extensive holiday development with moorings adjacent to bungalows and a boat harbour	Marina; water; electricity; fuel; several cranes; slipway
L'Escala (G)	Boat harbour	Club Nàutic; water; electricity; fuel; crane
L'Estartit (G)	Boat harbour	Club Nàutic; water; electricity; fuel; crane; slipway; workshop
Llanfranch (G)	Marina	Club Nàutic; water; electricity; fuel; crane; slipway
Masnou (B)	Marina	Club Nàutic; water; electricity; fuel; crane; slipway; workshop
Palamós (G)	Boat harbour	Club Nàutic Costa Brava; water; electricity; fuel; crane; slipway; workshop; customs
La Platja d'Aro (G)	Marina	Water; electricity; fuel; crane
El Port de la Selva (G)	Boat harbour	Club Nàutic; water; electricity; fuel; crane; workshop
Premiá de Mar (B)	Marina	Club Nàutic; water; electricity; crane; workshop
Roses (G)	Boat harbour	Water; fuel; crane; slipway; workshop
Sant Andres de Llavaneras (B)	El Balis Marina	Club Nàutic; water; electricity; fuel; crane; slipway; workshop
Sant Feliu de Guíxols (G)	Marina	Club Nàutic; water; fuel; crane; slipway; workshop
Santa Margarida (G)	Bungalows with moorings	Water; electricity; crane; slipway; workshop; customs in Port-Bou

(B) = Barcelona Province (G) = Girona Province

Motorcycle Rental

See Bicycle Rental

Museums

Spain

Note
For an alphabetical list of Spanish place names with their Catalan equivalents see p. 214.

Arenys de Mar
Museu d'Arenys de Mar/Museu de la Punta Frederic Marès (local museum)
Carrer de l'Eglesia 41

Badalona
Museu de Badalona (municipal museum)
Plaça Assemblea de Catalunya 1

Banyoles
Museu de Arqueològic Comarcal de Banyoles (Archaeological Regional Museum)
Plaça de la Font 11

Barcelona
Aquarium Barceloneta
Barceloneta, Passeig Nacional

Casa-Museu Gaudi (Gaudi Museum)
Parc Güell, Carrer Olot

Col-lecció d'Indumentària i Accessoris de Bomber (fire brigade equipment and uniforms)
Passeig Nacional 67

Exposició Permanent d'Odontologia (Dental Museum)
Carrer de Tapineria 10

Fundació Joan Miró (J. Miró foundation; modern art)
Parc de Montjuïc, Passeig de Miramar

Gabinet de Fisica Experimental Mentora Alsina (natural science collection)
on the road from Vallvidrera to Tibidabo

Galeria de Catalans Illustres (portrait gallery of famous Catalans)
Carrer del Bisbe Cassador 3

Institut Amatller d'Art Hispànic (collection of Spanish art)
Passeig de Gràcia 41

Institut Botànic (botanical institute, only for specialists)
Parc de Montjuïc, Avinguda dels Muntanyans

Museu Arqueològic (Archaeological Museum)
Parc de Montjuïc, Passeig de Santa Madrona

Museu d'Art de Catalunya (Museum of the Art of Catalonia)
in the Palau Nacional, Parc de Montjuïc

Museu d'Art Modern (Catalan art from the 19th c.)
Parc de la Cuitadella

Museu de les Arts de l'Espectacle (Theatre Museum)
in the Palau Güell, Carrer Nou de la Rambla 3

Museu d'Arts, Indústries i Tradicions Populars (craft work and traditional art)
in the Poble Espanyol, Parc de Montjuïc, Plaça Major 6

Museu dels Autòmates (Museum of Automata)
in the Parc d'Atraccions, Tibidabo

Museu de l'Automòbil (Antic Car Club de Catalonya; vintage cars)
Via Augusta 182

Museu del Calçat Antic (Shoe Museum)
Plaça de Sant Felip Neri

Museu de la Catedral (Cathedral Museum)
in the cathedral cloisters, Barri Gòtic, Carrer Santa Llúcia

Museu i Centre d'Estudis de l'Esport Dr Melcior Colet (Museum of Sport)
Carrer Buenos Aires 56–58

Museu de Cera (waxworks)
Passatge de la Banca 7 (at the harbour end of Ramblas)

Museu de Ceràmica (ceramics)
in the Palau Nacional, Parc de Montjuïc

Museu de la Ciència (Museum of Science)
Carrer Teodor Roviralta 55

Museu Clarà (work of the sculptor Josep Clarà, d. 1958)
Carrer de Calatrave 27–29

Museu Etnogràfic Andino-Amazònic (folk art of the Andes and Amazon areas)
Carrer Cardenal Vives i Tutó 16

Museu Etnològic (folk art)
in the Parc de Montjuïc, Avinguda de Santa Madrona

Museu de la Farmàcia Catalana (Museum of Pharmacy)
in the Pharmacological Institute of the University, Avinguda de la Diagonal

Museu del Futbol Club Barcelona (Football Museum)
in the stadium of FC Barcelona, Avinguda Aristides Maillol

Museu de Geologia (Geological Museum)
in the Parc de la Ciutadella, Passeig deis Til-lers

Museu d'Història de la Ciutat (Municipal Museum of History)
Carrer de Veguer

Museu de l'Institut de Criminologia (history of crime; only for specialists)
in the Faculty of Law of the University, Zona Universitària, Avinguda de la Diagonal

Museu Frederic Marés (formerly the art collection of the connoisseur F. Marés)
Carrer de Comtes de Barcelona 8

Museu Maritim (Maritime Museum)
in the Drassanes Reials, Porta de la Pau

Museu Militar (military and weapons)
Castell de Montjuïc

Museu Monestir de Pedralbes (religious art from the monastery of the Poor Clares of Pedralbes)
Baixada del Monestir 9

Museu de la Música (Museum of Music)
Avinguda de la Diagonal 373

Museu del Palau de Pedralbes (Gobelin tapestries, paintings)
Avinguda de la Diagonal 686

"A faun", by Picasso

Museu Parroquial de Santa Maria del Mar (Diocesan Museum)
Carrer Sombrerers 3

Museu del Perfum (Museum of Perfume)
Passeig de Gràcia 39

Museu Picasso (Picasso Museum)
Carrer Montcada 15

Museu de Pompes Fúnebres (Funeral Museum)
Carrer Sancho de Avila 2

Museu Postal (Postal Museum)
in the Palau de la Virreina, Rambles 99

Museu Taur de la Monumental (Museum of Bullfighting)
Gran Via de les Corts Catalanes 749

Museu del Temple Expiatori de la Sagrada Familia (history of the building of the Sagrada Familia)
Carrer de Mallorca 401

Museu Textil i d'Indumentària (textiles and clothing)
Carrer Montcada 12

Museu Verdaguer (memorabilia of the writer Jacint Verdaguer)
Carrer de les Planes, km 7

Museu de Zoologia (Zoological Museum)
in the Parc de la Ciutadella, Passeig dels Til-lers

Planetarium Barcelona
Carrer Escoles Pies 103

Blanes

Jardi Botànic Mar i Murtra (botanic gardens, Karl Faust foundation)
Carrer Sant Joan

Caldes de Montbui

Museu d'Història (Museum of History)
Carrer Santa Susanna 4

Museu Romàntic Deiger
Carrer Mossèn Delger 8

Calella de la Costa

Museu-Arxiu Municipal (local museum and archive)
Carrer Escoles Pies 34–36

Calonge

Museu Arqueològic (Archaeological Museum)
Castell de Calonge

Petit Museu Parroquial (Parochial Museum)
in Sant Marti Parish Church

Canet de Mar

Museu-Arxiu Parroquial (Parochial Museum and archives)
Plaça de l'Englesia 17

Castelló d'Empúries

Plaça Mossèn Cinto Verdaguer

Museu Monogràfic d'Empúries at the excavation site	Empúries
Teatre-Museu Dali (collection of works by Salvador Dali) Plaça Salvador Dali i Gala	Figueres
Museu de l'Empordà (regional museum of Ampurdán) Rambla 2	
Museu de Joquets (Toy Museum) Rambla 10	
Museu Arqueològic de Sant Pere de Galligants (Archaeological Museum) Carrer Santa Llúcia 1	Girona
Museu d'Art (Museum of Art) in the Episcopal Palace, Pujada de la Catedral 12	
Museu Capitular de la Catedral (Cathedral Museum) in the cathedral	
Museu Farmàcia de l'Hospital de Santa Catalina (Pharmacy Museum) Plaça Pompeu Fabra 1	
Museu d'Història de la Ciutat (Municipal Museum of History) Carrer de la Força 27	
Museu de Granollers (local museum) Carrer Anselm Clavé 40	Granollers
Museu-Arxiu de Santa Maria de Matoró (Church Museum and archives) in Santa Maria Basilica, Plaça del Fossar Xic	Mataró
Museu Comarcal del Maresme (area museum) Carrer el Carrerò 17–19	
Museu de Montserrat (paintings, archaeological exhibits) Plaça del Monestir	Montserrat
Museu Comarcal de la Garrotxa (countryside museum) Carrer Hospici 4 (scientific and volcanic department in the Parc Municipal, Avinguda Santa Coloma)	Olot
Museu-Tresor Parroquial (Parochial Museum and church treasury) in Sant Esteve's Church, Carrer de Sant Esteve	
Museu-Arxiu Municipal (Parochial Museum and archives) Carrer Cervantes 10	Palafrugell
Jardi Botànic de Cap Roig (botanical gardens) in Calella de Palafrugell, Cap Roig	
Museu Cau de la Costa Brava (paintings, collection of shells) Plaça del Forn 4	Palamòs

Pais — Museu d'Arqueologia Submarina (Museum of Underwater Archaeology)
in the Case de Cultura, Carrer de la Creu 7

Peralada — Museu del Castell de Peralada (Castle Museum)
in the Citadel

Ripoll — Museu-Arxiu Folklòric (museum and archive of folklore)
Plaça Abat Oliva

Sant Feliu de Guíxols — Museu Municipal (Parochial Museum)
Plaça del Monestir

Sant Joan de les Abadesses — Museu del Monestir de Sant Joan de les Abadesses (collection of ecclesiastical art)
Plaça de l'Abadia

Sant Pol de Mar — Museu de Sant Pol de Mar (local museum)
Plaça de la Vila 1

Torroella de Montgrí — Museu del Montgrí del Baix Ter (regional museum)
Carrer Major 31

Tossa de Mar — Museu de la Vila Vella i Museu Municipal (local museum)
Plaça Pinta Roig i Soler

Ullastret — Museu Monogràfic d'Ullastret (Archaeological Museum)
at the excavation site

Vic — Museu Arqueològic – Artistic – Episcopal (archaeological, artistic and ecclesiastical exhibits)
Plaça del Bisbe Oliba

Opening Times (Business Hours)

Museums, sights

The hours when museums and other buildings are open vary considerably. Basically it can be stated that most are closed at midday in France between noon and 3 p.m. and in Spain between 1 and 4 p.m.

Shops

In France and Spain there are no official shopping hours. Shops are generally open from 9 a.m. to 1 p.m. and from 3 to 7 p.m.; in summer they often remain open until late in the evening (especially food and tobacco shops).

Stores and shopping centres

France:
Shopping centres on the outskirts of large towns are generally open on weekdays including Saturday from 9 a.m. to 7 p.m. (sometimes even until 9 p.m.)

Spain:
The large stores and shopping centres are generally open Monday to Saturday from 10 a.m. to 8 p.m. continuously. A few, however, close on Monday morning.

Banks

France:
Normally French banks are open Monday to Friday between 9 a.m. and 4 p.m. (in some places they close on Monday).

Spain:
The banks are open Monday to Saturday between 9 a.m. and 2 p.m.; in tourist centres during the high season they are sometimes open in the afternoon.

Post offices

France:
Post offices are open for business Monday to Friday from 8 a.m. to 7 p.m. (sometimes with a fairly long midday closing) and on Saturday from 8 a.m. to noon.

Spain:
Hours when post offices are open vary and generally are displayed in the offices (on Monday they frequently do not open until 9 a.m.; there is a fairly long midday closing and most branches are closed on the many public holidays).

Post and Telephone

France

Post

Mail to be collected from post offices must be marked "Poste Restante".
Stamps (*timbres-poste*) can be obtained from post offices and also from tobacconists, stationers and souvenir shops.

Telephone

Long-distance and international calls can be conveniently made from public coin boxes.
Telephone codes:
from the United Kingdom to France 01033
from the United States and Canada to France 01133
from France to the United Kingdom 1944
from France to the United States and Canada 191

Spain

Post

Mail to be collected from post offices must be marked "Lista de Correos".
Stamps can be obtained from post offices and from most tobacconists (*estancos*).

Telephone

Long-distance and international calls can be conveniently made from public coin boxes. Since 25, 50 and 100 peseta coins are normally required (unless a notice in the call box indicates otherwise) a supply of small change is necessary. Five-peseta coins can only be used for calls within Spain!
Telephone codes:
from the United Kingdom to Spain 01034
from the United States and Canada to Spain 01134
from Spain to the United Kingdom 0744
from Spain to the United States and Canada 071

Public Holidays

France

Official public holidays	1 January	New Year
	1 May	Labour Day
	14 July	National holiday (storming of the Bastille 1789)
	15 August	Feast of the Assumption
	1 November	All Saints' Day
	11 November	Armistice Day 1918
	25 December	Christmas Day
Other public holidays	Easter Monday	
	Ascension Day	
	Whit Monday	

Spain

Official public holidays	1 January	Año Nuevo (New Year)
	8 January	Reyes Magos (Epiphany)
	19 March	San José (St Joseph's Day)
	1 May	Dia del Trabajo (Labour Day)
	14 June	San Juan (name day of the king)
	29 June	San Pedro y San Pablo (St Peter and St Paul)
	25 July	Santiago (St John the Apostle)
	15 August	Asunción (Feast of the Assumption)
	11 September	Diada Nacional de Catalunya/Fiesta Nacional de Cataluña (Catalonian National Feast Day)
	12 October	Dia de la Hispanidad (discovery of America)
	1 November	Todos los Santos (All Saints)
	8 December	Immaculada Concepción (Annunciation)
	25 December	Navidad (Christmas Day
Other public holidays	Viernes Santo (Good Friday)	
	Corpus Christi	

Radio and Television

France

Radio

In cases of great emergency the BBC (tel. 01–580 4468) will accept messages from near relations only, which will be broadcast in French on Radio France Inter (long wave 1829 m).

Television

The French television system differs from that in the United States and Great Britain and therefore British and American sets are of no practical use in France.

Spain

Radio and television

Spanish radio and television organisations have their headquarters in Madrid. The Ràdio Associació de Catalunya (UKW 105 MHz) and Catalunya Ràdio (UKW 88.4 MHz) broadcast in July and August, from Monday to Friday, news programmes for foreigners in English at 10.30 a.m.
In cases of extreme emergency the Spanish radio organisation Ràdio Nacional will transmit messages for tourists travelling in Spain. The motoring associations can provide information.

Restaurants

France

French cuisine is world-famous both for quality and variety. Since the French lay great store on a varied menu and allow one to two hours for the consumption of a meal, eating has become an important part of French daily life and the art of French cooking an element of French culture.

Lavish preparation, the use of only fresh ingredients (no tinned food) and of butter and cream (*crème fraîche*) are typical of discriminating French cooking (*haute cuisine*); herbs and spices are used in abundance and in many different combinations; the excellent sauces are also renowned. For a few years there has been much talk about *nouvelle cuisine*. This is distinguished by simplicity of preparation and at the same time by attention to the natural taste of fine fresh ingredients.
As well as "haute cuisine" country-style cooking (*cuisine régionale*) is of great importance and is much esteemed by gourmets.
Although meals take up a good deal of time, the visitor to France should conform to the national custom. It is a fact that even inconspicuous restaurants in the country can often produce a choice menu, and it is frequently customary and sensible to discuss the proposed meal with the proprietor. If no menu is provided, it is best to enquire about prices since a wide choice understandably leads to higher costs. Considering the quality and range of the menus the prices are in general not excessive.
A "menu" at a fixed price (usually including wine) is cheaper than an à la carte meal.

Restaurants in France (selection)

Amélie-les-Bains

Central, Avenue de Vallespir
Le Bogavanta, Quai G. Bosch

Perpignan

Delcros, Avenue Maréchal Leclerc 63
Relais St-Jean, Cité Bartissol 1
Le Supion, Avenue Maréchal Leclerc 71
Le Quai, Quai Vauban 37
François Villon, Rue Four St-Jean 1
Le Helder, Rue Courteline 1
La Serre, Rue Dagobert 2 bis

Spain

As everywhere else in Spanish tourist areas the resorts on the coast of Catalonia have a wide range of restaurants (*restaurantes*) of all categories from the simple beach restaurant, the *fonda* (country snack bar), the *casa de comida* (eating house) and the *mesón* to restaurants of superior style with international cuisine. Every eating place must offer a tourist menu of three courses at a fixed price, but understandably this is often inferior both in quality and quantity to meals taken à la carte which, of course, are somewhat more expensive. Meals in Spain are taken one to two hours later than in most other countries in Western Europe; hotel restaurants frequented principally by central European and British visitors often go to considerable trouble to meet the eating habits of their guests. In the case of fixed menus this unfortunately often means that the food offered is what the restauranteur thinks his customers prefer and tasty local dishes are missing. In restaurants in the interior of the country, however, one can often find traditional fare.

Restaurants in Spain (selection)

Arenys de Mar

Hispanier, Carrer Reial 54

Badalona

Obiols Prim, Carrer Prim 172

Barcelona

Beltxenea, Carrer Mallorca 275
Via Veneto, Carrer Ganduxer 10
Reno, Carrer Tuset 27
Neichel, Avinguda de Pedralbes 16
Finisterre, Avinguda Diagonal 469
Hostal des Sol, Passeig de Gràcia 44 (1st floor)
Botafumiero, Carrer Major de Gràcia 81
La Odisea, Carrer Copons 7
Azulete, Via Augusta 281
Eldorado Petit, Carrer Dolors Monserd 51
Ara-cata, Carrer Doctor Ferràn 33
Agut d'Avignon, Carrer Trinidad 3
Jaume de Provença, Carrer Provença 88
Hostal Sant Jordi, Travessera de Dalt 123
Siete Puertas, Passeig Isabel II 14

Begur

Mas Comangau, on the Fornells road

Besalú

Pont Vell, by the old bridge, Carrer Pont Vell 28

Blanes

Port Blau, Esplanada del Port 18
Casa Patacano, Passeig del Mar 12
Can Flores II, Esplanada del Port 3

Cadaqués

La Galiota, Carrer Narcis Monturiol 9

Caldes de Malavella

Can Geli, on the national road II

Calonge

Can Muni, Carrer Major 5

in Sant Antoni:
Costa Brava, on the road to Sant Feliu de Guíxols
Refugi dels Pescadors, Passeig Josep Mundet 43

Camprodón
Sayola, Carrer Josep Morer 4

Empúria Brava
El Bruel, Edificio Bahia II

L'Estartit
Els Tascons, Edificio Medas Park II
La Gaviota, Passeig Maritim

Figueres
*Mas Pau, on the Olot road

Girona
Cipresaia, Carrer Perhalta 5
Rosaleda, Passeig de la Devesa
Selva Mar, Carrer Santa Eugenia 81
Casa Marieta, Plaça de la Independencia 5

Granollers
L'Amperi, Plaça de la Font Verde
La Granolla, Carrer Girona 52
L'Ancora, Carrer Aureli Font 3

La Jonquera
Can Agusti, on the national road II

Llançà
La Brasa, Plaça de Catalunya

Lloret de Mar
La Bodega Vella, Na Marina 14
Taverna del Mar, Carrer Pescadors 5
Ca l'Avi, on the Vidreres road

Mataró
Gumer's, Carrer Novas Caputxinas 10
El Nou Cents, Carrer del Torrent 21
El Celler, on the national road II

Olot
Purgatori, Carrer Bisbe Serra 51

Palafrugell
in Calella:
Rems, Carrer del Pintor Serra 5
Can Pep, Carrer Lladó 22

in Llafranc:
San Sebastián (fine view), near lighthouse

Palamós
La Cuineta, Carrer Adrián Alvarez 111
Plaça Murada, Plaça Murada 5
La Gamba, Plaça Sant Pere 1
L'Art, Passeig del Mar 7
El Delfin, Avinguda Onze de Setembre 93

Pals
Sa Punta, 5 km E at the Platja de Pals

La Platja d'Aro
*Carles Camos – Big Rock, on the Masnou road
Mas Nou, in Masnou
Aradi, on the Palamós road

Portbou
L'Ancora, Passeig de la Sardana 3

El Port de la Selva
Ca l'Hermida, Carrer Isla 7
Comercio, Moll Balleu 3

Ripoll
Grill El Gall, on road 152

Roses
El Bulli, on the Platja Montjoi
La Llar, on the Figueres road
L'Antull, Plaça de Sant Pere 7

S'Agaró	Sant Jordi, on the Palamós road
Santa Coloma de Farners	Mas Sola, on the Sils road Can Gurt, on the Sils road
Sant Cugat del Vallès	La Marmita, Carrer Barcelona 15
Sant Feliu de Guíxols	Eldorado Petit, Rambla Vidal 23 S'Adolitx, Carrer Major 13 La Bahia, Passeig del Mar 18
Torroella de Montgrí	Elias, Carrer Major 24
Tossa de Mar	Es Moli, Carrer Tarull 5 Maria Angela, Passeig del Mar 10 Castell Vell, Plaça Roig i Soler Rocamar, Travessia Codolar 7 Can Tones, Plaça de l'Eglesia
Vic	L'Anec Blau, Carrer Verdaguer 21
Food and Drink	See entry

Roads

Note

Within the area covered by this guide motorways are practically only of use as access routes. The fairly high tolls and the fact that the motorway exits are very far apart make it advisable when travelling in this area to use the French and/or Spanish national roads.

France

France is served by a dense network of roads and even minor roads are usually in excellent condition. The motorways (*autoroutes*) which have been developed in recent years now have a total length of some 4000 km/2485 miles. Tolls are payable on motorways except on a few short stretches near large cities.

Most of the traffic, however, is still carried on the excellently engineered routes nationales, which are marked by red and white kilometre stones. The extensive network of roads means that as a rule they are not too crowded, though there may be considerable holdups during the holiday season.

Roads of lesser importance bear yellow and white kilometre stones; they are not much inferior to the routes nationales.

Spain

Since the improvement of main roads and the continuing development of motorways (*autopistas*) the Spanish road system is now generally good. Tolls are charged on the longer motorways such as the Autopista del Mediterráneo from the French-Spanish border to Barcelona.

The national highways (*carreteras nacionales*), numbered with the prefix N are mostly good modern roads. At fairly long intervals can be seen the huts of the maintenance men (*peones camineros*). Regional highways (*carreteras comarcales*), numbered with the prefix C, are also mostly reasonably good, at any rate on the main routes. Unnumbered minor roads may be in poor condition.

For suggested itineraries see p. 29.

Safety Precautions

In the main season, especially in Barcelona and the other large centres of tourism, an increase must be expected in thefts. Many a wallet has changed hands in a crowd and the detection rate is small.

If the police are informed of a theft or that something has been stolen from a vehicle, the victim will be treated with courtesy but will have little chance of any action being taken, for the authorities are simply overtaxed; however, a statement made to the police in the event of the complaint of a theft is necessary in the event of a claim under insurance.

It is advisable always to keep articles of value with you (identity documents, money, etc.) and to leave large sums of cash in the hotel safe or in the safe deposit of a camping site. It is also a good idea to have photocopies of passports and other important documents which should be kept separately from the originals. In the event of loss this will greatly facilitate replacement.

Note

The loss of Eurocheques, travellers' cheques, cheque cards, etc., should be immediately reported to the bank or other issuing office in order that replacements may be made available.

Shopping and Souvenirs

France

In France there are fine examples of hand-crafted articles such as basket work and things made of wood (especially olive wood); sometimes charming antiques can also be found. Most of the culinary specialities of the country can be obtained in tins and make a most acceptable present for connoisseurs. Visitors who wish to take wine home with them are advised to purchase it from a co-operative (*cave coopérative*) or directly from the producer. In France spirits are highly taxed and therefore no cheaper than they are in one's own country.

Spain

Spanish craft work has a long tradition and products based on old designs can be found as well as modern crafts. There

is a particularly good selection of ceramic work on sale in many places; in Catalonia most of this comes from the town of La Bisbal where there is also a technical school of ceramics. Of course goods aimed at the souvenir trade predominate; tasteful, practical and not expensive are the everyday ceramic articles of the region. Good modern leather work (shoes, clothing, accessories) can be bought in specialist shops and often directly from the factory; plenty of time should be allowed so that quality and price can be compared. Shoes made in Spain can, of course, be obtained in the UK and the advantage in price by buying them in Spain is not very great. In addition artistic articles made of glass should be mentioned. In Barcelona particularly charming little bottle ships completely made of glass are produced. The ships chandlers in the area of the port also sell attractive brass articles which also make good souvenirs.
Replicas of items exhibited can also be obtained in many museums (e.g. Museu de Arte de Catalunya in Barcelona). Glass, ceramics, leather, enamel articles, fashion jewellery and other crafted articles are produced in the workshops of the Pueblo Español (Spanish village) of the Montjuïc in Barcelona where they can also be purchased.
Spanish silver ware is very tasteful. In the better shops the visitor can find artificial pearls which cannot be distinguished from the real thing and the experts in their preparation are the people of Mallorca. These pearls are certainly not cheap fashion jewellery and they are sold not only in Spain but exported all over the world. The most noteworthy brand is "Perlas Majorica".

La Bisbal: a ceramic plate

Other popular souvenirs are Spanish sweets (including candied fruits, nougat and Turkish honey) some of which originated in the time of the Arab domination in Spain. The Moors were particularly fond of very sweet titbits, the taste of which is too strong for those from other countries. Ensaimadas, a sweet pastry made of light oatmeal dough and often with a filling, was originally a speciality of Mallorca; small ones are served for breakfast but larger ones can also be obtained.
Spain has good and cheap spirits, principally brandy. This is distilled from wine and resembles cognac but is fruitier in taste and has a stronger aroma than its French counterpart. The best brands are Lepanto and Duque de Alba; cheaper brands can also be obtained abroad. Aniseed liqueur is popular throughout the country and is drunk after meals – it makes the oily Spanish food more digestible.
For other details about Spanish drinks see Food and Drink and also Wine

Spanish and Catalan Place Names

Places in this guide book are arranged alphabetically according to their Catalan names. These often differ from the way they are written and pronounced in "High" Spanish (i.e. Castilian). Visitors may well be better acquainted with the Castilian forms than with the Catalan names, which have only fairly recently come into official use. In order to make it easier for the reader to locate a particular place (especially in the Practical Information section of this book), an alphabetical list of place names in Castilian together with their Catalan equivalents will be found below. Where no entry appears it may be assumed that the two forms do not differ.

Spanish	Catalan
Ampuriabrava	Empúria Brava
Ampurias	Empúries
Bagur	Begur
Bañolas	Banyoles
Caldas de Malavella	Caldes de Malavella
Caldas de Montbuy	Caldes de Montbui
Castellfullit de la Roca	Castellfollit de la Roca
Castelló de Ampurias	Castelló d'Empúries
Costa Dorada	Costa Daurada
Estartit	L'Estartit
Figueras	Figueres
Gerona	Girona
La Junquera	La Jonquera
Llansá	Llançà
Perelada	Peralada
Playa de Aro	La Platja d'Aro
Port-Bou	Portbou
Puerto de la Selva	El Port de la Selva
Rosas	Roses
San Feliú de Guixols	Sant Feliu de Guíxols
San Juan de las Abadessas	Sant Joan de les Abadesses
San Pedro de Roda	Sant Pere de Rodes
San Pol de Mar	Sant Pol de Mar
Santa Coloma de Farnés	Santa Coloma de Farners
Vich	Vic

Time

During the winter months (October to March) France and Spain observe Central European Time, e.g. one hour ahead of Greenwich Mean Time: six hours ahead of Eastern Standard Time in the United States. The clock is advanced by another hour during the summer months (March to September). It is probable that in the near future Great Britain may adopt the same time as the rest of Western Europe.

Tipping

France

Tipping (service) is generally included in hotel and restaurant bills (inclusive prices).
Tips (*pourboire*) are generally given as they would be in one's own country. In France guides in castles, museums and other sights expect tips as do taxi drivers and usherettes in theatres and cinemas.

Spain

Tipping (*servicio*) is replaced in hotels and restaurants by an addition to the bill, but waiters (*camarero*), room maids (*camarera* or *muchacha*), porters (few people carry their own luggage) and servants (both *mozo* in Spanish) expect a small tip (*propina*) especially when some particular service has been provided. Taxi drivers, supervisors in buildings visited, usherettes in theatres, cinemas and at bullfights expect a tip, so that it is advisable always to have some small change.

Traffic Regulations

France

As in all the countries of continental Europe vehicles travel on the right. Seat belts must be worn while travelling.
In general vehicles coming from the right have priority (often signed *priorité à droite*). When negotiating a roundabout vehicles entering the roundabout must wait (unless signs indicate otherwise). Roads with the right of way are signed "passage protégé" before crossings.
In built-up areas with sufficient street lighting side lights are prescribed; at night signals must be given with headlights and not with the horn.
Foreign vehicles are not forced to use the yellow headlights which are customary in France. Maximum speeds: on motorways 130 km/h (80 mph), on main roads 110 km/h (68 mph) and on national and country roads 90 km/h (55 mph). In built-up areas 60 km/h (35 mph). When it is raining the permitted speeds are reduced from 130 to 100 km/h (62 mph) and from 110 and 90 km/h to 80 km/h (50 mph). A driver who has not had a licence for at least a year may not travel faster then 55 mph.
The maximum permitted alcohol level in the blood is 8 milligrammes per millilitre.

Spain

In Spain, as in the rest of continental Europe, vehicles travel on the right. Seat belts must be worn while on the move; children under 10 years of age must travel in the rear seats.
In general vehicles coming from the right have priority (even from side roads in towns). Exceptions are specifically signed.
When turning to the right away from built-up areas, one must first travel on the right of the road and wait until the road is free, often at crossings the traffic lanes are correspondingly marked.
If a driver is turning left into a road which has high priority, he will often find that he must drive along an acceleration lane parallel to the main lane and from this he must then move right into the traffic.
When overtaking, a driver must first indicate with his left indicator and having passed the other vehicle indicate with the right one. While overtaking and when approaching

bends the horn must be sounded (and after dark a signal given with the headlights); this is obligatory.
Drivers should be particularly careful when overtaking lorries.
In well-lit streets (except main roads and motorways) side lights may be used instead of headlights. One should beware of vehicles travelling with no lights at all!
Parking in one-way streets is allowed on even dates on the side with even house numbers and correspondingly on the other side on odd dates.
In the evening when the streets in the town are crowded one will frequently find pedestrians unwilling to leave the roadway and also on cross-country roads with relatively little traffic, strict attention must be paid, for the country people often ignore the rules of the road and in addition many animals make the roads unsafe.
Signals by the police (*policia de tráfico*) in the towns and by the gendarmerie (*guardia civil*) in the country must be absolutely obeyed. If a motorist fails to observe their hand signals it is possible that the police may make use of the weapons they carry (there are frequent raids on terrorists).
Fines for breaking the traffic regulations have to be paid on the spot and are considerable. Towing away with a private vehicle is forbidden.
Maximum speeds: Motorways 120 km/h (75 mph), main roads 100 km/h (62 mph), other roads 90 km/h (56 mph) and in built-up areas 60 km/h (37 mph).
The maximum permitted blood alcohol level is 8 milligrammes per millilitre.

Travel Documents

France

Personal documents

Visitors from Britain and most Western countries require only a valid passport (or British Visitor's Passport) to enter France. Visitors from countries which do not belong to the European Community need an entry and transit visa. This insistence on a visa has been introduced by France to guard against terrorists.

Car documents

A national driving licence and car registration document are accepted in France and should always be carried when driving. Taking a green international insurance card is advisable. Vehicles must bear the oval nationality plate.

Spain

Personal documents

Visitors from the United Kingdom, the Commonwealth and the United States must have a valid passport. No visa is required by nationals of the UK, Canada and New Zealand for a stay of up to 3 months or by the US for a stay of up to 6 months provided in each case that they are not taking up any paid employment. An extension of stay can be granted by the Spanish police authorities.

Car documents

A national driving licence is accepted in Spain but must be

accompanied by an official translation stamped by a Spanish consulate; it is probably easier and cheaper to carry an international driving permit (which is, in any event, required for business trips). The car registration document must be carried as well as an international insurance certificate (green card) and a bail bond (issued by an insurance company with green card) should be taken out, since in the event of an accident the car may be impounded pending payment of bail.

Note

It is advisable to prepare copies of passports, driving licence, etc., before departure and to keep these separately from the originals. If papers are lost a photocopy makes it easier to obtain a replacement.

Walking

The hilly hinterland of the Côte Vermeille (France), the Costa Brava (Spain) and the Montseny region provide excellent country for walking. The low density of population and large areas of unspoiled landscape have a particular charm. Good maps (for example from the Institut Géographique National (France) and Alpina (Spain) and, if possible a compass are really indispensable.

Water Sports

The Côte Vermeille (France) and the Costa Brava and the Costa Daurada (Spain) are a paradise for every imaginable kind of water sport. In the more important holiday centres the necessary equipment can be rented.

Underwater sport

Both the Côte Vermeille and the Costa Brava are heavily indented and rocky, so that as well as many beaches suitable for bathing there are excellent places for diving, but these can often only be reached by boat. In some places, because of protected areas and strict regulations for underwater hunting, information should be obtained from tourist offices or from the resort itself. In the larger holiday centres and in ports there are diving schools and undertakings specialising in diving expeditions (generally with a compressor station). A sportsman who brings his own scuba gear will need an adaptor for attachment to air bottles which he can rent. It is easy to forget that, when snorkelling, salt water and sunlight can quickly cause serious sunburn; as a precaution a light cotton shirt or T-shirt should be worn when snorkelling. One should be careful of grasping clefts and hollows in the rock; a pair of stout rubber gloves is good protection against stings and nettle poison. Best of all is to wear a so-called wet suit, which also protects against too rapid cooling.
Sportsmen diving in Spain need in any case a diving licence. This can be obtained from the appropriate marine headquarters or will be supplied by a diving base for its customers.

Windsurfing, near El Port de la Selva

Swimming, surfing

In contrast to the above the Costa Daurada is almost flat; it is, therefore, better for windsurfers and ideal for families with children. Similar flat stretches of beach lie to the east of Perpignan. Windsurfing schools and places where equipment can be hired can be found almost everywhere.

Beach supervisory service

The most important bathing beaches in France and most of those in Spain are supervised; the conditions for swimmers are indicated by coloured pennants (green: bathing permitted without restraint; yellow: bathing dangerous; red: bathing forbidden).

Marinas

See entry

When to Go

The best times for visiting the Côte Vermeille, the Costa Brava and the Costa Daurada are in late spring and early summer. In high summer, during the school holidays, the resorts become so crowded that obtaining accommodation without pre-booking can be a problem. Summer heat is moderated by winds off the sea. In the higher places in the Pyrenees the summer months are also pleasant; on the northern side of the Pyrenees and in the Montseny the forests give protection and thus have a moderating effect on the temperature.

An extended visit to the Catalonian capital Barcelona is best made in spring or autumn; in summer the heat in the inner city can become rather oppressive.

Wine

France

Wine has always been the national drink of France, even though the consumption of beer has gone up in recent times. In addition to good local wines, superior vintages are also found in Roussillon, especially in the region of Banyoles. Here the vineyards are concentrated on the slopes of the Côtes du Roussillon near the coast and also in the gently undulating countryside of Corbières (Aude; here the emphasis is on the cultivation of particularly productive but less "noble" varieties of grape). Almost a third of all French wines are produced in this region. A speciality is the so-called *vin doux naturel* (natural sweet wine) which is normally prepared from Muscatel grapes. However, this is not the complete story. To attain a satisfactory residual sugar content as well as a sufficient concentration of alcohol the fermentation process is interrupted by the addition of alcohol.

Spain

On the lower southern slopes of the Pyrenees there are surprisingly very few vineyards and their produce has little importance outside the region. The largest wine-producing area of Catalonia is to the south of Barcelona, centred around Tarragona. Here the emphasis is on the production of red wine, the greater part of which is sold as blended wine. However, the production of sparkling wine is notable; probably the largest cellar in the world for sparkling wine is to be found here.

In hotels and restaurants the red, white and rosé wines (*vino tinto, blanco* and *rosado*) listed come primarily from other parts of Spain, the finest from the Rioja region in the south-western foothills of the Pyrenees.

Youth Hostels

Young people will find reasonably priced accommodation in Youth Hostels (French: *auberges de jeunesse*; Spanish: *albergues juveniles* or *albergues de la juventud*). Members of national youth hostel organisations affiliated with the International Youth Hostels Association can normally use the hostels from July to September. For an individual a stay in a hostel is limited to three nights; in the main season previous booking is advisable.

Youth Hostels prospectus

The International Youth Hostels Prospectus (volume 1 for Europe and countries bordering the Mediterranean) is issued every year. The publisher is the Youth Hostel Federation, Welwyn Garden City, Hertfordshire, England.

Index

Places in Spain are marked (E), those in France (F).
"ll", which in Spanish comes at the end of the alphabet, will be found in this index in its normal English position.

Index

Please turn the page for an order form and a list of additional Baedeker Guides.